COMPREHENSION OF GRAPHICS

ADVANCES IN PSYCHOLOGY

108

Editors:

G. E. STELMACH
P. A. VROON

NORTH-HOLLAND
AMSTERDAM • LONDON • NEW YORK • TOKYO

COMPREHENSION OF GRAPHICS

Wolfgang SCHNOTZ

Institute of Psychology
Friedrich Schiller University of Jena
Jena, Germany

Raymond W. KULHAVY

College of Education
Division of Psychology in Education
Arizona State University
Tempe, AZ, USA

1994

NORTH-HOLLAND
AMSTERDAM • LONDON • NEW YORK • TOKYO

NORTH-HOLLAND
ELSEVIER SCIENCE B.V.
Sara Burgerhartstraat 25
P.O. Box 211, 1000 AE Amsterdam, The Netherlands

ISBN: 0 444 81792 1

This book is printed on acid-free paper.

Printed in The Netherlands

With Contributions by

Linda C. Caterino, Michel Denis, Günter Dörr, Johannes Engelkamp,
August Fenk, Marie-Dominique Gineste, Camilla Gobbo,
Valérie Gyselinck, Michael Henninger, John R. Kirby,
Raymond W. Kulhavy, Abdellatif Laroui, Ulla Maichle,
Richard E. Mayer, Mark A. McDaniel, Gilbert Mohr, Phillip J. Moore,
Joan Peeck, Emmanuel Picard, Frédérique Robin, Jill Scevak,
Wolfgang Schnotz, Norbert M. Seel, William A. Stock, Hubert Tardieu,
Paula J. Waddill, Bernd Weidenmann, William Winn,
Hubert D. Zimmer, Michael Zock

Preface

Graphic displays like charts, graphs, diagrams, and maps play today an important role in the design and presentation of instructional materials education. There is also a strong need in scientific, technical and administrative fields to visually present certain facts, laws, principles etc. In recent years, the use of computer-based learning environments has also become an important field where the visual presentation of information plays a central role. Despite the importance of graphical displays as a means of communication and despite the fact that research about learning and cognition has advanced rapidly in the last two decades, the comprehension of graphics is still a rather unexplored area. Many studies have shown that graphics can make communication and learning more effective, but we have only recently begun to understand better why and under what conditions they are really effective. The comprehension of graphics is not only a stimulating topic in the fields of science and instructional psychology, but also of related disciplines like semiotics, and artificial intelligence. Research on the comprehension of graphics complements the scientific investigation of cognitive processes in text comprehension, which has contributed much to our understanding of human cognition and learning. Ultimately, a better understanding of the cognitive processes involved in the comprehension of graphics will have an impact not only on cognitive theory, but also on educational practice.

In order to stimulate theoretical and applied research on comprehension of graphics, a conference on Comprehension of Graphics was held at the Learning Research Department in the German Institute of Distance Education at the University of Tübingen from October 29 till 30, 1991. The aim of this conference was to provide an opportunity for scientists from different countries to exchange theoretical approaches and empirical findings and to discuss new research perspectives on the comprehension and knowledge acquisition from graphics. In addition, the conference was initiated to stimulate international co-operation within this field of investigation. Participants of this conference came from Australia, Austria, Canada, France, Germany, Italy, the

Netherlands, and the USA. The conference was initiated and organized by the first editor, and financed by the Volkswagen foundation.

The conference was organized as a working meeting with research presentations followed by discussions involving all participants. The papers presented in this volume are the result of these presentations and the subsequent discussions. The papers have been grouped into four sections: (a) graphical codes and graphics processing, (b) graphics and mental representations, (c) differential and developmental aspects, and (d) instructional aspects.

Graphical codes and graphics processing

The first section concerns the relation between visual codes appearing in stimulus materials and cognitive processes that are triggered by these codes during the comprehension of graphics. In chapter 1, Winn provides an overview of the state of the art in research on graphics comprehension. He describes the interaction between the preattentive processes of detection, discrimination, and configuration of visual signs on the one hand and the concept-driven, schema-directed attentive processes on the other hand. Winn points out the relevance of culture-specific processing habits, like, reading from the left to the right, which strongly influences the understanding of graphics. Referring to his own studies, he demonstrates that graphics can considerably enhance problem solving behaviors by providing individuals with a two-dimensional display of problem structures.

In chapter 2, Weidenmann analyses different kinds of graphic codes and their relevance for graphics comprehension. A basic disctinction is made between depicting and directing codes. Whereas depicting codes have a representational function, directing codes guide cognitive processing without directly representing depicted facts. Since graphics are often processed only superficially and their semantic content is only vaguely described verbally, the special function of directing codes is to trigger certain kinds of cognitive processing. Weidenmann points out that directing codes should not be interpreted as eqiuvalent to the schemata of general perception. Rather, the learner has to grasp the communicative intentions of the author by mentally reconstructing the author's visual argument. A better understanding of the function of graphical codes can be considered as an essential basis to enhancing visual literacy and to adequately combining verbal and pictorial information during instruction. For future research, Weidenmann suggests investigations of the relation between various graphic codes and subsequent cognitive processes that these codes activate during graphic comprehension.

In chapter 3, Fenk analyzes a special aspect of graphical codes: their relation to the metaphorical content of natural language. Referring to Peirce's distinction between symbolic signs, iconic signs, and indexes, Fenk demonstrates that so-called logical pictures like graphs and charts do not have an arbitrary structure entirely determined by conventions. According to his point of view, graphical codes should be considered as externalized spatial metaphors derived from language. In two studies, Fenk demonstrates that the closer the structure of a logical picture corresponds to an appropriate metaphor of language, the easier it can be understood. Such a relation between logical pictures and linguistic spatial metaphors is not only relevant for our understanding of graphics comprehension, it can serve also an important heuristic function. One implication of Fenk's position is that graphic designers should refer more explicitly to the predominant linguistic spatial metaphors in their culture.

In chapter 4, Kirby examines the question of how graphical maps are cognitively processed. He proposes a distinction between holistic and analytical strategies of map processing. In the former strategy, a map is considered as a coherent spatial structure, wherein structure is processed visually with special consideration of spatial relations between its elements. In the latter strategy, a map is processed using verbally-oriented mechanisms that target various elements in the map. Different levels are assumed within both kinds of strategies. Kirby relates the holistic and the analytical strategy to different dimensions of cognitive processing, which can also be combined to each other. The ability to switch flexibly between holistic and analytic processing or to combine them flexibly according to actual demands seems to be a central point in comprehending graphics. Kirby points out that learners seem to have difficulties spontaneously carrying out higher order holistic and analytical processing.

In chapter 5, cognitive processing of graphics is approached from another perspective: Denis, Robin, Zock, and Laroui examine how individuals analyze and verbally describe visual displays of different complexity. The authors demonstrate that generating a verbal description of a holistic two-dimensional structure is subject to the constraints of cognitive economy: When describing non-linear graphical structures, individuals try to reduce the required cognitive processing capacity by minimizing the number of elements to be stored in working memory and by keeping storage time as short as possible. Denis and his colleagues demonstrate that optimal descriptive sequences require a sufficient analysis of the graphical display by the subject. Finally, the authors outline a computer model for describing complex graphical displays, and which can serve as a tool for the examination of psychological assumptions about graphics processing by combining simulations and experiments.

Graphics and mental representations

The contributions of the second section investigate relations between cognitive processing initiated by graphical codes and mental representations constructed as a result of this processing. A central point of this section is the question of how graphical information is mentally represented. In chapter 6, Zimmer examines a multimodal memory model developed with Engelkamp. The model distinguishes between a visuo-spatial subsystem, a conceptual subsystem and a motor subsystem. Zimmer assumes that the visuo-spatial subsystem can be used for the processing of visual as well as the processing of verbal input. Accordingly, learners can construct similar mental representations using either verbal or graphical information. Processing proceeds differently, however, depending on whether information about features or about spatial relations is more important. Zimmer demonstrates that graphical information is automatically processed in the visual subsystem, but that use of the resulting mental representation depends on the task at hand. Accordingly, Zimmer argues that the use of graphics does not, per se, facilitate learning. The essential point is which cognitive subsystem encodes which kind of information and to what extent the resulting mental representation is suited for coping with the respective problem. Zimmer also points out that it remains unanswered whether learners create exocentric representations for some problems and egocentric representations for others or whether exocentric representations are generally preferred.

In chapter 7 Engelkamp and Mohr examine how different forms of visual and verbal information about size differences affect memory. The assumption is made that such information can be mentally stored both in a spatial representation of the visual display as well as a spatial representation of the entailed size differences. Accordingly, both forms of representation can be congruent or incongruent with each other. The authors demonstrate that with incongruent representations the data are similar to results yielded by using verbal representations only. The authors interprete their results as follows: graphical information on size differences can be directly encoded in a visuo-spatial code and then be directly read from it. Further, dual encoding in visual and verbal forms does not always take place, or such dual encoding won't be used in every case. Thus, graphics offer the possibility of constructing both a spatial mental representation and a propositional representation, but in order to ensure that this possibility is efficient, it is important that the learner has access to the required mental representation.

In chapter 8, Mayer examines the question under what conditions graphics aid learners to understand the function of technical devices. He assumes that learners understand the function of such devices when they are able to construct appropriate mental models. Such models entail representations of the components of the device and causal relations between these components, so that a change of the state in one component leads to a change of state in other component. The author argues that the formation of such a model requires that the learner constructs representational links between graphical information and the respective mental representation, representational links between verbal information and the respective verbal mental representation and, finally, referential links between the two types of mental representations. According to Mayer, graphics support the understanding of a technical device under the following conditions: First, the learning material needs to contain information on cause and effect relations underlying the device. Second, the graphical presentations must show various system states and their interrelations. Third, the referential links between verbal and graphical information need to be supported by contiguity. Fourth, the learner is infamiliar with the function of the device. These principles obviously apply both to graphics in written text and to animated graphics combined with auditory verbal explanations.

In chapter 9, Gyselinck and Tardieu investigate to what extent an already existing mental model may be further reinforced through the presentation of a related graphic. They describe an empirical study, in which an experimental group of subjects first read a text and then was given a graphical display. A control group read the same text twice. No substantial difference was found between the two groups concerning the course of learning. The authors conclude that a mental model needs to reach a certain degree of consolidation before it can be further elaborated with graphical information. Another interpretation could be that, in this case, readers construct a mental model from the text and that this model does not correspond well to the subsequently presented graphic. These discrepancies could have caused interference between the graphic and the mental model. Accordingly, a possible conclusion could be that graphics should be presented from the beginning of a verbal description because this allows a learner to construct an outline of a mental model which can then be subsequently elaborated.

In chapter 10, Kulhavy, Stock and Caterino examine the conditions under which maps are an efficient aid for recalling text information. They assume that maps are encoded as intact images with a specific spatial structure. If such an image is in working memory, information contained in the map can be quickly located and used as a retrieval cue for the respective text information. According to the theory of conjoint processing developed by Kulhavy and his associates, maps increase the amount of information remembered when the maps are presented as organized visual displays, when subjects actually process the map, and when the text information to be remembered is directly related to the map. The authors raise the question whether the feature information and the structure information contained in a map contribute to the same extent to the retention of the respective text information. They demonstrate that feature information has no substantial effect on recall, wherease clear positive effects can be found for structure information. Accordingly, the mnemonical function of graphics is based upon their global structural characteristics and not upon their feature information.

Differential and developmental aspects

The topic in the third section is the influence of individual differences in prior knowledge and cognitive abilities, as well as developmental differences, on the comprehension of graphics. In chapter 11, McDaniel and Waddill examine how differences in reading ability modify the influence of graphics on recall of text information. A distinction is made between detail and relational information, essentially corresponding to the distinction between feature and structure information. McDaniel and Waddill discuss two views of the function of graphics, the first of which treats graphics as serving a compensatory function, i.e., that graphics help low ability readers. The second view treats graphics as serving an enrichment function, i.e., that graphics support high ability readers. According to the empirical findings of McDaniel and Waddill the compensating function of pictures seems to play a minor role, in that mainly high ability readers benefitted from graphics. High ability readers took advantage both of pictures presenting detail information and of pictures presenting relational information whereas low ability readers had higher recall of detail information only after having seen pictures with detail information. The authors conclude that graphical displays support encoding and retrieval of information, which is focussed on by the individual him/herself, as well as of information, which is difficult to encode only verbally. This applies, however, only if the individual has the necessary cognitive prerequisites. Therefore, both individual differences concerning the individual perspective of processing as well as differences concerning the cognitive abilities will affect the degree of success that individuals have comprehending graphics.

In chapter 12, Schnotz, Picard, and Henninger examine what factors make a difference that leads to deeper understanding of graphics and texts. The authors present a theoretical framework in which the comprehension of graphics is considered as a process of structure mapping between a graphic and an analog mental model. Accordingly, graphical entities are mapped onto mental entities and visuo-spatial relations are mapped onto semantical relations. The authors then report results from an empirical study which suggest that more successful learners interpret graphics more comprehensively, and, accordingly, achieve a more consistent mapping between the graphic and their mental model. The more successful learners also are more adapt in retrieving relevant text information at the right time. Finally, the authors discuss possibilities for improving graphics comprehension by giving students adequate processing strategies, such as aids for coordinating graphics and text information, and by selecting and sequencing learning tasks.

In chapter 13, Maichle examines differences exist between good and poor readers of line graphs. Using a thinking aloud method, she demonstrates that both good and poor graph readers are able to determine point values or single trends in a line graph. However, good graph readers do significantly better in extracting more complex, higher order information patterns. Furthermore, good graph readers invest more time and effort in orientation activities before extracting specific information from a line graph. These activities include informing themselves about the kind of information presented and about scale characteristics of the coordinate axes etc. Obviously, good graph readers use more elaborate graph schemata which enable them to parse a line graph in the appropriate way, to direct their attention to the relevant aspects and to transform perceptual patterns into the according semantical information. Poor graph readers, on the contrary, seem to possess only general graph schemata. Maichle discusses several implications of her results for the diagnosis of graph comprehensionabilities and for the design of effective instructional programs to foster these abilities.

While the contribution of Maichle is concerned with understanding line graphs by adult learners, in chapter 14 Gobbo examines the kinds of problems that exist among younger subjects in the comprehension of line graphs. She demonstrates that learners of age 12 often have difficulties correctly understanding the interplay of the coordinate axes with the function curves being depicted. Furthermore, Gobbo points out that even adequately designed graphics do not insure greater understanding. Rather, the interpretation of a graphic can turn into a specific, cognitively demanding task and, as a result, the learner possesses fewer processing resources that can be directed to the learning of the instructional material. Obviously, in cases where people lack expertise with graphics, there is a trade-off between demands for processing the presentational form and demands for processing the actual instructional content.

In chapter 15 Gineste examines the effects of a pictorial presentation of analogies on the knowledge acquisition of young school-children. With reference to Piaget's concept of cognitive development, she demonstrates that a pictorial presentation significantly improves the understanding of analogies as compared with verbal presentation. Gineste concludes that a basic conceptual understanding of analogies has developed by this age, and that both the conceptual knowledge and the format in which analogies are presented are relevant factors for comprehension. Graphical presentation of analogies seems to facilitate the performance of younger school-children because it allows them to directly and visually depict the relevant semantic relations.

Instructional aspects

The last section addresses the instructional possibilities at graphics. In chapter 16, Seel and Dörr investigate whether the ability to spatially interprete technical drawings can be improved through special computer-based training programs. Starting out from Salomon's supplantation hypothesis, which postulates that mental processes can be supported through external simulation, Seel and Dörr have developed a training program in which the spatial projections in technical drawing are made manifest as shiftings and rotations with the help of a computer. The authors report an experiment in which learners using this training program performed better than learners using pure imagining instruction. Furthermore, Seel and Dörr found that it was easier for the subjects to transform three-dimensional objects into two-dimensional projections than vice versa. The results indicate that future experiments on fostering graphic comprehension skills should take into account more explicitly the issue of encoding specifity and of learning transfer.

In chapter 17, Peeck analyses to what extent the instructional possibilities of graphics can be better employed by learners through providing them with explicit guidance for their cognitive processing. He discusses various possibilities, including: a simple invitation for the learner to look at a graphic, specific tips as to what part of a graphic should receive special attention, and tasks which require the learner to produce an external, controllable result. Based on his own studies, Peek concludes that learners are more successful when they are asked to identify what information from the text is being visualized with the graphic and how this is being accomplished. He points out, however, that learners are sometimes willing but not able to follow such instructions for the handling of texts and graphics. In particular, younger learners seem to need a lot of coaching before strategic training makes learning more efficient.

In chapter 18 Moore and Scevak examine whether improved comprehension of graphics and texts can be achieved when learners receive specific guidance about how to link text and graphic information. The authors report an experiment in which learners had to indicate after each text paragraph which part of a related tree diagram corresponded to the respective text paragraph. For these subjects the intensity of the linking and the learning result were positively correlated. On the whole, however, those subjects did not achieve as high levels of comprehension as subjects who received the text and the graphic without being asked to link them. The results indicate that positive consequences of employing certain processing strategies are possibly neutralized because these strategies require too much cognitive processing capacity. Too frequent mental switches from text information to graphic information and vice versa might, for example, interfere with global coherence formation. Moore and Scevak therefore emphasize the necessity of developing and teaching strategies that contribute to the construction of knowledge that is coherent both at the local and the global level.

In their concluding remarks, Schnotz and Kulhavy outline some general perspectives for future research. They conclude that the comprehension of graphics is a promising field for future research, in which cognitive psychology, educational psychology, semiotics, linguistics, and artificial intelligence can engage in a fruitful collaboration. Such research from different perspectives would provide a fairly good chance to attain a better theoretical understanding of graphics comprehension and a better basis for adequate practical decisions. A broader and deeper knowledge about this topic will become even more relevant in the future, when developments in multimedia, computer-based learning environments, and man-machine interfaces with strong emphasis on the visualization of information, will play ever larger roles in human life.

Wolfgang Schnotz   Raymond W. Kulhavy

Acknowledgements

The editors would like to thank a number of persons whose support contributed to the organization of the conference and to issuing this volume. We are very grateful to Steffen-Peter Ballstaedt, Helmut Felix Friedrich, Aemilian Hron, and Emmanuel Picard for their assistance in preparing and organizing the conference as well as to Christel Jansen, Hildegard Preißer and Margot Stoll for taking care of the various technical arrangements. Without their support, the meeting could not have been implemented successfully. We are also grateful to Claudia Petruch for the layout work on the completed manuscripts. Furthermore, we thank Michael Pfeiffer and Thomas Zink for supporting the work on the subject and author index. Our special thanks goes to the Volkswagen foundation which made this conference possibe through its financial support.

List of Contributors

Linda C. Caterino
Walker Research Institute, 2441 East Edgewood Ave, Mesa, Arizona
85204 - 4601, USA

Michel Denis
Laboratoire d' Informatique pour la Mécanique et les Sciences de
l'Ingénieur, Centre National de la Recherche Scientifique,
PB 133, F-91403 Orsay Cedex, France

Günter Dörr
Pädagogische Hochschule Weingarten, Kirchplatz 2, D-88250
Weingarten, Germany

Johannes Engelkamp
Fachrichtung Psychologie im FB 6 der Universität des Saarlandes,
Universitätscampus Bau 1.1, D-66123 Saarbrücken, Germany

August Fenk
Institut für Psychologie der Universität für Bildungswissenschaften
Klagenfurt, Universitätsstraße 65-67, A-9022 Klagenfurt, Austria

Marie-Dominique Gineste
Laboratoire d' Informatique pour la Mécanique et les Sciences de
l'Ingénieur, Centre National de la Recherche Scientifique, PB 133,
F-91403 Orsay Cedex, France

Camilla Gobbo
University of Padova, Department of Psychology, Via B. Pellegrino 26,
I-35137 Padova, Italy

Valérie Gyselinck
Laboratoire de Psychologie Cognitive de la Communication, Ecole
Practique des Hautes Etudes, 3ème Section, 28 rue Serpente, F-75006
Paris, France

Michael Henninger
Lehrstuhl für Empirische Pädagogik und Pädagogische Psychologie,
Universität München, Leopoldstraße 13, D-80802 München, Germany

John R. Kirby
Queen's University, Faculty of Education, Kingston Ontario, Canada
K7L 4L9, Canada

Raymond W. Kulhavy
Arizona State University, College of Education, Divison of Psychology
in Education, Tempe, Arizona 85287-0611, USA

Abdellatif Laroui
Laboratoire d' Informatique pour la Mécanique et les Sciences de
l'Ingénieur, Centre National de la Recherche Scientifique,
PB 133, F-91403, Orsay Cedex, France

Ulla Maichle
Institut für Test- und Begabungsforschung der Studienstiftung des
deutschen Volkes, Koblenzer Straße 77, D-53177 Bonn, Germany

Richard E. Mayer
University of California, Department of Psychology, Santa Barbara CA
93106, USA

Mark A. McDaniel
Purdue University, 1346 Psychology Bldg., Room 3156, West Lafayette,
IN 47907-1364, USA

Gilbert Mohr
Fachrichtung Psychologie im FB 6 der Universität des Saarlandes,
Universitätscampus Bau 1.1, D-66123 Saarbrücken, Germany

Phillip J. Moore
University of Newcastle, Department of Education, Rankin Drive,
Shortland, Newcastle, NSW 2308, Australia

Joan Peeck
University of Utrecht, Deptartment of Psychology, Heidelberglaan 2,
3584 CS Utrecht, The Netherlands

Emmanuel Picard
Deutsches Institut für Fernstudien an der Universität Tübingen,
Arbeitsbereich Lernforschung, Konrad-Adenauer-Straße 40, D-72072
Tübingen, Germany

Frédérique Robin
Laboratoire d' Informatique pour la Mécanique et les Sciences de
l'Ingénieur, Centre National de la Recherche Scientifique,
PB 133, F-91403, Orsay Cedex, France

Jill Scevak
University of Newcastle, Department of Education, Rankin Drive,
Shortland, Newcastle, NSW 2308, Australia

Wolfgang Schnotz
Friedrich-Schiller-Universität Jena, Institut für Psychologie, Abteilung
Pädagogische Psychologie, Am Steiger 3/Haus 1, D-07747 Jena,
Germany

Norbert M. Seel
Technische Universität Dresden, Fakultät für Erziehungswissenschaft,
Mommsenstraße 13, D-01062 Dresden, Germany

William A. Stock
Arizona State University, College of Education, Divison of Psychology
in Education, Tempe, Arizona 85287-0611, USA

Hubert Tardieu
Laboratoire de Psychologie Cognitive de la Communication, Ecole
Practique des Hautes Etudes, 3ème Section, 28 rue Serpente, F-75006
Paris, France

Paula J. Waddill
Department of Psychology, University of Scranton, Scranton,
Pennsylvania 18510 - 4596, USA

Bernd Weidenmann
Universität der Bundeswehr München, FB Sozialwissenschaften,
Werner-Heisenberg-Weg 39, D-85579 Neubiberg, Germany

William Winn
University of Washington, 412 Miller DQ-12, Seattle, Washington
98195, USA

List of Contributors

Hubert D. Zimmer
Fachrichtung Psychologie im FB 6 der Universität des Saarlandes,
Universitätscampus Bau 1.1, D-66123 Saarbrücken, Germany

Michael Zock
Laboratoire d' Informatique pour la Mécanique et les Sciences de
l'Ingénieur, Centre National de la Recherche Scientifique,
PB 133, F-91403, Orsay Cedex, France

Content

PART I   GRAPHICAL CODES AND GRAPHICS PROCESSING

PART II   GRAPHICS AND MENTAL REPRESENTATIONS

PART III   DIFFERENTIAL AND DEVELOPMENTAL ASPECTS

PART IV   INSTRUCTIONAL ASPECTS

PART I

GRAPHICAL CODES
AND GRAPHICS PROCESSING

Chapter 1

Contributions of Perceptual and Cognitive Processes to the Comprehension of Graphics

William Winn

University of Washington, Seattle, USA

ABSTRACT

This chapter describes perceptual and cognitive processes that are involved in the organization, interpretation and comprehension of graphics. The notational symbol system of graphics provides an unambiguous one-to-one relationship between each symbol and a referent in the content domain as well as relatively clear indications of the relations among symbols. Perceptual processes, operating on these symbols and inter-symbol relations, allow the viewer to detect, discriminate among and configure graphic symbols into patterns. Cognitive processes, to some extent influenced by the organization imposed by perception, operate iteratively on information organized by perception leading to the identification, interpretation and comprehension of what has been perceived. Studies that illustrate the operation of these processes are described. Research questions for future study are offered as a conclusion.

Comprehension occurs when a symbol system used to convey a message interacts with psychological processes active in the person who receives it (Salomon, 1979). In the case of graphics, the symbol system is highly notational (Goodman, 1968). This means that it consists of discrete symbols, each of which 1) bears a unique and unambiguous relationship to an object in the domain the graphic describes; and 2) has a unique set of spatial relations with other symbols in the graphic. The comprehension of graphics therefore involves processes by means of which a person identifies the objects for which the graphic symbols stand and interprets the spatial relations among the symbols as specifying relations among objects in the domain of reference.

Symbols and the spatial relations shown among them may refer by direct representation to concrete objects and real-world relations, or, by analogy, to abstract concepts and conceptual relations. Maps are an example of the former (Schlichtmann, 1985). Map symbols refer directly to real features in a real territory, such as buildings, mountains and lakes. To be useful for navigation, the relative distances among symbols on maps must, at a reduced scale, correspond to the relative distances among the features of the territory. By contrast, diagrams often illustrate abstract domains of reference (Winn, 1989). For example, the symbols used in a flowchart represent the steps in a procedure, not physical objects. The lines joining the symbols show the sequence of steps, not physical connections.

The purpose of this chapter is to offer an account of how people come to understand the information presented in graphics. This requires a careful analysis of the symbol system used in graphics. It also requires an explanation of how perceptual and cognitive processes act on the symbolic elements of graphics and are influenced by them. Research supporting the account will be described and an agenda for further research will serve as a conclusion.

The processes involved

The symbol system of graphics consists of two elements. First are symbols that bear an unambiguous one-to-one relationship to objects in the domain of reference. Objects may be represented as words, dots, boxes or other geometric shapes, icons, drawings, or any of a host of other symbols. Second are spatial relations of the symbols to each other and to the whole graphic. A symbol may be close to or far from, above or below, to the left or right of another symbol. The symbol may also be near the edge of the graphic or close to its center, at the top or the bottom, to the left or to the right. Relations may be shown by using any of a number of devices, including lines or arrows that connect symbols together and boundaries that surround symbol groups.

Figure 1 shows how the symbol system of graphics interacts with viewers' perceptual and cognitive processes. As a prerequisite for comprehension, the symbols in a graphic have to be detected by the

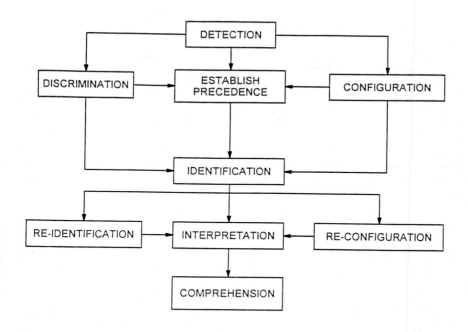

Figure 1. An overview of the processes involved in the perception and comprehension of graphics.

perceptual system. Also, the spatial organization of the symbols, implicit in the patterns formed by the varying distances among them and by the links and boundaries that group them, has to be discerned. These tasks are achieved through the operation of processes for the detection of symbols, the discrimination of one symbol from another, and the configuration of symbols into patterns. Detection determines whether a symbol is present at a particular location. Discrimination establishes whether it is the same as or different from other symbols. Configuration determines which other symbols are associated with it. These are pre-attentive perceptual processes. As such, they are not open to the influence of a person's existing knowledge (Pylyshyn [1984] calls them "cognitively impenetrable"). They operate rapidly because they work in parallel and draw little upon cognitive resources (Treisman, 1988; Uttal, 1988). However, the organization they impose on the information conveyed by a graphic predisposes the viewer to certain interpretations as we shall see.

The subsequent attentive scrutiny of information organized by perception involves a number of top-down cognitive processes. Important are processes for the identification of symbols, for their re-identification, and for the reconfiguration of inter-symbol relations. Through identification, the viewer attempts to match objects and relations to existing knowledge. Identified objects and relations are also interpreted in light of existing knowledge. If objects are identified while perceived inter-object relations make no sense, the viewer may reconfigure the relations among the objects so that they are meaningful. Likewise, objects may also be re-identified to fit interpretable configurations. Interpretation, re-identification and re-configuration recur iteratively until the graphic makes sense. Comprehension is therefore achieved when the viewer's interpretation can be accomodated by existing knowledge schemata (Rumelhart & Norman, 1981).

Two points need to be stressed. The first is that variations in the symbol system are potentially meaningful. Whether two symbols can be discriminated from each other will determine, initially at least, whether the two objects they represent are understood to be the same or different. Whether two symbols are configured to belong in the same or different clusters will affect the way viewers understand how objects are related and interact. Second, the influences on symbol discrimination and configuration occur before any process capable of attaching meaning to symbols and symbol patterns has had a chance to operate. Thus perceptual organization is influenced by the structural characteristics of the graphic. Attentive processing introduces semantic influences on interpretation. However, since difficulties in interpretation may incur re-identifcation of symbols and reconfiguration of inter-symbol relations, attentive processing is also influenced by structural aspects of graphics. Comprehension is obviously affected by both.

Pre-attentive processing

I turn now to a more detailed examination of pre-attentive perceptual processing of graphics. To simplify matters, I will assume that the viewer is capable of detecting the symbols in a graphic, and I will therefore confine the discussion to discrimination and configuration. This section examines how configuration and discrimination work, and what influences them.

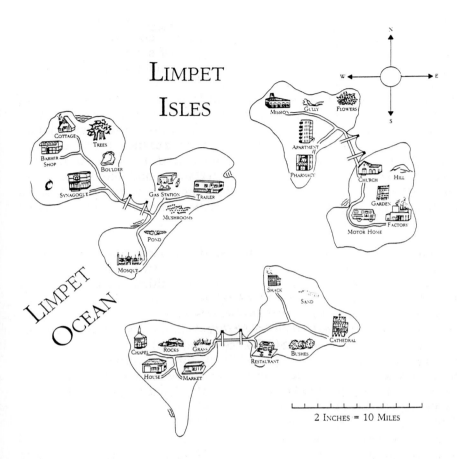

Figure 2. Materials used in the study by Schwartz and Phillippe (1991). The symbols are configured into groups by proximity, by their enclosure in boundaries (coastlines), and by explicit links (bridges). Precedence determines whether the reader begins by seeing individual symbols (cottage, cathedral, gully), six islands, or three pairs of islands. From Contemporary Educational Psychology, 1991, Vol. 16, No. 2, p. 174. Copyright by Academic Press. Reprinted by permission.

So far, I have stated that the basic unit of analysis in graphic comprehension is the symbol that bears an unambiguous relation to an object in the domain of reference. But what is a symbol and what is an object? At first sight, it might appear that the identity of symbols and objects is self-evident. The conventional symbols used on maps obviously meet the criterion of unambiguously representating single objects. Yet this is not always, or even usually, the case, as the map in Figure 2 shows.

Examination of Figure 2 shows that the map may be organized perceptually at several different levels. At one level, the units of analysis are the three pairs of islands, meaning the map has but three symbols. At the next level are the symbols for the six separate islands. Next are the symbols representing the five features found on each island. Finally are the lines and shapes that make up each feature's symbol, such as the steeple on the chapel, the door of the house or the leaves on the trees. Each feature on this map can serve as a symbol for an object in its own right, or as a part, with others, of a larger symbol.

The hierarchical nature of parts of symbols, symbols and clusters of symbols points out an important interdependency between configuration and discrimination. The way the parts of a symbol are configured affects the viewer's ability to discriminate among them. The thirty features on the map in Figure 2 are easily perceived as being different because they are composed of different sets of parts. If they had all been shown as boxes, they would have been impossible to discriminate without labels. What is more, because the thirty features are easily discriminable, the viewer will most likely consider them to be the units of analysis for this map, analogous to the "basic categories" proposed by Rosch (1978; Rosch & Mervis, 1975) for the classification of concepts in the natural world.

Pomerantz (1986; Pomerantz, Pristach & Carson, 1989) has provided a criterion for what constitutes such a basic perceptual category, or symbol. The unit of analysis for the perceptual system is any group of parts among which our attention is not divided. Thus, when we perceive a triangle, we see the whole figure rather than its three lines and three angles (Pomerantz, Sager & Stover, 1977). The "triangleness" of a triangle arises as an emergent property (Rock, 1986) of its parts. The same is true of the symbols for features in Figure 2. We see the bushes, gas station and mission, not the individual lines that make them up.

There are situations when we see undivided clusters of symbols and treat them as higher-level symbols, as when we see each island as a whole. By the same token, to discriminate among symbols, we must notice whether their parts are different or the same, and therefore divide our attention among smaller parts of the graphic. The inclusiveness of the groups of symbols or parts over which our attention

```
S           S
S           S
S           S
SSSSSSS
S           S
S           S
S           S
```

Figure 3. Experimental material of the type used by Navon (1977) in his study of precedence. Reaction times depended on whether subjects had to detect the presence of the large letter, or of the small letters that made them up.

is not divided can therefore vary considerably. This variation affects the precedence with which symbols are treated in perception. A symbol has precedence if we perceive it first when we look at a graphic. Precedence therefore determines what we first discriminate as separate symbols and is extremely important in perceptual organization. For example, do you see the big H or the little s's when you first look at Figure 3. Navon (1977) found that his subjects saw the H first. He concluded that this gave evidence of global precedence in perception, that people see the forest before the trees.

Navon's claim for global precedence as the norm in perception has been challenged. Paquet and Merikle (1984) found that the predendence of the global form, reported by Navon, disappeared at longer exposures. (Navon presented his material tachistocopically.) Also, the nature of the small features affects whether they are perceived before the big picture (Lesaga, 1989). In particular, their discriminability from each other and familiarity are important (Winn, 1988). What people expect to see and the visual strategies people use is also important (Kinchla, Solis-Macias & Hoffman, 1983). Above all, the size of the symbols determines their precedence. Kinchla & Wolfe (1979) found evidence for local precedence when figures like Navon's were enlarged. When the large letter subtended a visual angle of more than nine degrees, subjects reported attending to the smaller letters first. (Navon's figures subtended smaller visual angles.) Antes & Mann (1984) reported similar results for drawings rather than letters. They proposed that precedence was determined by the amount of detail in a given area, optimally four contour crossings per degree of visual angle. In order to keep the optimal amount of detail constant, a viewer is therefore "drawn into" a graphic to give precedence to smaller symbols when the amount of detail within them increases.

While a number of factors, affecting precedence, determine what we perceive as symbols, a number of other factors help determine how we configure these symbols into patterns. The most basic of these factors is inter-symbol distance. Intuitively, we assume that objects that are physically close to each other in a graphic form groups and are seen as somehow belonging together. Pomerantz & Schwaitzberg (1975) reported that the likelihood that attention between parts of a symbol would be divided increased as the distance between the parts increased. One of my students is exploring this phenomenon (Duong, 1991). The experimental procedure is as follows. Four-by-four matrices of simple shapes, shown in Figure 4, are divided either vertically or horizontally into two equal groups of eight shapes. The distance between the groups is varied randomly from 0 to 80 minutes of visual arc. Over repeated trials, the patterns are presented tachistoscopically to subjects and masked so as to preclude attentive processing. Subjects press one of two keys to indicate whether they see one or two groups. As the angle separating the two groups increases, response latencies at first increase, then decrease. There are always in fact two groups of shapes. When the two groups are close together, rapid "one-group" reponses occur. When they are far apart, subjects give quick "two-group" responses. At around 20 minutes of visual angle, responses slow significantly, indicating uncertainty as two whether one or two groups are present. This suggests that two groups start to become discernible at around 20 minutes of angle. Figure 5 shows these results. We are now in a position where we can examine the effect of many factors on configuration in the pre-attentive perception of graphics.

A second important determinant of configuration is the use of boundaries to enclose groups of symbols that, without boundaries, would not be configured into groups. The power of boundaries to structure information has been demonstrated in experiments (McNamara, 1986) that use priming to determine encoded structures. In a typical study, symbols representing objects, or objects themselves, are placed at various distances from each other and divided into groups by boundaries. Subjects learn the displays to mastery. On a test trial, recall of items is better if they are primed by items enclosed within the same boundary then when primed by items enclosed within a different boundary. This is true even when the two items are physically far apart within the same boundary or very close but within different boundaries.

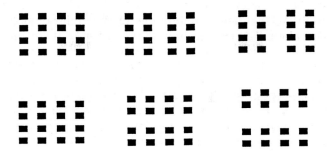

Figure 4. Materials used by Duong (1991) in her study of perceptual gruping. Subjects pressed keys to indicate whether they saw one or two groups of squares. Separation between the groups of eight squares was varied by increments of two pixels.

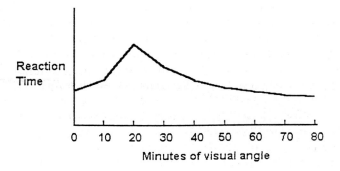

Figure 5. Results of Duong's (1991) study. Response latencies were short when it was clear that either one or two groups were present. At around 20 minutes of visual angle, subjects were less certain and took longer to detect the presence or absence of two groups.

A third determinant of configuration is symmetry. In Pomerantz's research (see Pomerantz, 1986 for an overview), attention was divided between the parentheses arranged as (but undivided for ((and ().
The latter two pairs of symbols possess the Gestalt property of "symmetry" (Wertheimer, 1938). The first pair does not. More generally, if symbols form symmetrical patterns, it is likely that they will be configured together in pre-attentive perception.

In this section, I have discussed some of the factors that affect how people determine the nature of symbols representing objects, how they discriminate among them, and how they configure them into groups. I have suggested that the precedence of symbols in perception has a great deal to do with this. It is evident that a great deal of perceptual organization goes on pre-attentively. How this affects top-down attentive processing and ultimately comprehension is discussed in the next section.

Attentive processing

Comprehension is the result of the interaction between top-down, knowledge-driven processes, and bottom-up, data-driven processes (Neisser, 1976; Rumelhart & Norman, 1981). Graphics are interpreted in terms of what viewers already know, what they expect the graphic to mean, and so on. Pre-attentive processing can therefore be considered to prepare raw perceptual data for attentive scrutiny by detecting, discriminating and configuring symbols in a graphic. Comprehension succeeds or fails to the extent that the information organized by pre-attentive processes can be assimilated to existing schemata, or that schemata can be altered to accomodate that information. This section examines some of the factors that enable or inhibit assimilatory and accomodative mechanisms that operate on graphics.

First, however, I would like to stress the importance of pre-attentive organization on interpretation and comprehension. Owen (1985a, 1985b) asked her subjects to identify ambiguous pictures, like the "young or old woman" or "mouse or boy" pictures, shown in Figure 6. Prior to each picture, subjects were primed with versions of the same picture that had been rendered unambiguous through some simple changes. These primes were presented tachistoscopically and masked so as to preclude attentive interpretation. Nonetheless, subjects' interpretations of the pictures presented supraliminally were consistent with the unambiguous tachistoscopically presented pictures. The pre-attentive organization of the information in the unambiguous pictures clearly predisposed the subjects to interpret the pictures in particular ways. It is the nature and extent of this predisposition that determines how, or even whether, a graphic can be given a meaningful interpretation.

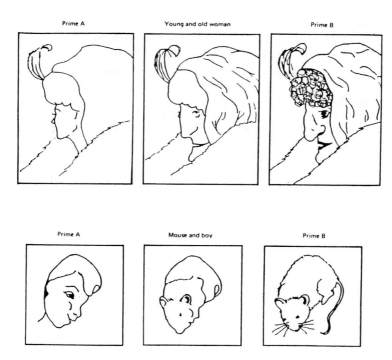

Figure 6. Figures used by Owen (1985a). The left- and right-most figures were used as tachistoscopic primes for the central, ambiguous, figure. Identification of the ambiguous figure depended on the prime. Copyright by The Britisch Psychological Society. Reprinted by permission.

Interpretation of a graphic begins with the identification of the symbols it contains. Identification of something presented to the visual system depends on the successful recognition of a critical number of its parts (Biederman, 1987; Hoffman & Richards, 1984; Marr, 1982). This, rather than template-matching (see Pinker, 1985), allows people to identify objects or their representations that are new examples of known categories, or representations of famliar objects from novel points of view. If symbols are not identified at a first attempt, other interpretations are tried iteratively until an identification is made (Palmer, 1975), or the conclusion is drawn that the symbol is entirely new and therefore cannot be identified. Note that often, as in the map in Figure 2, identification is aided by the attachment of verbal labels to the symbols. Once the symbols have been identified, interpretation proceeds as the viewer determines whether or not the objects and the relations among them, represented by the symbols as configured in the graphic, are compatible with existing knowledge of the graphic's domain of reference.

The assimilation of information, obtained from the graphic by pre-attentive processing, to existing knowledge is greatly affected by the viewer's knowledge of graphic conventions. Knowledge about the graphic structures themselves can affect interpretation and comprehension that might otherwise have been based solely on existing knowledge about the content domain. The studies described in the following section illustrate this for interpretation, recall, comprehension and problem-solving.

Graphic conventions

In a study by Winn & Solomon (1991), subjects were shown pairs of nonsense words in boxes joined by lines in various configurations. A forced-choice binary response indicated subjects' preferred interpretation of the simple diagram. Thus, in the first example shown in Figure 7, subjects had to choose between "a zogwit causes yutcur" or "a yutcur causes zogwit". Striking, not just significant, biases were consistently found in subjects' interpretations. For example, the object to the left was almost always seen as the cause rather than the effect of the object on the right. The object in the inner box was nearly always interpreted as an attribute of the object in the outer box. The diagrams were semantically neutral because the words were meaningless. Thus, the biases in interpretation resulted exclusively from the structural properties of the diagrams. Each particular bias could be explained in terms of the conventions of written English, such as moving from left to right and down the page, subjects preceding verbs in active sentences, and so on.

A second experiment compared performance on nonsense words with meaningful words. "A zogwit causes yutcur" was matched with "a dentist causes pain". When the graphic (dentist on the left) conformed to the sense of the English sentence ("a dentist causes pain"), the same biases were found as with the nonsense words, and were frequently more pronounced. When the graphic did not conform to the sense of the sentence, with "dentist" in the right-hand box, the biases disappeared

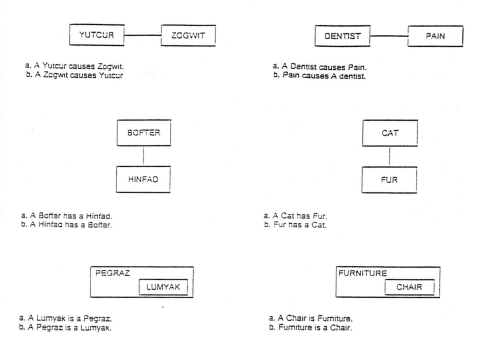

Figure 7. Materials used by Winn and Solomon (1991) in their study of bias caused by graphic conventions. In the nonsense version, the interpretation was (sentence a or b) made on the basis of graphic conventions. With the English sentences, the same biases were found when one of the sentences conformed to a graphic tradition. In other cases, selection of either one of the pair was no different from chance.

completely, with roughly half of the subjects choosing the interpretation implied by the graphic ("pain causes a dentist"), and half favoring the semantic interpretation. In the few cases where biases were found, they were reversed from the biases found for nonsense words, favoring the semantic interpretation.

The conclusion that these biases are attributable to the way we read English is supported by the findings of a study by Zwaan (1965) of the interpretations of figures by Dutch and Israeli subjects. In a series of experiments, Zwaan established that Dutch subjects associated the left-hand side of the perceptual and visual fields with the concepts "proximity", "past" and "self". He argued that people who read from left to right have learned that the starting point of displays is on the left,

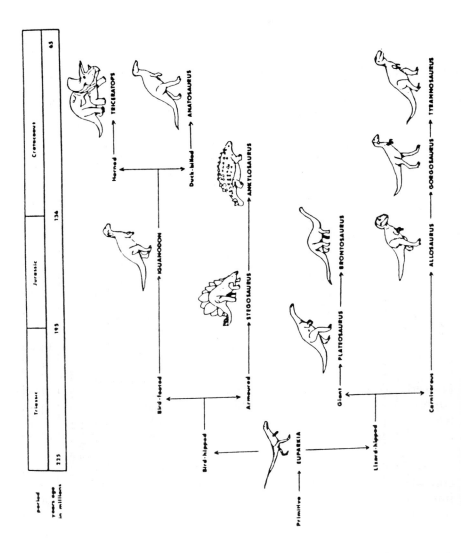

Figure 8. Materials used by Winn (1982, 1983). The second, reversed, version proved to be difficult to learn from. Records of subjects' eye movements showed that they looked in the wrong places for the information they needed to answer questions. From Winn, W. D., & Holliday, W. G., Design Principles for Diagrams. In D. H. Jonassen (Ed.) (1982), The Technology of Text (pp. 287, 288). Englewood Cliffs, NJ: Educational Technology Publications. Copyright by Educational Technology Publications. Reprinted by permission.

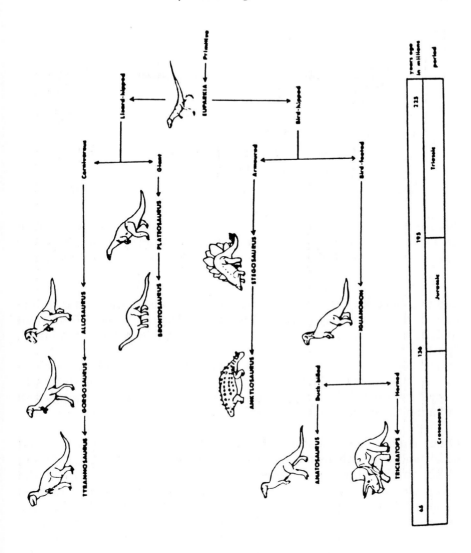

Figure 8 (continued).

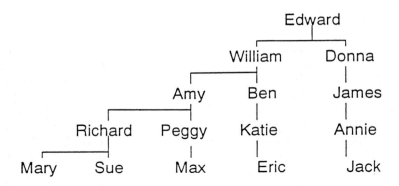

Figure 9. Materials used by Winn, Li and Schill (1991). Subjects given no kinship rules to apply were quicker at finding a person's relatives than subjects given a fictitious rule or even those given the correct rule.

and that material to the right is unknown, yet to be learned, afar. In the case of the Israeli subjects, whose language, Hebrew, is read from right to left, the associations were exactly the opposite, with "proximity", "past", "self" and the starting point for inspection on the right. His conclusion that how people inspect visual material is largely determined by the way their langauge is read apply equally well to our studies of simple two-word diagrams. These conventions are very strong, and violating them can seriously impede the interpretation of graphics.

Other studies have established relationships among conventions and recall and comprehension, not just interpretation. In one study (Winn, 1982), high school students studied a diagram that described the evolution of dinosaurs. For some, the diagram showed the animals evolving left to right across the page. For others, the diagram was reversed, running from right to left and violating other conventions as well (see Figure 8). On tests of evolutionary sequence and tests that required students to classify dinosaurs into families, violating the conventions significantly reduced recall and comprehension. A subsequent study (Winn, 1983) had students answer questions while viewing the same normal and reversed diagrams. Their eye movements were recorded. The data showed that the recall and comprehension difficulties caused by the reversed diagram arose from scanning errors. Graphic conventions determine where subjects who know them will look, and in what sequence. Violating the conventions means that learned scanning strategies no longer work and people look in the wrong places for information.

Other evidence suggests that when graphics have a conventional structure, they make it simpler or even unnecessary to apply rules to solve problems. Winn, Li & Schill (1991) used materials shown in Figure 9 to test aspects of Larkin & Simon's (1987) production-system model of diagram processing. Subjects saw a series of family trees and were given English kinship rules, nonsense kinship rules, or no rules to apply to them. They were then asked such questions as "Is Jack Mary's second cousin?" For more distant relationships, which would involve a great deal of computation if the rule were applied, subjects given no rules arrived at correct responses more rapidly than subjects given either English or nonsense rules. This finding, coupled with analysis of solution strategies described by subjects, suggested that knowledge of the graphical conventions of family trees was sufficient to allow subjects to find answers to the questions readily and accurately. Rather than tracing up the tree and down again to look for particular links between people, subjects simply applied their ready knowledge that cousins are shown on the same level as oneself, two branches over. Being forced to apply rules describing nonsense relationships, or choosing to apply English rules, increased the amount of processing required to arrive at an answer. These studies demonstrate the power of structural conventions to affect the interpretation of graphics and the negative impact of violating them. To some extent they also demonstrate the re-configuration of symbols during attentive processing that is sometimes necessary for graphics to be understood. For example, in the second dinosaur study, after a few trials, subjects started out by looking at the bottom right-hand corner ofthe reversed diagram rather than the top left-hand corner, where they had started out looking. They had reconfigured the diagram so that it ran right to left rather than left to right.

Other studies illustrate reconfiguration more convincingly. Hirtle & Mascolo (1986) had subjects learn the locations of labelled features shown on maps, like the one shown in Figure 10. Although all features are approximately equidistant from each other, you will notice that allof the public buildings are grouped together as are all the recreational facilities. The map has no spatial structure, but a definite semantic one. On a distance estimation task, subjects tended to under-estimate the distances among features in the same semantic cluster. Hirtle & Kallman (1988) found the same "constriction effect" for maps whose features were shown as pictures. On the basis of the identifications of the

BEACH

PARK

POOL

MARINA

STADIUM   BANK

POST OFFICE   TOWN HALL

LIBRARY

HOSPITAL

Figure 10. Materials of the kind used by Hirtle and Mascolo (1986).
Although evenly spaced, the items tended to cluster in recall according
to whether they were recreational or business facilities.

features the subjects made, the structure of the map was reconfigured to
reflect its semantic organization.

This group of studies has shown that semantic and structural features of
graphics influence each other, often in ways that the subject is unaware
of. Instructional designers are interested in how the comprehension of
graphics can be improved by manipulating the structure of graphics,
and by exploiting graphic conventions. I therefore conclude this section
by looking at studies that have deliberately used the mutual influence of
structural and semantic features of diagrams to improve
comprehension.

Graphics in instruction

There is considerable evidence that creating graphical representations of
information by arranging it into spatial structures improves people's
ability to recall and understand it. This is true for free recall of words
(Bellezza, 1983, 1986; Decker & Wheatley, 1982), recall of verbal

information about labelled features in maps (Kulhavy, Caterino & Melchiori, 1989; Kulhavy, Lee & Caterino, 1985), or recall of relationships among labelled concepts in diagrams (Winn, 1982). This effect is typically accounted for by some form of "dual coding" (Paivio, 1971, 1983; Clark & Paivio, 1991) which proposes that spatially-arranged material is encoded both as images and as words, providing redundancy that improves retrieval. Specifically, Bellezza (1986) concluded that his subjects recalled more words when they were presented in visual patterns because the patterns were stored as intact images in memory and were retrieved intact in response to cue words. The patterns then served as cues to the retrieval of the individual words embedded within them. Similarly, Kulhavy's "conjoint retention" theory (Kulhavy, Lee & Caterino, 1985; Schwartz & Kulhavy, 1987, 1988) proposes that maps are encoded and retrieved as complete images. The spatial information, provided by the image of the map, supports recall of verbal information by providing "second stratum cues" that subjects use when direct recall of verbal information fails. In a typical study (Schwartz & Kulhavy, 1981), subjects studied a map while listening to a narrative. On a posttest, subjects who saw the map recalled more verbal information related to map features than no-map controls. Map subjects' performance was no different from that of the control group on items not related to map features showing that the effect was confined to spatially presented information.

It is likely that creating structural arrangements improves recall and comprehension of information in graphics by helping subjects configure the information. When subjects view spatial layouts, they encode the objects they see in clusters. These clusters vary in their degree of inclusiveness. Thus, the information in spatial layouts is stored as hierarchies in memory (Hirtle & Jonides, 1985; McNamara, 1986). McNamara, Hardy & Hirtle (1989) constructed ordered trees from the sequence in which subjects recalled objects they had seen in a spatial layout. The trees identified the hierarchical clusters into which subjects grouped the objects. Their subjects took a recognition test in which each targeted item was primed by an item that was either in the same cluster in the tree or in another. Response latencies were faster for items primed by objects from the same cluster than for items primed by objects outside the cluster. Inspection of McNamara et al.'s (1989) data shows that, for the most part, the contents of each cluster and the place of clusters within the hierarchy were determined by the spatial proximity of the objects in the array. Objects close together tended to appear in the same cluster.

The advantages accorded encoding, retrieval and comprehension by the spatial structuring of semantic information has also been exploited instructionally in a variety of "semantic mapping" strategies (Armbruster & Anderson, 1982, 1984; Dansereau et al., 1979; Johnson, Pittelman & Heimlich, 1986; Schwartz & Raphael, 1985). Here, students are taught to draw diagrams that map the semantic structure of a body of information, typically text. Though different in their appearance, techniques, goals and conceptual bases, all of these mapping techniques exploit grouping through proximity, links or boundaries in order to convey semantic structure graphically.

The studies described in the preceding sections show that creating graphics that facilitate pre-attentive and attentive processing improves performance on a variety of tasks. Careful spatial construction makes it easier for people to configure the symbols and objects graphics represent into meaningful groups. If graphics conform to established conventions, they can reduce the amount of processing required to interpret them. Dual coding makes it easier to recall and understand them. Finally, students can be taught to construct their own graphic maps of content they are to learn. This activity also improves recall and comprehension.

Conclusion

I have argued that pre-attentive perceptual organization, drawing on the structural properties of graphics that affect the discrimination and configuration of symbols that stand for objects, predispose people to interpret graphics in particular ways. I have presented data from several studies that have examined this phenomenon and have illustrated the ways in which people attempt to assimilate the information they find in graphics with what they already know. The theory about how processes implicated in pre-attentive and attentive processing act and interact requires further experimental research. In particular, the following questions need answers.

1.   Are any other processes, in addition to detection, discrimination and configuration, involved in pre-attentive processing of graphics?
2.   To what extent do people compromise either existing knowledge of a domain or existing knowledge of the conventions of graphics before they decide that a graphic is uninterpretable?

3. To what extent are the conventions of graphics culture-specific? Are the processes that enable detection, discrimination and configuration universal?
4. Do graphic conventions act with the force of syntactic "rules", or are they merely what Salomon (1979) has called "conventions of coherence"? To what extent, then, can graphics be relied upon to convey information in a consistent manner?
5. Is it possible to develop prescriptions for graphic design that affect discrimination and configuration in predictable ways?

These questions cover both descriptive and prescriptive instructional theory. It is necessary to address both if we are to understand how graphics function and how they can be used instructionally. We know that graphics work. We need to know why they work if we are to continue to improve their use for communication and instruction.

RÉSUMÉ

Ce chapitre décrit les processus perceptifs et cognitifs qui sont impliqués dans l'organisation, l'interprétation et la compréhension des graphiques. Le système de symboles notationnels des graphiques fournit aussi bien une relation terme à terme entre chaque symbole et un référent dans le domaine du contenu, que des indications relativement claires sur les relations parmi les symboles. Les processus perceptifs, opérant sur ces symboles et sur les relations inter-symboles, permettent à la personne qui regarde de détecter, de discriminer et de configurer les symboles graphiques en patterns. Les processus cognitifs, influençés jusqu'à un certain point par l'organisation imposée par la perception, opèrent de façon itérative sur l'information organisée par la perception, aboutissant à l'identification, l'interprétation et la compréhension de ce qui a été perçu. Des études qui illustrent la mise en oeuvre de ces processus sont décrites. En conclusion, des questions de recherche sont proposées pour des études futures.

References

Antes, J.R., & Mann, S.W. (1984). Global-local precedence in picture processing. *Psychological Research*, *46*, 247-259.

Armbruster, B.B., & Anderson, T.H. (1982). *Idea mapping: The technique and its use in the classroom, or simulating the "ups" and "downs" of reading comprehension.* Urbana, Illinois: University of Illinois Center for the Study of Reading. Reading Education Report #36.

Armbruster, B.B., & Anderson, T.H. (1984). Mapping: Representing informative text graphically. In C.D. Holley & D.F. Dansereau (Eds.). *Spatial Learning Strategies.* New York: Academic Press, 189-209.

Bellezza, F.S. (1983). The spatial arrangement mnemonic. *Journal of Educational Psychology*, *75*, 830-837.

Bellezza, F.S. (1986). A mnemonic based on arranging words in a visual pattern. *Journal of Educational Psychology*, *78*, 217-224.

Biederman, I. (1987). Recognition by components: A theory of human image understanding. *Psychological Review*, *94*, 115-147.

Clark, J.M., & Paivio, A. (1991). Dual coding theory and education. *Educational Psychology Review*, *3* (3), 149-210.

Dansereau, D.F., Collins, K.W., McDonald, B.A., Holley, C.D., Garland, J., Diekhoff, G., & Evans, S.H. (1979). Development and evaluation of a learning strategy program. *Journal of Educational Psychology*, *71*, 64-73.

Decker, W.H., & Wheatley, P.C. (1982). Spatial grouping, imagery, and free recall. *Perceptual and Motor Skills*, *55*, 45-46.

Duong, L.V. (1991). *Perceptual Grouping.* Seattle: University of Washington, unpublished report.

Goodman, N. (1968). *The languages of art.* Indianapolis: Hackett.

Hirtle, S.C., & Jonides, J. (1985). Evidence of hierarchies in cognitive maps. *Memory and Cognition*, *13*, 208-217.

Hirtle, S.C., & Kallman, H.J. (1988). Memory for the locations of pictures: Evidence for hierarchical clustering. *American Journal of Psychology*, *101*, 159-170.

Hirtle, S.C., & Mascolo, H.F. (1986). Effect of semantic clustering on the memory of spatial locations. *Journal of Experimental Psychology: Language, Memory and Cognition*, *12*, 182-189.

Hoffman, D.D., & Richards, W.A. (1984). Parts of recognition. *Cognition*, *18*, 65-96.

Johnson, D.D., Pittelman, S.D., Heimlich, J.E. (1986). Semantic mapping. *Reading Teacher*, *39*, 778-783.

Kinchla, R.A., & Wolfe, J. (1979). The order of visual processing: Top-down", "bottom-up", or "middle-out"? *Perception and Psychophysics, 25*, 225-230.

Kinchla, R.A., Solis-Macias, V., & Hoffman, J. (1983). Attending to different levels of structure in a visual image. *Perception and Psychophysics, 33*, 1-10.

Kulhavy, R.W., Caterino, L.C., & Melchiori, F. (1989). Spatially cued retrieval of sentences. *The Journal of General Psychology, 116*, 297-304.

Kulhavy, R.W., Lee, J.B., & Caterino, L.C. (1985). Conjoint retention of maps and related discourse. *Contemporary Educational Psychology, 10*, 28-37.

Larkin, J.H., & Simon, H.A. (1987). Why a diagram is (sometimes) worth ten thousand words. *Cognitive Science, 11*, 65-99.

Lesaga, M.I. (1989). Gestalts and their components: Nature of information precedence. In B.E. Shepp & S. Ballesteros (Eds.) *Object perception: Structure and process*. Hillsdale, NJ: Lawrence Erlbaum Associates, 165-202.

Marr, D. (1982). *Vision*. New York: Freeman.

McNamara, T.P. (1986). Mental representations of spatial relations. *Cognitive Psychology, 18*, 87-121.

McNamara, T.P., Hardy, J.K., & Hirtle, S.C. (1989). Subjective hierarchies in spatial memory. *Journal of Experimental Psychology: Learning, Memory and Cognition, 15*, 211-227.

Navon, D. (1977). Forest before trees: The precedence of global features in visual perception. *Cognitive Psychology, 9*, 353-383.

Neisser, U. (1976). *Cognition and reality*. San Francisco: Freeman.

Owen, L.A. (1985a). Dichoptic priming effects on ambiguous picture processing. *British Journal of Psychology, 76*, 437-447.

Owen, L.A. (1985b). The effect of masked pictures on the interpretation of ambiguous pictures. *Current Psychological Research and Reviews, 4*, 108-118.

Paivio, A. (1971). *Imagery and verbal processes*. New York: Holt, Rinehart and Winston.

Paivio, A. (1983). The empirical case for dual coding. In J.C. Yuille (Ed.). *Imagery, memory and cognition*. Hillsdale: Lawrence Erlbaum, 310-332.

Palmer, S.E. (1975). Visual perception and world knowledge. In D.A. Norman and D.E. Rumelhart (Eds.), *Explorations in Cognition*. San Francisco: Freeman.

Paquet, L., & Merikle, P.M. (1984). Global precedence: The effect of exposure duration. *Canadian Journal of Psychology, 38*, 45-53.

Pinker, S. (1985). Visual cognition: An introduction. In S. Pinker (Ed.), *Visual cognition*. Cambridge, MA: MIT Press.

Pomerantz, J.R. (1986). Visual form perception: An overview. In E.C. Schwab & H.C. Nusbaum (Eds.) *Pattern recognition by humans and machines. Volume 2, Visual perception*. New York: Academic Press.

Pomerantz, J.R., Pristach, E.A., & Carson, C.E. (1989). Attention and object perception. In B.E. Shepp & S. Ballesteros (Eds.) *Object perception: Structure and process*. Hillsdale, NJ: Lawrence Erlbaum Associates, 53-90.

Pomerantz, J.R., Sager, L.C., & Stover, R.J. (1977). Perception of wholes and their parts: Some configural superiority effects. *Journal of Experimental Psychology: Human Perception and Performance, 3*, 422-435.

Pomerantz, J.R., & Schwaitzberg, S.D. (1975). Grouping by proximity: Selective attention measures. *Perception and Psychophysics, 18*, 355-361.

Pylyshyn Z.W. (1984). *Computation and cognition: Toward a foundation for cognitive science*. Cambridge, MA: MIT Press.

Rock, I. (1986). The description and analysis of object and event perception. In K.R. Boff, L. Kaufman & J.P. Thomas (Eds.) *The handbook of perception and human performance, Volume 2*. 33-1 - 33-71.

Rosch, E. (1978). Principles of categorization. In E. Rosch & B.B. Lloyd (Eds.) *Cognition and categorization*. Hillsdale NJ: Lawrence Erlbaum, 27-48.

Rosch, E., & Mervis, C.B. (1975). Family resemblances: Studies in the internal structure of categories. *Cognitive Psychology, 7*, 573-605.

Rumelhart, D.E., & Norman, D.A. (1981). Analogical processes in learning. In J.R. Anderson (Ed.), *Cognitive Skills and their Acquisition. Hillsdale*, NJ.: Lawrence Erlbaum.

Salomon, G. (1979). *Interaction of media, cognition and learning*. San Francisco: Jossey Bass.

Schlichtmann, H. (1985). Characteristic traits of the semiotic system "Map symbolism". *The Cartographic Journal, 22*, 23-30.

Schwartz, N.H., & Kulhavy, R.W. (1981). Map features and the recall of discourse. *Contemporary Educational Psychology, 6*, 151-158.

Schwartz, N.H., & Kulhavy, R.W. (1987). Map structure and the comprehension of prose. *Educational and Psychological Research, 7*, 113-128.

Schwartz, N.H., & Kulhavy, R.W. (1988). Encoding tactics in the retention of maps. *Contemporary Educational Psychology, 13,* 72-85.

Schwartz, N.H., & Phillippe, A.E. (1991). Individual differences in the retention of map. *Contemporary Educational Psychology, 16(2),* 171-182.

Schwartz, R.M., & Raphael, T.E. (1985). Concept of definition: A key to improving students' vocabulary. *The Reading Teacher, 39,* 198-205.

Treisman, A. (1988). Features and objects: The fourteenth Bartlett Memorial Lecture. *Quarterly Journal of Experimental Psychology: Human Experimental Psychology, 40A,* 210-237.

Uttal, W.R. (1988). *On seeing forms.* Hillsdale NJ: Lawrence Erlbaum Associates.

Wertheimer, M. (1938). *Laws of organization in perceptual forms in a source book for Gestalt psychology.* London: Routledge and Kegan Paul.

Winn, W.D. (1982). The role of diagrammatic representation in learning sequences, identification, and classification as a function of verbal and spatial ability. *Journal of Research in Science Teaching, 19,* 79-89.

Winn, W.D. (1983). Perceptual strategies used with flow diagrams having normal and unanticipated formats. *Perceptual and Motor Skills, 57,* 751-762.

Winn, W.D. (1988). Recall of the patterns, sequence and names of concepts presented in instructional diagrams. *Journal of Research in Science Teaching, 25,* 375-386.

Winn, W.D. (1989). The design and use of instructional graphics. In H. Mandl and J.R. Levin (Eds.). *Knowledge Acquisition from text and pictures.* North Holland: Elsevier, 125-144.

Winn, W.D., Li, T.Z., & Schill, D.E. (1991). Diagrams as aids to problem solving: Their role in facilitating search and computation. *Educational Technology Research and Development, 39,* 17-29.

Winn, W.D., & Solomon, C. (1991). *The effect of the rhetorical structure of diagrams on the interpretation of simple sentences.* Seattle, WA: University of Washington, unpublished manuscript.

Zwaan, E.W.J. (1965). *Links en rechts in waarneming en beleving.* (Left and right in visual perception as a function of the direction of writing). Doctoral Thesis, Rijksuniversiteit Utrecht, The Netherlands.

Chapter 2

Codes of Instructional Pictures

Bernd Weidenmann

University of the Armed Forces, Munich, FRG

ABSTRACT

The author argues that research on learning with graphics would greatly benefit from a systematic analysis of graphic codes. Instructional graphics are conceived as "visual arguments", created intentionally by a graphic author using graphic codes. Within this framework, learning with graphics is a problem solving activity with the aim of reconstructing the visual argument by interpreting the codes in an adequate manner. Two classes of graphic codes, i.e. "depicting codes" and "directing codes", are described and illustrated. Depicting codes are devices to construct a surface structure which is processed in analogy to real world perception. Directing codes are used by a graphic author to direct the picture processing of complex visual arguments in order for learners to perceive and process them sufficiently. Therefore, directing codes deserve the special interest of illustration research. The article ends with a prospectus of future research on codes of instructional graphics.

The main purpose of this chapter is to direct attention to the fact that illustration theory and research need a systematic analysis of graphic codes. Effective learning with pictures and graphics depends on the competence of a learner to "read" an illustration in a way that fits with the instructional intentions of a graphic designer. Graphic codes are the essential means of this communication process, but we know very little about the richness of instrutional graphic codes, about the ways illustrators use them, and about the cognitive demands and impacts of these codes with respect to the learner. The following considerations are a first attempt to structure the field.

Recent theory and research on learning from pictures shows a growing interest in explaining the evident instructional effectiveness of pictures (Willows & Houghton,1987; Mandl & Levin,1989). Levie (1978, p. 26) states efforts toward a "psychology of pictorial learning". New theories on knowledge acquisition, especially the theory of mental models, are invading illustration research (see Schnotz et al., and Tardieu & Gyselinck in this volume). More and more studies are designed to analyze how learners use and comprehend instructional pictures and graphics, and to identify the cognitive processes involved in these activities (see Maichle, Kirby, Seel & Dörr in this volume). This current approach is a further differentiation of earlier considerations on the relationship between instructional methods and cognitive operations (Salomon, 1979; Wittrock, 1979; Bovy, 1981). Traditional research so far has favoured the analysis of memory for pictures and illustrated texts.

It should be noted that the quality of the pictorial stimuli changed with the new approach. Today researchers prefer pictorial material which is more complex and more abstract than it used to be years ago. Representational pictures (Knowlton, 1966) have decreased in favour of logical pictures and pictorial analogies, because the present illustration research examines learning from pictures in the context of problem solving activities.

This new orientation in illustration research can be evaluated as important progress. At the same time a distinctive learner-orientated perspective runs the risk of neglecting the specific condition of the stimulus material. In the research on learning from texts, we find a variety of methods to analyse a text, for example its readability, cohesion, sequential order and information content (main ideas). The description of the stimulus material is an important prerequisite for the determination of a reader's performance, since there is a chance to identify the so-called encoding gap (Hannafin, 1988), the difference between intended and interpreted meaning, if the structure and content of a text is clear. Such careful analysis of the stimulus material seems to be regarded as needless effort in the research on learning from pictures and graphics. It is common practice to assess effects of illustrations without prior analysis of the graphic structure and message. This practice may be acceptable as long as only global effects of illustrations on the understanding of texts are under investigation. But an accurate analysis of the graphic stimulus is indispensible when the processing of instructional pictures and their use by learners is under exploration. The analysis of illustrations with respect to their structure and content turns out to be a definite problem for present research.

In order to analyze the structure of pictures, it is necessary to analyze their function. Instructional pictures are designed for communication. They convey information about specific content, which is mediated through a designer's knowledge of the content and through her or his ability to conceive an effective form of representation. Therefore instructional graphics can be analyzed from two perspectives. First, as externalizations of the designer's knowledge with respect to the content. Second, as an intentionally created means of communication. From the first perspective, an instructional picture or graphic may be more or less correct with respect to the specific content field. From the second perspective, a picture or graphic may be more or less effective with respect to the instructional intention.

Instructional pictures and graphics as visual arguments

In the process of designing an instructional illustration, the communicator transforms mental representations into graphic representations. Figure 1 is an illustration from a text on the system of blood pressure (Levin, Anglin & Carney, 1987, p. 60).

Obviously, this picture externalizes a dynamic mental model of the circulatory system with its component parts heart (pump), vessels, blood and arm. These components show a dynamic interplay while in two phases the heart presses blood through the vessels. The mental model shown in this illustration is far from being a complete representation of the knowledge about blood pressure and blood circulation. It doesn't consider the pulmonary system, the complete heart (which contains two pumps), the rhythmic expansion and contraction of the blood vessels. The mental model visualized by this picture is an incomplete and highly simplified representation of the state of affairs.

Unfortunately, we don't know the mental model of the author of this picture, but we can assume that illustrations in general are visualized interpretations of a domain by the author. For the preparation of an instructional graphic, the graphic communicator selects parts of his/her

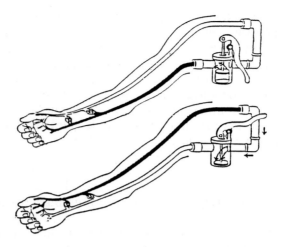

Figure 1. Illustration of the blood pressure system (Levin, Anglin & Carney, 1987). From A. Eisenberg & H. Eisenberg (1979), Alive and well: Decisions in health. New York: McGraw-Hill. Copyright by McGraw-Hill. Reprinted by permission.

mental representations and treats some parts as more important than others. These decisions are influenced by suppositions about the users of the picture. In figure 1, the illustrator interpreted and accentuated the function of the heart as a pump. She or he visualized this concept by choosing the metaphor of a hand-pump as part of a water pipe. We may assume that this graphic device was developed in order to facilitate the comprehension of the heart function by novices in physiology. At the same time, the designer expects that the readers are acquainted with hand-pumps and water pipes.

The decision to draw part of the illustration as a pictorial analogy (pump, water pipe), means to select a specific instructional method. Such conceptual and methodical decisions should be conceived as formulation of an argument. In order to visualize it, the designer has to transform it into a graphic language. Professional designers have a great number of graphic skills and graphic codes at their disposition. In figure 1 we see the effect of graphic skills in the depiction of the pump, the water pipe and the fingers. Additionally several pictorial codes like contour, symbolic colours (not to be seen in this reproduction), and arrows are used.

The expertise of a graphic designer is difficult to describe. "Using the visual to interpret the content for an effective message" (Abed, 1989, p. 30) is a very complex task, which becomes obvious by the choice of numerous solutions with equal value. This complexity and the lack of clear rules for creating instructional pictures and graphics is apparently no invitation for researchers to explore the design process. In this situation, a useful step is the reduction of complexity by adequate descriptive categories and fruitful research questions. The following two paragraphs are an attempt.

Means of graphic design: depicting codes and directing codes

Several authors tried to reduce the complexity of the graphic domain by taxonomies. Predominant are listings of picture types with respect to functions or purposes (Macdonald-Ross, 1977; Duchastel, 1978; Levie & Lentz, 1982; Levin, Anglin, & Carney, 1987). So we find pictures with iconic purpose, data display purpose, explanatory purpose, or operational purpose. Instructional graphics are classified as useful for a representational function, or an organisational and an interpretational function with respect to the learning of texts. Four possible functions of text illustrations are given: attentional functions, affective functions, cognitive functions, and compensatory functions.

Such classifications may serve as useful heuristics to explain empirical effects of instructional pictures and graphics. But if we take a design-oriented perspective we must look for categories which describe essential features of visual arguments. Figure 2 offers an example.

Most instructional illustrations contain depicting and directing features. Depicting codes are devices for constructing a surface structure which is processed by a perceiver in analogy to real world perception. Depicting codes simulate contour, shadow, perspective and other characteristics of object perception. The assumption that these codes are processed in analogy to real life experiences is the result of considerable experimental research. Here are two impressive examples. Kraft (1987) managed to show how pictures of persons recorded from different camera angles affected the viewers' comprehension and memory according to real-life-consequences of the induced viewer positions. Intraub and Richardson (1989) found that the subjects' recall and recognition of photographed scenes reveal a pronounced extension of the picture's boundary.

depicting features of instructional graphics	directing features of instructional graphics
aim: to facilitate perception of content	aim: to facilitate understanding of the visual argument
means: depicting codes - contour - shadowing - perspective - natural colors - natural size and proportions	means: directing codes - accentuations - principles of montage (contrast, spatial arrangement) - special cues (arrows, symbolic colors)
strategy: - conventional representation of reality - simulation of real perception	strategy: - unconventional representation of reality - cueing by logical and symbolic signs
task of the learner: attention to and use of the depicting codes in order to identify the content	task of the learner: attention to and use of the directing codes in order to understand the visual argument

Figure 2. Features of instructional graphics

Directing codes are a second class of codes in instructional graphics. Illustrators use them to convey a visual argument, which goes beyond the depicting of an object or a situation. Typically, directing codes appear as a deviation from real world appearance. With the help of these codes the graphic designer tries to direct the picture processing of the perceiver. In figure 1 we see some examples. Beneath the depicting codes which simulate the real world perception of an arm or a pump we notice several directing codes which facilitate the grasping of the central

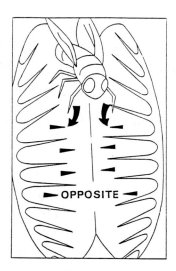

Figure 3. Example of visual cueing by directing codes. The arrows direct the viewers attention to the symmetric hairs of a Venus flytrap. From Beck, C.R. (1984). Copyright by Association for Educational Communications and Technology. Reprinted by permission.

visual argument which is that blood pressure is a function of the pump's position. This argument is accentuated by the arrangement of the two identical arms which show different phases of blood pressure, by the contrasting colour of the blood vessels, and by the arrows. These codes are used to direct such cognitive processes as comparing, generating inferences, and imagining motion. Other directing codes which are quite common in instructional graphics are special colours with a signaling function (for example in logical pictures) or exaggerations of special picture elements (for example size or thickness of contour) to accentuate importance.

In some publications (for example Beck, 1984) some of these codes are discussed under the label of visual cueing strategies. These authors restrict the functions of directing codes to a prompting of the learner's attention to relevant picture details. Figure 3 shows an example from the Beck study (1984, p. 210).

The arrows here are prompts to concentrate attention on the symmetric hairs of a Venus flytrap. But the richness of graphic directing codes cannot be grasped by analyzing only their "attentional function" (Levie & Lentz, 1982). In addition to these functions, graphic designers use them to stimulate and direct a great diversity of perceptual and cognitive processes.

Processing instructional pictures and graphics: a problem solving activity

Learners process depicting codes and directing codes in a different way. Levie states that "people' s responses to pictures seldom go beyond a simple labelling response accompanied by a fleeting affective reaction" (1978, p. 35). But with this he describes only the automatic processing of depicting codes. Pettersson describes this low-level-processing as follows: "1. The subject looks at the image. A few rapid eye fixations are made. 2. The information is handled as a "whole" in parallel, simultaneous, tentative, rough, holistic, and fast processing. 3. A "wholeness interpretation" occurs, recognition and meaning of the image content is formed very quickly- "immediately". 4. This interpretation is expressed by the use of a very limited number of words" (Pettersson 1988, p. 53). This "direct mode" of processing in analogy to real-world-perception is so salient, that some learners even process logical pictures as if they were representational. Mokros & Tinker (1987) call it the graph-as-picture-confusion.

If perceivers process directing codes they cannot use routines acquired by natural perception. Instead, directing codes shape picture processing into a problem solving activity. The problem to be solved is to find out what the graphic designer had intended to convey with the help of the chosen directing codes. The learner has to reconstruct the intentions and decisions of the designer, i.e. the full visual argument.

How successfully learners work on this problem solving task depends on individual specific variables as pictorial literacy (acquaintance with pictorial codes), attention or interest, and domain specific knowledge. In most cases, authors of instructional pictures or graphics seem to doubt these prerequisites, because they add verbal captions. But captions are seldom designed in a systematic way. Figure 2 could serve as a heuristic to formulate captions more purposely. First, captions can be written to safeguard depicting codes against an incomplete or incorrect identification. For example, such a caption could be necessary if a familiar object is depicted in an unconventional perspective, or if a previously unseen object is shown (for example the pump in figure 1). Second, a caption can be designed as a verbal reformulation of the visual argument or of several directing codes.

This approach could be an interesting perspective for future research on the effect of captions on the understanding of instructional pictures and graphics. Until now, only few studies have explored the effect of different sorts of captions. Recently, Bernard (1990) varied two types of captions. The descriptive captions "contain verbal information that overlap the illustration as exactly as possible", whereas the so-called instructive captions "were designed to aid in processing the illustration by suggesting people pathways through the illustrations" (Bernard, 1990, p. 219). On the basis of our approach, the first type of caption can be seen as a verbal cue for the learner to attend to the depicting codes. The second type of captions seems to verbally reformulate some graphic directing codes ("the pathways through the illustrations" are graphically signaled by arrows). The results show a remarkable effect of both types of captions. And, as in a former study by Weidenmann (1989), the illustrations-without-captions-condition did not outperform the text-only-condition. Mayer (1989) reported on a similar result with an illustrated text on the functioning of a hydraulic brake. Providing only pictures (without corresponding labels) did not allow students to build useful mental models of the system (p. 244). Such studies (see Peeck in this volume) reveal that many learners need captions or labels to extract the relevant pictorial information This seems to be especially the case for information presented by graphic directing codes.

Exploring the codes of instructional pictures and graphics

The analytic approach outlined in this chapter may stimulate some new research. First, we should investigate the process of designing instructional pictures or graphics with a combination of observational and explorational methods. The aim of this research is "getting the know-how of the master performer" (Macdonald-Ross, 1989, p. 146). Research on expertise is done in many domains, but we know nearly nothing about knowledge base and production decisions of professional graphic communicators. Rankin (1987) made a first step in asking authors of instrutional illustrations four questions: 1. What is the purpose of the illustration? 2. What is the message? 3. Could you briefly summarize the main points being made? 4. To what other purpose could the illustration be used?

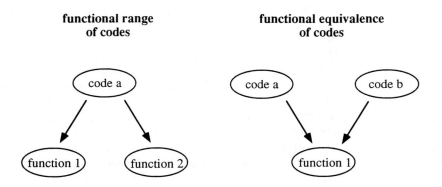

Figure 4. Two paradigms for exploring instructional codes

Research on graphic expertise is difficult to do for several reasons. What are the characteristics of a master performer? How are we able to make her or his implicit knowledge explicit? Are creative, idiosyncratic graphic solutions generalizable?

A second line of research with respect to the current approach is the empirical investigation of relations between graphic codes and modes of processing (modes in the sense of Pick & Saltzman, 1978). Here, two paradigms should be favoured (see Figure 4).

The first paradigm explores the functional range of codes or graphic signs with respect to the processing they stimulate in the learner. An arrow, for example, may induce a specific scanning direction (arrow as symbol for direction), or a movement image (arrow as symbol for motion) or an attention of focussing (arrow as sign). These are quite different cognitive processes activated by the same sign. The second research paradigm explores the functional equivalence of codes or graphic signs. Attention focussing, for example, can be achieved by an arrow, by a special color, by a thickened contour, by a frame, or other stimuli. This paradigm explores, how different graphic codes or signs are able to stimulate the same cognitive process. Both paradigms should be explored two-fold, from the viewpoint of graphic designers as well as from the perspective of learners. In the first case, conventions shared by graphic professionals will be investigated. In the second case, the learners way of processing specific graphic signs and graphic codes will be empirically described. The comparison between the two will reveal possible encoding gaps.

A typical encoding gap could be shown in a recent study by the author (Weidenmann, 1990). The material consisted of a highly illustrated biography of Hitler. The book was developed especially for juvenile readers (Bedürftig & Kalenbach, 1989). The graphic designer used a great number of graphic directing codes to convey complex visual arguments. For example, in illustrating the burning of banned books in May 1933, he placed the faces of some banned poets and writers into the smoke cloud of the burning books. With this montage, he wanted to visualize the statement of one of the banned poets, Heinrich Heine, who wrote the following a hundred years ago: "Where books are burned human beings will find the same end." An analysis of the processing of the text and illustrations revealed a rather disappointing processing quality of pictorial directing codes. For example, a cued recall procedure tested how precisely the readers remembered main ideas of pictures expressed essentially by directing codes. The mean score of this test proved to be very low. This is surprising considering that unfamiliar elements in pictures and deviations from real-life experience (this was typical for the chosen pictures) are supposed to be processed more vividly and remembered better (Loftus, 1976; Loftus & Mackworth, 1978; Friedman, 1979). A further analysis of the relations between diverse process and product variables revealed an interesting difference between the processing of text and pictures. With respect to text processing, we found the expected significant correlation between invested mental effort and knowledge acquisition. However this was not the case for the processing of the pictures. Students who reported having invested considerable mental effort toward understanding the pictures did not remember more pictorial main ideas than students who reported only a weak effort. Together with other data, this supports the interpretation that most students failed to process the directing codes in an adequate manner. So, many visual arguments expressed by the graphic communicator remained unnoticed.

Such results point out the importance of systematic research on codes of instructional pictures and graphics. The analytic approach which was roughly sketched in this chapter may serve as one possible approach to this complex task.

RÉSUMÉ

L'auteur défend l'idée que les recherches sur l'apprentissage à l'aide de graphiques bénéficieraient grandement d'une analyse systématique des codes graphiques. Les graphiques instructionnels doivent être considérés comme des "arguments visuels", où l'auteur du graphique utilise intentionnellement certains codes graphiques. Dans cette perspective, apprendre à l'aide de graphiques est une activité de résolution de problèmes ayant pour but de reconstruire l'argument visuel en interprétant les codes de manière adéquate. Deux classes de codes graphiques, les "codes qui dépeignent" et les "codes qui orientent", sont décrits et illustrés. Les codes qui dépeignent sont des moyens pour construire une structure de surface, qui est traitée de façon analogue à la perception du monde réel. Les codes qui orientent sont utilisés par l'auteur du graphique pour guider le traitement du dessin d'arguments visuels complexes afin que les apprenants les perçoivent et les traitent suffisamment. Pour cette raison, les codes qui orientent devraient faire l'objet d'un intérêt spécial dans les recherches sur les illustrations. L'article s'achève sur des propositions de recherches à venir sur les codes des graphiques instructionnels.

References

Abed, F. (1989). What training institutions should know about visual designers. *Educational Technology, 29*, 27-31.

Beck, C.R. (1984). Visual cueing strategies: pictorial, textual, and combinational effects. *Educational Communication and Technology Journal, 32* (4), 207-216.

Bedürftig, F., & Kalenbach, D. (1989). *Hitler* Bd. 1. Hamburg: Carlsen.

Bernard, R.M. (1990). Using extended captions to improve learning from instructional illustrations. *British Journal of Educational Technology, 21* (3), 215-255.

Bovy, R.C. (1981). Successful instructional methods: A cognitive information processing approach. *Educational Communication and Technology Journal, 29* (4), 203-217.

Duchastel, P. (1978). Illustrating instructional texts. *Educational Technology, 18*, 36-39.

Friedman, A. (1979). Framing pictures: The role of knowledge in automatized encoding and memory for gist. *Journal of Experimental Psychology: General, 108*, 316-355.

Hannafin, M.J. (1988). The effects of instructional explicitness on learning and error persistence. *Contemporary Educational Psychology, 13*, 126-132.

Intraub, H., & Richardson, M. (1989). Wide-angle memories of close-up scenes. *Journal of Experimental Psychology: Learning, Memory, and Cognition, 15* (2), 179-187.

Knowlton, J.Q. (1966). On the definition of picture. *Audiovisual Communication Review, 14*, 157-183.

Kraft, R. (1987). The influence of camera angle on comprehension and retention of pictorial events. *Memory and Cognition, 15* (4), 291-307.

Levie, W.H. (1978). A prospectus for instructional research on visual literacy. *Educational and Communication Technology Journal, 26* (1), 25-35.

Levie, W.H., & Lentz, R. (1982). Effects of text illustrations: A review of research. *Educational Communication and Technology Journal, 30*, 195-232.

Levin, J.R., Anglin, G.J., & Carney, R.N. (1987). On empirically validating functions of pictures in prose. In D.M. Willows & H.A. Houghton (Eds.). *The psychology of illustration*, Vol. I (pp. 51-85). New York: Springer.

Loftus, G.R. (1976). A framework for a theory of picture recognition. In R.A. Monty, & J.W. Senders (Eds.). *Eye movements and psychological processes* (pp. 499-534). New York: Wiley.

Loftus, G.R., & Mackworth, N.H. (1978). Cognitive determinants of fixation location during picture viewing. *Journal of Experimental Psychology: Human Learning and Memory, 4*, 565-576.

Macdonald-Ross, M. (1977). Graphics in texts. *Review of Research in Education, 5*, 49-85.

Macdonald-Ross, M. (1989). Towards a graphic ecology. In H. Mandl & J.R. Levin (Eds.). *Knowledge acquisition from text and pictures* (pp. 145-154). Amsterdam: North Holland.

Mandl, H., & Levin, J.R. (Eds.). (1989). *Knowledge acquisition from text and pictures*. Amsterdam: North-Holland.

Mayer, R.E. (1989). Systematic thinking fostered by illustrations in scientific text. *Journal of Educational Psychology, 81* (2), 240-246.

Mokros, J.R., & Tinker, R.F. (1987). The impact of microcomputer-based labs on children's ability to interpret graphs. *Journal of Research in Science Teaching, 24* (4), 369-383.

Pettersson, R. (1988). Interpretation of image content. *Educational Communication and Technology Journal, 36*, (1), 45-55.

Pick, H.L., & Saltzman, E. (1978). Modes of perceiving and processing information. In H.L. Pick & E. Saltzman (Eds.). *Modes of perceiving and processing information* (pp. 1-20). Hillsdale, NJ: Erlbaum.

Rankin, R.O. (1987). The development of an illustration design model. *Educational Technology - Research and Development, 37*, 25-46.

Salomon, G. (1979). *Interaction of media, cognition and learning.* San Francisco: Jossey Bass.

Weidenmann, B. (1989). When good pictures fail: An information-processing approach to the effect of illustrations. In H. Mandl, & J.R. Levin (Eds.). *Knowledge acquisition from text and pictures* (pp. 157-170). Amsterdam, NY: Elsevier.

Weidenmann, B. (1990). *Lernen mit einem Sachcomic.* Abschlußbericht zu einer Studie im Auftrag der Stiftung Lesen und der Bundeszentrale für politische Bildung. (in press).

Willows, D.M., & Houghton, H.A. (Eds.). (1987). *The psychology of illustration.* New York: Springer.

Wittrock, M. (1979). The cognitive movement in instruction. *Educational Researcher, 8*, (2), 5-11.

Comprehension of Graphics
W. Schnotz and R. W. Kulhavy (Editors)
© 1994 Elsevier Science B.V. All rights reserved.

Chapter 3

Spatial Metaphors and Logical Pictures

August Fenk

University of Klagenfurt, Austria

ABSTRACT

This paper studies the following, closely related questions: Where do "logical" pictures said to be arbitrary and non-representational get their form? And what makes them an appropriate cognitive and communicative instrument? Obviously these pictures do not portray visible objects and they cannot portray invisible mental models. Thus, logical pictures cannot be classified as "iconic", if the term "iconic" is reserved for cases of similarity established by imitating or simulating that which ist represented. It is more likely that they are transformations of spatial metaphors into visual analogues, mapping the spatial allusion of the verbal metaphor into a two-dimensional representation. This visual analogue increases the efficiency of the metaphor as a heuristic tool in providing visual control of the construction of mental models. And if we are familiar with the verbal metaphor, the "arbitrary" picture determined by this metaphor is to a certain degree "self-explanatory". Two simple experiments, conducted by students, are reported: They demonstrate the application of guessing-game techniques in order to measure text-picture-transinformation, and their results indicate that the degree of enhancement of text-comprehension yielded by the logical picture depends on the success of the translation of the spatial metaphor into the illustration.

Several authors suggest a classification of instructional pictures as representational, analogical, or arbitrary. According to Alesandrini, arbitrary pictures include graphs, diagrams, flowcharts and, in particular, graphic organizers, hierarchies and networks "representing important relationships in the text such as comparing and contrasting concepts." (Alesandrini, 1984, p. 71). Arbitrary pictures are also termed "non-representational" or "logical" pictures "because those highly schematized visuals do not look like the things they represent but are related logically or conceptually." (ib., p. 70). But which "things", if any, do they represent? And where do they get their shape from, if they are "arbitrary" and "non-representational"? What links them up with the language system and and makes them useful for text comprehension?

Weidenmann (1988) argues that texts as well as pictures should be regarded as "objectivations of mental models" (p. 40), and that for an operative pictorial effect, i.e. in order to influence the mode of processing, logical pictures are the most appropriate choice (p. 163). But why are precisely those pictures which are said to be "non-representational" assumed to be the most appropriate ones in the control and self regulation of mental processes and operations?

In order to answer such questions, this paper emphasizes the relations between logical pictures and metaphors - without losing sight of the convention (cf. Mac Cormac, 1985, p. 143) according to which the term "metaphor" is reserved for verbal expressions. These relations can best be illustrated by means of "logical pictures" in a narrow sense, i. e. in the sense of graphics used to depict those ("logical") relations between concepts which are prerequisites for, or part of, definitions and categorical syllogisms. Pure graphical components and pure graphical configurations are not apt to explain themselves, because they cannot achieve self-referential levels or metalevels of discourse (cf. Fenk, 1990, p. 367). Nevertheless they are useful within such a metalevel discourse: when linguistic expressions are used to state or explicate relations between other linguistic expressions - as it is the case in definitions and in semiotic discourse, where certain symbols (usually words) are used to describe the function of the "symbol" and of other signs - these relations can be made transparent by logical pictures.

The following brief survey presents the stages in our argument. Drawing on quotations from Peirce (1906, 1976) as well as Ogden & Richards (1923), Thesis 1 establishes the premise that "pure" symbols as well as "pure" icons are "incomplete". With the help of logical pictures, an attempt is made in Thesis 2 to sharpen the concept of the "icon" and, as a further step, to develop the concept of the "diagram": while the iconic symbol realizes both the symbolic and the imitative function, these two functions complement each other by means of special elements in the diagram. Thesis 3 maintains that these abstract drawings are not imitative in a strict sense; on the other hand they are not really "arbitrary" but motivated by our spatial metaphors: diagrams and logical pictures in general are two-dimensional figures capturing the figural allusions of our figures of speech. The metaphor's virtual space is materialized in a spatial, two-dimensional analogue. This analogue prevents abstract propositional and mathematical thinking from losing its firm foundation in topological thinking. Expressed with another metaphor: this analogue provides a form for formal operations, and it provides visual control of the construction of "mental models". A pilot-study reported in section 3.2 demonstrates that a literal translation of the metaphor's spatial references into a picture format increases text-picture coherence and the extent to which the picture reduces the cognitive load of processing the text and vice versa. The last section of the paper compares different views of the relation and co-evolution of external and internal representations. To sum up Thesis 4: spatial methaphors seem to play the role of a cognitive tool which we can use to create new tools, i.e. new metaphors and graphic analogues.

"Pure" symbols and "pure" icons are incomplete

Peirce on the one hand and Ogden & Richards on the other hand are sometimes (e.g. von Glasersfeld, 1982, p. 194) referred to as proponents of conflicting semiotic positions. But the following quotations from these authors read like different versions of the doctrine of a triadic nature of sign and of the thesis stated above.

Peirce distinguishes three qualities and/or classes of signs, called "symbol", "icon" and "index", and characterizes them as follows: "They seem to be all trichotomies, which form an attribute to the essentially triadic nature of a Sign. I mean because three things are concerned in the functioning of a Sign; the Sign itself, its Object and its Interpretant" (1906, p. 496 f.). "(Strictly pure Symbols can signify only things familiar, and those only insofar as they are familiar)" (ib., p. 513).

"A pure icon /.../ asserts nothing. /.../ A pure index simply forces attention to the object /.../ An icon can only be a fragment of a completer sign" (1976-edition, p. 242). "But a symbol, if sufficiently complete always involves an index, just as an index sufficiently complete involves an icon" (ib., p. 256).

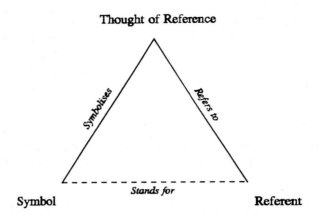

Figure 1. The Ogden & Richards - diagram, simplified, (Ogden & Richards, 1923/1985, p. 11).

Ogden & Richards (1923) comment on their famous triangle (see figure 1) as follows:

"Between the symbol and the referent there is no relevant relation other than the indirect one, which consists in its being used by someone to stand for a referent. Symbol and Referent, that is to say, are not connected directly (and when /.../ we imply such a relation, it will merely be an imputed, as opposed to a real, relation) but only indirectly round the two sides of the triangle" (ib., p. 11 f.) ". An exceptional case occurs when the symbol used is more or less directly like the referent for which it is used, as for instance, it may be when it is an onomatopoeic word, or an image, or a gesture, or a drawing. In this case the triangle is completed; its base is supplied /.../ Its greater completeness does no doubt account for the immense superiority in efficiency of gesture languages /.../ Standing for and representing are different relations". (Footnote in Ogden & Richards, 1923, p. 12)

The remarks by Ogden & Richards on the efficiency of gesture language, and by Schopenhauer (n.d., p. 142 f) on the relationship between gesticulation and logics, might suggest that logical pictures - like the Ogden & Richards triangle - complete texts in the way gestures complete speech. Could it be the case that the form of gestures and the form of logical pictures have a common (mental? metaphorical?) origin? Or do the pictures take their form from gestures, as if they were a recording of them? This possibility would merely shift the focus of our question: where does the form of gestures originate? At least with regard to the form of pictures we have a tentative answer (s. Thesis 3). The route to this answer leads via an analysis of two different modalities in which symbolic and iconic functions may complement and complete one another.

"Symbolising" and "imitating" fall together in the "iconic symbol" and complement each other, with special elements, in the diagram

The picture story in figure 3 (see also Fenk, 1990, p. 367) was partly inspired by the Ogden & Richards diagram, but here the term "thought" (Peirce's "interpretant") is replaced by the term "Concept" at the top of the triangle. In this way, the left side of the triangle can be associated with the intension of concepts while the right side is associated both with the extension of concepts (falling) and with the process of concept formation (rising).

The picture story is also inspired by Peirce's terminology, but "symbol" and "icon" refer explicitly to different functions and not to different classes of sign. The distinction between "index", "icon" and "symbol" cannot be upheld if we mean distinct classes (instead of functions) of signs (Fenk, 1992b). Since we interpret every event as an indication of something else (of causes, correlations, etc.) the concept of "sign" becomes empty when it includes "indices" (in the sense of indications and symptoms). Moreover, similarity is neither a sufficient nor even necessary condition for "reference" (cf. Goel, 1991, p. 41) nor for "representation" and for "signs" subsumed under "representation"; only when similarity is achieved by imitation, can we speak of a case of external "representation" (s. fig. 2). The necessary and sufficient condition for the symbolic function (and, depending on the interpretation of this term, also for the sign-function in general) is the encoding of a concept or proposition. We may speak of iconic symbols when symbols - as in the case of pictograms and onomatopoetic words - imitate or simulate the objects that fall under the encoded concept. Logical pictures and diagrams, however, must be considered as combinations of separate graphic and symbolic elements; the graphic elements take on their significance, or their context-related meaning only be means of the symbolic elements.

A. Fenk

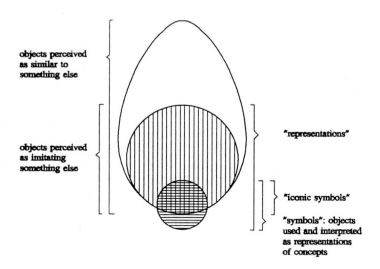

objects perceived
as similar to
something else

objects perceived
as imitating
something else

"representations"

"iconic symbols"

"symbols": objects
used and interpreted
as representations
of concepts

Figure 2. A logical picture concerning relations between semiotic concepts.

"Pure" symbol:
As illustrated in the first triangle at the top of figure 3, the "pure" symbol, first of all, denotes (the "intension"? of) a concept.

The concept is the result of cognitive processes like the detection of invariants, like abstraction and classification - including the classification of an object as a symbol, and the detection of what is invariant in the contexts where this object is used to depict other "objects". "Objects" is used here in a broad sense, comprising even "symbols" which are "objects" interpreted as referring to a concept and thus functioning as symbols (see figure 2); each symbol, and also the symbol "symbol", can become the referent of another symbol. In self-referential or meta-level discourse the direct connection between S and O proves to be superficial, or "imputed".

"Pure" icon:
The situation changes in the case of a representation, which we here call "imitative". What is meant is the essence of terms such as "imitating", "simulating", "picturing", "modelling", "enacting" ... - all of which are processes where the goal and the result is similarity between representation and represented.

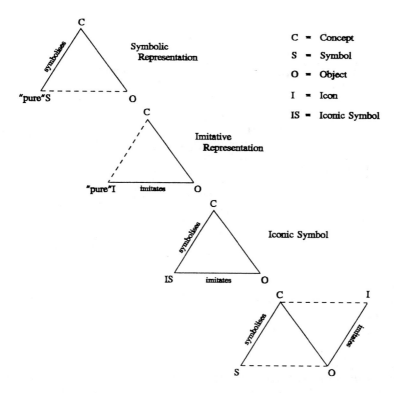

Figure 3. A puicture story, ending with a diagram of the diagrammatic function. From Fenk, A. (1990, p. 367). Copyright by Leuchtturm-Verlag. Reprinted by permission.

Similarity, however, as we know, is often caused by processes other than imitative as well; the reflection of a tree in water resembles the tree, but no one can maintain that the water is "imitating" or "simulating" the tree. (Even in a landscaped garden where the reflection of a tree or a castle in a pond is deliberately arranged by the architect, the similarity between the castle and its reflection is a result of natural laws and not of imitation). Such common features or similarities are neither necessary nor sufficient for representation. But this is only a negative "definition" of representation. Our positive argument says: When similarity is established by imitation, this is a sufficient condition for representation and for the kind of representation we call "iconicity".[1]

But even in those cases when similarity is achieved by imitation, imitation is not directly referring to a concept. For this imitative representation we construct a similar triangle as for the symbolic representation; in this second triangle (in figure 3) the connection with the concept is "imputed" (shown by the dotted line in the diagram).

Iconic symbol:
If we superimpose our triangle 2 on triangle 1, we see three solid sides. The symbol is, in Peirce's terminology, "completed"; symbolic function and imitative function coincide. This is the case in "iconic symbols", like onomatopoetic words or pictograms. This third triangle in our picture-story is, in some way, "authorized" by Ogden & Richards (see their footnote quoted under Thesis 1). But their expression "representing" was not adopted to depict the base line of our triangle, because nowadays this term is currently used in a broader sense, including symbolising, imitating, and "standing for".

Diagram:
When the two triangles are unfolded along the "C-O" axis, S and I are in diametrically opposite positions, namely as those functions which are only conceptually separable in the case of the iconic symbol and are realised by separate and complementary elements in the diagram: Graphic elements take on the imitative function, symbols (like "I", "O") give meaning to the graphic elements.

Eco (1985, p. 213) maintains that a picture does not resemble the object represented but merely our "perceptive model of the object". If we read the "O" of our parallelogram as the "perceptive model of the object" (or as the mental image), two types of internal representation oppose one another along the short diagonal (C,O), between which according to Winn (1988, p. 63) the "mental model" proposed by Johnson-Laird (1983) would be located, while on the long diagonal (S, I) there are two types of external representation each linked to a direct partner in the internal representation.

Our attempt to develop a concept of the "diagram" from the concept of iconicity can only be considered successful if one follows Peirce in calling "pure forms" "iconic" and regards "iconicity" as an extremely broad term. If, however, the concept of iconicity is reserved for instances of a perceived similarity between representation and represented, achieved by simulation, then the concept of "object" and of "simulation" must be broadly defined so that such pictures can be classified as "iconic". For which (mental?) "object" e.g. in our triangular diagram (fig. 3) is "simulated"? The triangles which were used to explain the concept of iconicity cannot portray, simulate or be isomorphic with this or any other concept of iconicity. Hence the form of logical pictures cannot be seen to be the result of direct imitation or simulation. Nevertheless their form is obviously not completely arbitrary. But what precisely is the origin of their particular form?

Logical pictures are determined by spatial metaphors

Theoretical considerations

An analysis of the semantic function of logical pictures might follow a line of arguments concerning (a) some special qualities of metaphors and (b) their function on the meta-level of discourse where (c) the use of logical pictures concretizing spatial metaphors activates our visual "surveying-system" and (d) induces "analogical" interpretations with a minimum of cognitive costs:

(a)   Schroeder (1989, p. 14) points out that Peirce introduced the term "hypoicon" in order to describe the icon as something, which is not only like anything else, but is used as a sign (of that thing), in which, says Peirce, "likeness is aided by conventional rules."[2] These hypoicons comprise images (likeness is the most prominent feature), diagrams (in a very broad sense) and "metaphors" (see figure 4).

According to Peirce metaphors are those hypoicons "which represent the representative character of a representation by representing a parallel in something else". But if reckoned among (hypo)icons at all, metaphors seem to play a very special role there: apart from a direct interaction with the extralinguistic world, only metaphors offer a possibility of generating new concepts (Rauh, 1989, p. 258 f). And because of their "intralinguistic" origin (Rauh, 1989, p. 261), "likeness" has a very special quality in metaphors.

(b)   The majority of our expressions for "phenomena" in cognition and communication is metaphorical (e.g. Waltz, 1978, Johnson & Lakoff, 1982), and according to Macdonald-Ross (1979, p. 233) "all our metaphors of knowledge are spatial". (One might even doubt whether these expressions, which apply spatial concepts to other aspects of 'reality', should be classified as metaphors, because there are no non-

figural alternatives: "The language, whatever it is, leaves us no choice."
Miller, 1985, p. 154)

(c)   In illustrations, abstract ideas can be concretized via spatial
metaphors (Winn, 1988, p. 59); and "all our knowledge, when placed in
a diagram becomes thus spatial, and thus amenable to pattern-
recognition capability inherent in our perceptual system."(Macdonald-
Ross, 1979, p. 232 f.)

(d)   For those who are acquainted with a certain verbal metaphor (or
metaphor theme), the visuals determined by this metaphor are not
arbitrary and - like metaphors - are "self-explanatory" to a certain
degree. Logical pictures induce - without demanding too many legends
and explanatory notes - an interpretation of graphic figures "by
analogy" to the relevant figure of speech (and an interpretation of
propositions by analogy to graphical figures). They constitute suitable
material for "comprehension", if "comprehension" is the detection and
construction of correspondences between different representations.

Take, for example, the visuals in this paper. Figures 1 - 4 are "logical"
pictures in a rather literal meaning of "logical" picture, i.e. in the sense
of graphics applicable in semiotics and in class logic. They try to make
relations between semiotic concepts transparent by superimposing
graphic figures on our figures of speech:

Figure 4 refers to the metaphor of conceptual hierarchies and
subsumptions. And figure 2, showing the symbol coming out of the
shell, refers to the metaphor of concepts including less extensive
concepts; the overlap cannot exceed the size of the narrow concept, and
only the circle with the larger circumference and diameter - only the
wider or broader concept - can contain or include the other one. The
triangles (figures 1 and 3) allude to the metaphor of the direct (straight
and short) or indirect ways in which concepts are connected. Metrical
properties become even more important in figure 5 which refers to
empirical (rather than "logical") stated relations: Only if one is used to
think of concepts like "time" or "relationship" as a quantity or a
dimension or a scale is one able to construct and correctly interpret
such more or less Cartesian diagrams (Fenk, 1987, p. 30). Again, the
linear scale is sometimes referred to as a special case of the path
metaphor (see Rice, 1991).

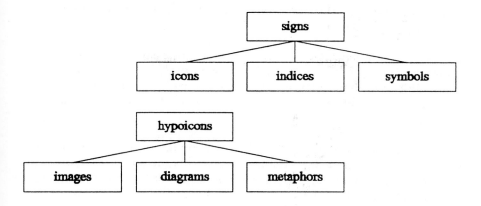

Figure 4. Peirce's subdivision of "signs" and "hypoicons".

The results of a pilot-study

Two simple experiments were carried out in order to demonstrate the influence of the metaphorical expressions in a text on text-picture composition (Exp. 1) and to test the assumption that the closest translation of the spatial metaphor into the two-dimensional representation would be the most effective one for reducing the informational content of a given text (Exp. 2). The basic idea for an economical experimental design of both experiments was to create a situation where the hypothesized influence of the metaphor comes into conflict with other tendencies determining the diagram, so that the metaphor's influence would become apparent in interacting with, and perhaps overcoming the conflicting factor.

Since our common front and back terms (and our forward and backward gestures) for the future and the past do not readily offer themselves for a direct transformation into a two-dimensional representation of the time axis, the direction of the time axis might be inspired by the content-specific metaphors in the corresponding text. If, for instance, the diagram refers to the evolution of species, the use of the metaphorical expression "phylogenetic tree" and of associated expressions in the corresponding text is expected to induce a tendency to an upward ordering of the time axis, i.e. in the vertical direction in which trees usually grow.

A candidate for a conflicting factor is the direction of text-processing: In European languages the written text "grows" and reads from left to right within the line. Remembering Traugott's (1975, p. 214) remark that verbal "left-right expressions for time are virtually nonexistent", this text-direction - instead of any metaphors - should be made responsible for the strong tendency found in English speakers, as compared to Hebrew and Arabic speakers, "to portray temporal concepts from left to right" (Tversky et al., 1991, p. 529) when drawing a diagram. Moreover, this text-direction might be responsible for the fact, that the left-to-right orientation of the time axis and of flow diagrams became the "normal" format, from which the (English speaking) subjects in the experiments of Winn (1982, 1983) extracted information faster and more accurately than in the case of an "unanticipated format" ordering the evolution of dinosaurs from right to left.

Experiment 1

Sixteen "experimenters" - I am indebted to the students attending a lecture on empirical methods in media research (winter 91/92) - asked a total of 84 subjects, which one of four given drafts they would combine with a given text on the evolution of Hominoidea. These drafts were four different orientations (upward, downward, to the right, to the left) of a phylogenetic tree (figure 5); the names of the species (Pongo, Pan, Gorilla, ...) were always written in horizontal position within a circle at the end of the "branches".

The upward-orientation was expected to be preferred, followed by the downward-version, i.e. the tree's mirror-inverted counterpart, which might also benefit from another direction of text-processing - from line to line and from top to bottom - and from the fact, that this is a quite "normal" format of genealogical tables in history books. The right-to-left version was assumed to be worse, because neither trees (nor their root-stocks) nor texts "grow" from right to left. (These hypotheses have been stated in a theoretical study by the author, 1991, p. 14, and were examined in Fenk, 1992a.)

The results: The hypothesized rank order proved to be valid with the exception that the left-to-right version surpassed the downward version. The four versions with the number of choices in brackets: upward (42), to the right (20), downward (16), to the left (6). Hence, 69% of the subjects (58 out of 84) chose one of the two vertical orientations, and

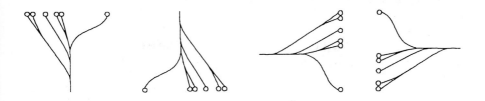

Figure 5. Four different orientations of a phylogenetic tree. From Fenk, A. (1992a, p. 162). Copyright by Leuchtturm-Verlag. Reprinted by permission.

50% of the subjects chose the upward version - despite the fact, that the upward ordering neglects both directions of text-processing as well as the usual direction of the time axis in diagrams, and presumably due to the spatial metaphors occuring in the corresponding text. (For instance: "Die stammesgeschichtliche Entwicklung und Ausdifferenzierung bis in die Gegenwart herauf ..." - "The phylogenetic evolution and differentiation up to the present ..."). The right-to-left order, which does not map with any direction of "growing" in anything relevant (trees; texts; time axis in "normal" diagrams) marks the endpoint of the rank order.

Experiment 2

In this experiment a more time-consuming performance score was used in order to measure picture-text-"transinformation", or, to be more precise, to measure the reduction of the subjective text-information (in bits) induced by a given picture. This performance score is in some respects similar to Goldsmith's (1984) "impoverished text" method measuring the "predictability" of a text, but quantifies "predictability" in terms of information theory. Only the two extreme positions of the hypothesized rank order (see experiment 1) were compared. Three students tested thirteen subjects. 8 of the subjects were shown the upward position, 5 of them the right-to-left position. Then all subjects were presented with the corresponding text. This time, a few crucial words (a total of 54 letters) in the text were omitted and had to be guessed letter by letter; there was only one guess per letter, and in cases of a wrong response the experimenter answered with the correct letter (The guessing game and accompanying formula to calculate information

A. Fenk

Table 1. The results of a guessing game (see text. Source: Fenk, 1992a, p. 165)

	mean number of errors	informational content	mean time taken for guessing
upward group	13.75	1.525 bit	9.87 min
right-to-left group	17.40	1.859 bit	10.20 min

content from the relative frequency of errors is taken from Weltner, 1973)[3].

The hypothesis that the "upward-group" would perform better than the "right-to-left group" was verified (see table 1). This indicates that the upward growing phylogenetic tree was more "successful" in reducing the cognitive costs of processing the corresponding text. And the subjects of the "right-to-left group", as compared to the "upward group", did not take much notice of the diagram during the cloze procedure; obviously, they did not expect as much help for their guessing-performance.

Spatial metaphors are heuristic tools and are used to create new metaphors and visual analogues

Let us return to the point that logical pictures (like our figures 1-5) do not directly imitate or simulate any reference-object existing in our perceptual world, and that they do not imitate or simulate any perceptive model of such an object. On a more general level, this problem might be discussed within a theory of "structural representation" and "surrogative reasoning" (Swoyer, 1991). Instead of that we will adhere to our focus and advance the question, what might be "representational" and "iconic" in "non-representational" pictures. Some lines of argument relevant to our question are:

(a)   Diagrams are viewed as "externalised" mental models and mental operations. (Suggestions of this type are discussed in Fenk, 1991).

Sometimes they are regarded as "simulating" mental processes. This view corresponds to Salomon's "supplantation"-hypothesis:
"Thus, to the extent that a symbol system entails coding elements that simulate (or can be made to simulate) a hypothesized internal process of elaboration, it can supplant the process and become internalized for use as a mental tool /.../ Yet, there is no theoretical reason to believe that overt modeling, or supplantation, of an elaborative transformation could not also be accomplished by nonnotational systems. To the extent that specific mental elaborations are of the logical-verbal rather than imagery type, nonnotational overt modeling should be capable of supplanting them and hence make them available to learning by observation" (Salomon, 1979, p. 234).

This view of diagrams as well as Weidenmann's (1988) view of pictures as "objectivations" of mental models assume that there is, in some way, an "isomorphic" relation between internal and external representations. On the other hand: Mental processes, even when dealing with forms and shapes, do not have any form or shape that might be externalised or simulated. (Only in our metaphors on mental "phenomena" is there talk about the form, or structure, or architecture of such "phenomena". See point c).

(b)   Peirce's theory disposes of this problem in a very radical way. In this theory, the division "internal/external world" is more or less abolished, and the term "sign" is broad enough to comprise thoughts. And the term "iconicity" is broad enough to comprise the syntactical form of sentences and syllogisms:

"For Reasoning, nay, Logic generally, hinges entirely on Forms. You, Reader, will not need to be told that a regularly stated Syllogism is a Diagram /.../ No pure Icons represent anything but Forms! no pure Forms are represented by anything but Icons." (Peirce, 1906, p. 513).

Our logical pictures, without the symbols completing them, might then be classified as "pure icons".

(c)   We regard logical pictures as the descendants of spatial metaphors and as visual analogues of more or less "self-explanatory" metaphors. (This view seems to hold - irrespective of the role we ascribe to gesticulation: Logical pictures accompanying written texts on abstract thoughts, as well as the more dynamic gestures accompanying the spoken text, may be seen as direct transformations of spatial metaphors; but gestures might also be seen as mediators in the process mapping spatial metaphors into logical pictures.) The advantages of this view: We do not need to make any assumptions about the "form" of thoughts. And it does not afford an "overextension" of the concept of "iconicity". Metaphorical expressions (like "overextension of concepts") may be "figurative" and "graphical" in a metaphorical sense - but they are not "iconic" in our restricted sense of the word, because they do not produce perceptual similarity.

This "economic" view leaves out the question as to the origin of the spatial metaphors determining our logical pictures. A probable answer to the question follows:

It is our spatial thinking that has invented spatial metaphors as an appropriate tool for metalevel cognition and communication and that has created logical pictures for just the same purpose. These pictures are a very recent cultural achievement (Tversky et al., 1991), and so they could go back to the spatial allusions of already existing metaphors. (Some of our metaphors in contemporary scientific language again seem to be inspired by already existing logical pictures.) From this point of view the metaphor of language as the "Procrustean bed" of thinking should be replaced by the metaphor of language as a tool of cognition and communication: this instrument or tool determines thinking, but is in turn created - and permanently modified - by our cognitive system. Spatial metaphors seem to play a key-role in this co-evolution of language and thinking and in the co-evolution of mental modelling and overt symbolic manipulation: with the aid of metaphors we produce new metaphors and visual analogues in just the way we use tools to manufacture new tools.

Our considerations have been of a merely terminological and theoretical character. But together with the experiments reported they provide at least one recommendation for the designer of instructional "text-picture compositions": In order to achieve high text-picture coherence, one should put stress on "viable" figures of speech and design pictures precisely mapping these spatial metaphors! These pictures then increase the efficiency of the metaphor as a heuristic instrument in providing a form or a matrix permitting direct visual control of the admissability of mental drafts, models, and operations. Thus, logical pictures in context are apt to activate that deeply rooted and highly developed potential for topological orientation, which has created our spatial metaphors.

Notes

1 A second possibility of developing a simple and sound concept of iconicity (Fenk, 1987, 1990) should be mentioned in passing here. In one respect it essentially boils down to Peirce's considerations: "pure" icons do not really exist! However, in other respects, this second posibility implies a radical rejection of Peirce's distinction between signs (see fig. 4): given the premise that symbolicity, i.e. the function of denoting a concept or a proposition, is a necessary and sufficient condition for "sign", iconicity is not more than a possible attribute of signs. The provocative consequence: nothing but a symbol can be iconic!

2 In our "iconic symbols", likeness is also aided by conventional rules. (Each symbol has to follow some conventions regarding its form in order to be identifiable as a certain symbol.) If one wanted to classify iconic symbols as hypoicons (see fig. 4), this would mean neglecting their function as symbols and cause additional difficulties: should, for example, pictograms and onomatopoetic words be classified as diagrams or even as metaphors? Or rather as "images": but how could we then claim that in pictograms or in onomatopoetic words "likeness is the most prominent feature"?

3 Actually, Weltner's procedure is not standardized for small gaps. Hence, for the main experiment a different procedure (cf. Fenk & Vanoucek, 1992) with a more global scope is applied.

RÉSUMÉ

Cet article étudie les deux questions suivantes, étroitement liées: où les dessins "logiques", dits arbitraires et non représentationnels, prennent-ils leur forme ? Et qu'est-ce-qui en fait un instrument cognitif et de communication approprié ? De toute évidence, ces dessins ne représentent pas d'objets visibles et ne peuvent figurer des modèles mentaux invisibles. Les dessins logiques ne peuvent donc pas être classés comme "iconiques", si on considère que le terme iconique est réservé aux cas de similarité établie par imitation ou par simulation du représenté. Il est plus probable qu'il s'agisse de transformations de métaphores spatiales en analogues visuels, mettant en correspondance l'allusion spatiale de la métaphore verbale avec une représentation bi-dimensionnelle. Cet analogue visuel augmente l'efficacité de la métaphore en tant qu'outil heuristique, fournissant un contrôle visuel de la construction des modèles mentaux. Et pour qui est familier avec la métaphore verbale, l'image arbitraire déterminée par cette métaphore est, dans une certaine mesure, "auto-explicative". Deux expériences simples, conduites par des étudiants, sont rapportées. Elles montrent l'application de techniques type devinette pour mesurer l'information qui transite entre texte et dessin. Leurs résultats indiquent en outre que le degré d'amélioration de la compréhension atteint avec le dessin, dépend du succès de la traduction de la métaphore spatiale en illustration.

References

Alesandrini, K.L. (1984). Pictures in adult learning. *Instructional Science, 13*, 63-77.

Eco, U. (1985). *Einführung in die Semiotik* (5th ed.). München: Fink.

Fenk, A. (1987). Zum Verhältnis von "Darstellung" und "Aussage". Am Beispiel der "didaktischen Visualisierung". In H. Kautschitsch & W. Metzler (Eds.), *Schriftenreihe Didaktik der Mathematik* (Vol. 15). Wien: Hölder-Pichler-Tempsky/Stuttgart: B.G. Teubner.

Fenk, A. (1990). Graphische Darstellung und kognitive Repräsentation. In N. Derner, C.D. Heinze, F. Klaus & A. Melezinek (Eds.), *Schriftenreihe Ingenieurpädagogik* (Vol. 25, Referate d. Int. Symposiums Ingenieurpädagogik '89). Alsbach: Leuchtturm-Verlag.

Fenk, A. (1991). Sprachbilder - Bildsprachen. In H. Kautschitsch & W. Metzler (Eds.), *Schriftenreihe Didaktik der Mathematik* (Vol. 20), Wien: Hölder-Pichler-Tempsky/Stuttgart: B.G.Teubner.

Fenk, A. (1992a). Pilotstudien zur Text-Bild-Interaktion. In A. Melezinek (Ed.), *Schriftenreihe Ingenieurpädagogik* (Vol. 30, Referate d. Int. Symposiums Ingenieurpädagogik 92). Alsbach: Leuchtturm-Verlag.

Fenk, A. (1992b). Zur Klassifikation von Symbolen. *Information und Classification.* 16th Annual Meeting of the Gesellschaft für Klassifikation, Abstract Volume, Dortmund.

Fenk, A., & Vanoucek, J. (1992). Zur Messung prognostischer Leistung. *Zeitschrift für experimentelle und angewandte Psychologie, 39* (1), 18-55.

Goel, V. (1991). Spezifikation und Klassifikation von Repräsentationssystemen. *Klagenfurter Beiträge zur Technikdiskussion* (Vol. 46).

Goldsmith, E. (1984). *Research into illustration.* Cambridge: Cambridge University Press.

Johnson, M., & Lakoff, G. (1982). *Metaphor and communication.* L.A.U.T., A-97, Trier.

Johnson-Laird, P.N. (1983): *Mental models: towards a cognitive science of language, inference, and consciousness.* Cambridge: Harvard University Press.

Mac Cormac, E.R. (1985). *A cognitive theory of metaphor.* Cambridge: MIT Press.

Macdonald-Ross, M. (1979). Scientific diagrams and the generation of plausible hypotheses: An essay in the history of ideas. *Instructional Science, 8* (3), 233-234.

Miller, J. (1985). *Semantics and syntax.* Cambridge: Cambridge University Press.

Ogden, C.K., & Richards, I.A. (1923). *The meaning of meaning.* London: Routledge & Kegan.

Peirce, C.S. (1976). KaÁva oÁoÁxeÁa. In C. Eisele (Ed.), *The new elements of mathematics* (Vol. IV). Paris: Mouton Publishers/ Humanities Press, Atlanta Highlands N.M.: Humanities Press.

Peirce, C.S. (1906). Prolegomena to an Apology for Pragmaticism. *The Monist, IV* (4), 492-546.

Rauh, G. (1989). Präpositionengesteuerte Metaphorik. In C. Habel, M. Herweg & K. Rehkämper (Eds.), *Raumkonzepte in Verstehensprozessen.* Tübingen: Niemeyer.

Rice, S. (1991). The concept "scale" as a grammatical metaphor. In C. Saalmann & H. Schulte (Eds.), *Abstracts of the papers to be held at the Second International Cognitive Linguistics Conference.* L.A.U.D., A-312, Duisburg.

Salomon, G. (1979). *Interaction of media, cognition and learning.* San Francisco: Jossey-Bass Publishers.

Schopenhauer, A. *Psychologische Bemerkungen.* München: Hyperionverlag, n.d.

Schroeder, C. (1989). Sprachlicher Ikonismus: Theoretische Grundlagen und Beispiele aus dem Türkischen. *Papiere zur Linguistik, 41* (2), 3-76.

Swoyer, C. (1991). Structural representation and surrogative reasoning. *Synthese, 87*, 449-508.

Traugott, E.C. (1975). Spatial expressions of tense and temporal sequencing: A contribution to the study of semantic fields. *Semiotica, 15* (3), 207-230.

Tversky, B., Kugelmass, S., & Winter, A. (1991). Cross-cultural and developmental trends in graphic productions. *Cognitive Psychology, 23* (4), 515-557.

von Glasersfeld, E. von (1982). Subitizing: The role of figural patterns in the development of numerical concepts. *Archives de Psychologie, 50,* 191-218.

Waltz, D.L. (1978). On the interdependence of language and perception. In D.L. Waltz (Ed.), *Theoretical issues in natural language processing, II.* Association for Computing Machinery. New York.

Weidenmann, B. (1988). *Psychische Prozesse beim Verstehen von Bildern.* Bern: Huber.

Weltner, K. (1973). *The measurement of verbal information in psychology and education.* Berlin: Springer.

Winn, W.D. (1982). The role of diagrammatic representation in learning sequences, identification and classification as a function of verbal and spatial ability. *Journal of Research in Science Teaching, 19* (1), 79-89.

Winn, W.D. (1983). Perceptual strategies used with flow diagrams having normal and unanticipated formats. *Perceptual and motor skills, 57,* 751-762.

Winn, W.D. (1988). Die Verwendung von Graphiken für Instruktion: Eine präskriptive Grammatik. *Unterrichtswissenschaft, 16,* 58 - 76.

Chapter 4

Comprehending and Using Maps:
Are there Two Modes of Map Processing?

John R. Kirby

Queen's University, Kingston, Ontario, Canada

ABSTRACT

Geographical maps are one of the most common types of graphical displays, yet relatively little is known about how we process or produce the information contained in a map. This paper reviews recent evidence regarding the cognitive processes involved in map use. Recent research points toward two approaches to map processing, holistic and analytic. In the holistic strategy, maps are dealt with spatially, as concrete objects. In the analytic strategy, maps are dealt with more verbally and abstractly. Three studies are reviewed which bear on this issue. It is argued that holistic and analytic are dimensions of map processing, and that the optimal strategy is usually one in which holistic and analytic processing are integrated and used flexibly.

One of the most common graphic displays encountered is the geographic map. Maps have been used in many societies for many years, yet we know little about how we mentally process or understand them. There is growing evidence that people may process the information represented on geographical maps in two qualitatively distinct modes, one predominantly holistic, the other analytic. My purpose here is to explore the cognitive processes involved in map comprehension and use, with the ultimate goal being to discover ways to overcome the difficulties faced by many map users.

It is important to remember that maps are abstract representations, employing complex codes and conventions to convey information in a form very different from the terrain or objects being represented. Maps present only certain information, which has been selected and distorted to communicate certain messages; as Monmonier (1991, p. 1) says, "Not only is it easy to lie with maps, it's essential". Comprehension processes are required to make any sense of a map, and especially if the map user wants to make some particular sense of it.

Holistic and analytic processing

One suggests two modes of processing with some trepidation, as such suggestions are easily over-extended or misunderstood. I am not suggesting that there are "two kinds of people", or that cognition is easily divisible into two types. What I am suggesting is that people's strategies in map processing can be analyzed along two dimensions (see Figure 1). Characteristic patterns may be observed, which can be summarized as two qualitatively different approaches, even though every person may employ both types of processing to some degree. The two modes are emphasized for clarity, without intending to indicate that these are the only two options. The two strategies call upon distinct cognitive processes, which form and interact with distinct types of mental representations.

Hunt (1974) proposed two strategies for solving Raven Progressive Matrices items, gestalt (holistic) and analytic (see also Kirby & Das, 1978). In the holistic strategy, the subject focuses on the display as a whole object rather than breaking it down into parts or features. In the analytic strategy, the subject considers distinct features or parts of the display in question when attempting to arrive at a solution. Lawson and Kirby (1981) demonstrated that these two strategies were successful for different test items, and Kirby and Lawson (1983) showed that each strategy could be taught. Boulter and Kirby (1991) identified holistic and analytic strategies in geometry problem solving. Conceptually similar strategies have been identified by other researchers with respect to other spatial tasks (see for example Cooper, 1976, 1990).

The analytic strategy is distinguished by its relative reliance upon verbal (as opposed to spatial), abstract (as opposed to concrete), and digital (as opposed to analogue) processes and representations (cf. Paivio, 1986). Whereas the analytic strategy deals with displays as though they were lists of features, the holistic strategy deals with displays as objects (of

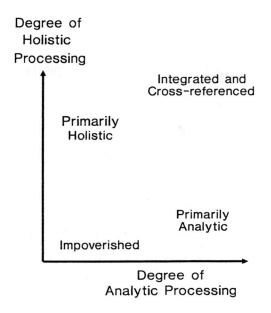

Figure 1. Holistic and analytic dimensions of map processing.

two or three dimensions). While the two strategies may be distinguished conceptually, they clearly rely upon many common processes (e.g., in map processing, both require visual perception). The situation is made more complicated by the use of terms such as "spatial": both strategies may be said to deal with "spatial" information, but only the holistic strategy deals with it in a "spatial" manner, as a real object in space. The two strategies may depend upon distinct spatial abilities, the holistic strategy upon "spatial orientation" ability (assessed by mental rotation tasks in which images of shapes must be rotated rigidly and compared with other images), the analytic strategy upon "spatial visualization" ability (assessed by spatial tasks in which the subject must analyze and assemble shapes) (see Kirby, 1990; Kirby & Schofield, 1991).

As is indicated in Figure 1, degrees of complexity may exist within each strategy, and the two may work together. For example, a superficial holistic representation may contain the information that a figure has sharp points, whereas a more complex representation may comprise a detailed three-dimensional image. Similarly a low level analytic representation may be "it's pointy", as opposed to a more complex one such as "it's an isosceles triangle with base = 5 cm". The most complex representations combine holistic and analytic features: for example, a three-dimensional image in which parts are both identifiable as units and exist in specified relations to each other.

Hunt (1974) suggested that the holistic strategy appeared developmentally earlier than the analytic; Kirby and Lawson (1983) observed that the analytic strategy often relied upon school-learned information (e.g., counting, names of patterns). In spite of this developmental sequence, each strategy has its appropriate uses. The verbal coding of the analytic strategy should be ideal for remembering sequences of easily distinguished and easily named items, whereas the holistic strategy should be more useful in remembering items which differ less dramatically (e.g., different shapes or line slopes), and when sequence is not essential. Subjects may differ in their capacity to employ these abilities or strategies, and in their willingness to do so (Kirby, Moore & Schofield, 1988), and may also shift strategies during a task. It seems likely that subjects able to employ a strategy in which both sets of processes are employed flexibly will perform best.

Map processing

Maps and map tasks vary considerably. For example, the map may be physically present or only remembered, or you may try to draw one; the area represented on the map may be small or large; and the surface portrayed on the map may vary in complexity, ease of encoding, and in artificiality (i.e. natural vs. constructed). The environment may be rich in cues, for instance written signs, or more barren. The map and area may be more or less familiar to you, as it may to the person asking directions. How we perform these tasks, and thus the degree to which holistic and analytic processes are employed, depend upon the nature of the map and our specific purpose in the task.

Consider three different maps: (a) a city street map, (b) a topographical map of a mountainous region, and (c) a map of the Atlantic Ocean. How would you process the information shown on these maps? Five of the many issues which come to mind are:

1. Do you think in two or three dimensions? You probably do not for the street or ocean maps, because height is usually not represented, and is seldom important in tasks for which such maps are used. You may or may not choose to do so with the topographical map,

for instance to "see" the relative heights of mountain chains and valleys; height information is more likely to be important in such environments, for instance in planning a route. In two dimensional processing, you may form a mental image of the map in which features maintain their spatial relationships (holistic representation) or deal with the features on the map as discrete items (analytic).

2.   Do you focus upon landmarks, or do you impose an abstract framework (such as a grid system) upon the map? With the street map, you could describe a route relying largely upon landmarks ("Follow this street until you get to the park, then go left until you see the church ...") or in terms of the grid system ("Go east for 3 km, then south ..."). Landmarks may be more difficult to identify on the topographical map, because of the absence of distinct features with unambiguous labels. The ocean map would of course lack landmarks in the central area; many abstract grid systems, such as those employing the magnetic north pole, the stars, and longitude and latitude, were developed to deal with the lack of landmarks at sea. (It is not surprising that the English word "navigate" comes from the Latin word "to sail".) Use of landmarks is a characteristic of lower-level analytic processing, while abstract grid systems (or other imagined frames of reference) characterize higher-level analytic processing.

3.   Do you think in terms of directions? If so, how? For instance, you may look for compass directions (north-south-east-west) on the map, and/or use these directions in describing the map. An alternative would be to provide directions which are self-oriented (e.g., "on my left ..."); in this case you may also imagine yourself on the map and describe a path in the same way ("on my right I can see ...; I turn to the left ..."). Some map processors attempt to rotate the map to make it match the orientation of the world, while others are content to perform the rotation mentally, or not perform it at all. The use of compass directions, like the use of an abstract grid system, is more analytic, while the use of self-oriented directions is more holistic. Holistic processing would be required to mentally rotate the map to match the environment.

4.   The size and complexity of the unit referred to can vary greatly: for the topographical map it may be a single turn in the path, or an entire mountain range; for the street map, a particular building or an entire suburb. This corresponds to amount of processing, in either holistic or analytic modes.

5.   Do you describe the map verbally to yourself, or maintain it as an image, or reprocess it as a three-dimensional terrain? The first would be analytic, the second lower-level holistic, and the third higher-level holistic. In imagining a path, an analytic approach would be to list a verbal chain of turns or landmarks, whereas a holistic approach would be to imagine a series of movements on a visualized representation.

These five issues do not exhaust the topic; they clearly overlap, and each is dependent upon the individual subject's mental abilities, experience, and purpose in the task, as well as the nature of the map involved. In the remainder of this paper I review evidence regarding landmarks and map inspection strategies, map learning, and position location on a map. Landmarks and map inspection.

Subjects vary in their use of landmarks in inspecting, describing, and remembering maps. For example, Dart and Pradhan (1967) found a difference between Nepalese and American children's drawings of maps of their route from home to school. The American children typically drew a grid of streets, in which angles and intersections between streets were accurately depicted, and the student's house and school were represented by symbols. In contrast, the Nepalese children drew pictures of their house and school, connected by a line "which seems to denote the process of going from one to the other, not the spatial relationship of one to the other" (Dart & Pradhan, 1967, p. 653, emphasis in original). The connecting path did not take into account changes in direction or choice-points. One could speculate that the two groups of children have different interpretations of the task, different experience of distance measures, live in quite different environments (natural vs. constructed), and so on. The point here is that one group produced a more analytic product (the American grid maps), whereas the other produced essentially a less analytic temporal string, in which the units were more representational. The former group concentrated upon the abstract relationships among the features, and the second upon the features themselves. Both strategies are combinations of holistic and analytic elements.

Others have explored sex differences in reliance upon landmarks. Galea and Kimura (1991) had male and female university students study a route on a map. Males learned more quickly and made fewer errors. However, females had better recall of landmarks either on or off the route learned, while males recalled better the "euclidean" properties of the map (relative location in two dimensions). Again both strategies are analytic-holistic composites, with females focussing upon the features, males upon the more abstract relationships among the features.

In 1985, I reported a study in which university students read a text (presented on a computer screen, one sentence at a time) that described a fictitious Himalayan trek. After reading each sentence, the subject could procede to (a) the next sentence, or (b) a map related to the text, or (c) a summary of the text, or (d) a statement by the author about why the text was written. A subsequent study employed high school students as subjects. Both studies are described in Kirby and Schofield (1991). The results presented here concern only the map inspections, which were not related to options (c) or (d).

The text sentences were divided into four overlapping categories: (a) those in which a geographical overview statement was made (e.g. "we had crossed the first of three mountain ranges"), (b) those in which a place name was mentioned for the first time, (c) those in which a place name was mentioned that had been mentioned before, and (d) those which made no reference to geography. Categories overlapped, in that a single sentence could contain, for instance, an old and a new place name. Map inspection following the overview statements should indicate that subjects were mentally constructing a spatial overview, while inspection after the new or old place names indicates that they were following a route, from landmark to landmark.

The proportions of sentences in each category which were followed by a map inspection are shown in Figure 2. The pattern of results is similar for both groups, map inspections being most common following the mention of a new place name. While there is some indication of overview construction (12.6% of these statements are followed by a look at the map for university students, 8.4% for high school students), the dominant strategy appears to be landmark following.

The landmark strategy can be described as a low-level analytic strategy; in it, features are dealt with as the important entities, not the spatial relations among them. This form of processing may be suited for remembering a sequence of places, as found on a route, but not for remembering the spatial relations of the map. The other strategy is also analytic, but at a higher level, in that the representational system is abstract as opposed to concrete; however this strategy also has a holistic element because the spatial relations among the elements are retained.

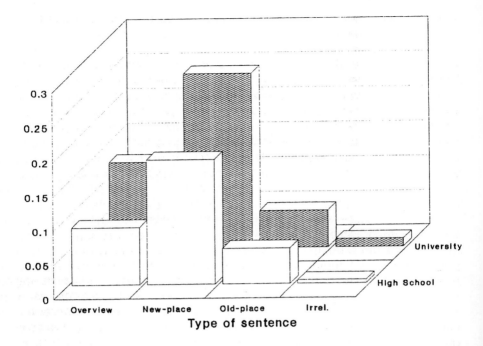

Figure 2. Proportions of sentences of each type followed by a map inspection in high school and university groups.

Verbal and spatial processes in map learning

Kirby and Lanca (submitted) studied the effects of verbal and spatial processing on map learning. University students were asked to study a topographical map under one of four conditions: in the Spatial condition, subjects were instructed to imagine the cross-sectional profile of the terrain, as seen from certain points; in the Verbal condition, subjects read a short narrative which involved the locations shown on the map, while they studied the map; in the Combined condition, subjects performed both the Spatial and Verbal tasks while studying the map; and in the Control condition, subjects studied the map without any additional imposed task. In terms of the present paper, the Spatial condition was intended to increase spatial (holistic) processing, the Verbal condition to increase verbal processing of landmarks; it was anticipated that optimal performance would be under the Combined condition.

Subjects were later tested for their knowledge of the map. Questions were of two types, relating either to three-dimensional (3D) information (the shape of the terrain), or to two-dimensional (2D) information (including the names of landmarks and their two-dimensional location). Retaining the three-dimensional information can be argued to require holistic processing in the form of elaborate imagery, while landmark information is more verbal; we opted to include two-dimensional location information in the latter group because we thought it could be recalled by verbal cues alone. At the very least, two-dimensional information is more likely than three-dimensional information to be retained by verbal processing.

The results failed to show any straight-forward evidence for the superiority of combined processing. What was apparent was a trade-off between spatial and verbal processing. Subjects in the conditions which received the additional spatial task (i.e. the Spatial and Combined groups) performed better on the 3D questions than they did on the 2D questions, while the opposite trend was found for the subjects who did not receive the spatial task (i.e. the Control and Verbal groups).

The results also contained an interesting sex difference. We had anticipated that males would score more highly in the Control condition, but that sex differences would be less apparent in the additional spatial processing groups. Our argument for this was that females may normally tend to deal with the map verbally, ignoring the more holistic and three-dimensional aspects; this strategy would be effective for retaining 2D, but not 3D, information. The interaction of sex and spatial task indicated, to the contrary, that the sexes performed similarly, except with additional spatial processing. Additional spatial processing helped males, not females; males performed significantly better with additional spatial processing, while the females' scores did not differ.

These results suggest that the strategies used by female subjects are quite successful under normal conditions, as long as complex spatial (e.g. 3D) information is not required. This of course would be a major disadvantage with topographical maps, and may extend to other maps in which information about a third dimension (such as population or agricultural statistics) is included, or in which complex spatial relationships are critical. Females may normally adopt a low-level analytic approach, which they are either unwilling or unable to discard; males may begin with a similar approach (they did not differ in the

Control group), but they do switch to a more holistic-spatial approach when encouraged to do so.

Position location

Schofield and Kirby (in press) studied the effects of strategy instruction upon subjects' ability to locate a position on a topographical map, after having been shown that position on an accurate three-dimensional model of a portion of the terrain represented by the map. The subjects for this study were 60 male Australian Army personnel, who were randomly assigned to three groups. The verbal and visual strategy instruction groups were intended to encourage, respectively, analytic and holistic processing; the third group was an uninstructed control group.

Verbal strategy training directed subjects to verbally identify the main features of the terrain from the model, and to rehearse them while inspecting the map. A two step scanning process was taught, subjects being directed to scan initially for the location of the whole model on the map, and then for the specific location provided. Systematic (left to right, top to bottom) scanning and checking were encouraged.

In visual strategy training, subjects were instructed to identify the prominent features, but to visualize how the features would appear on a contour map. Visual relationships between features were emphasized and shapes and slopes were described with hand gestures. Verbal labels or descriptions of features were avoided and discouraged. The two stage scanning process was again used, but when the general area had been identified the checking procedure which was implemented emphasised visualization.

Subjects did not necessarily adopt the strategy of the group to which they were assigned. Because we were interested in the strategies they used, we reassigned 12 subjects according to the strategies they were observed using. Subjects spontaneously adopting the verbal strategy tended to be of high spatial ability, while those opting for the visual strategy tended to be of low spatial ability (see Schofield & Kirby, in press, for details).

The central result was that subjects who used the verbal strategy were faster in position location than either the visual strategy or control groups. This demonstrates the power of the analytic approach, though it does not deny that other examples of visual-spatial training may be more effective, or that the visual strategy may be superior for other skills.

This study argues for the importance of analytic training in map processing. The visual training may have required a level of holistic processing which was beyond the ability of the subjects. Our interpretation was that the verbal strategy allowed subjects to process the map information beyond their habitual superficial level, which may have been either holistic or verbal, but certainly was not deep or elaborate. Because all map processing requires some sort of spatial-holistic base, it seems unlikely that the verbal strategy subjects processed the maps verbally instead of spatially. It seems more likely that the verbal-analytic strategy facilitated integrated processing, in which verbal and spatial codes were richly cross-referenced.

Conclusions

In the end, does it make sense to say that there are two modes of map processing? My answer is yes, as long as that is not taken to mean that there are only two possible choices. I see analytic and holistic processing as two dimensions along which processing may vary (see Figure 1). Most research has tended to emphasize the upper left and lower right corners of this figure, where processing is predominantly one or the other. While it is in these corners that the nature of each form of processing is seen most clearly, it is likely that the most useful processing is integrated or at least cross-referenced. (Although the Lanca and Kirby study failed to show this, it remains a reasonable position; more extensive training of the subjects, especially the females, may well have produced more convincing results.) Seen from the perspective of individual differences, this figure emphasizes the importance of having both types of skill, and of being able to switch between types of processing flexibly.

What implications are there for instruction? At the risk of overgeneralizing and going beyond the evidence presented above, most subjects (a) seem to not know how to perform sophisticated holistic processing (e.g., being able to visualize complex land forms), (b) do not spontaneously adopt verbal-analytic processing beyond the level of identifying place-names or features, and (c) do not integrate their holistic and analytic processes. For particular tasks, specific training programs could be devised to improve performance. For example, the Schofield and Kirby training program could be extended to teach map reading and map learning. Such specific programs would demonstrate holistic and analytic strategies of increasing sophistication, perhaps leading subjects first to analyze the map into components (major features), then to visualize each, then to describe (verbally-analytically) the relations between the features, and lastly to visualize the relationships between features. Switching between holistic and analytic processing would be encouraged, and extensive practice supplied. Physical models and computer-based simulations could be used to help subjects develop their representational processes, and to demonstrate the relationships between different forms of representation.

However, the use of maps is merely one example of the domain of complex spatial tasks, and addressing tasks one-by-one for adults may be missing the greater opportunity. The elementary and secondary school curricula (at least as I know them in the English-speaking world) do not try very hard to teach children to deal with complex spatial tasks, much less to address alternative strategies. Students are only likely to receive such instruction if they pursue studies in mathematics or physical science, but only those students who have already developed advanced spatial skills are likely to follow those paths. There is a need to address spatial skills earlier in school, for all students. If spatial instruction is to succeed, teachers and students will need to understand more about how spatial processing works; I suggest that the holistic-analytic framework presented in this paper is a worthwhile starting point.

RÉSUMÉ

Bien que les cartes géographiques constituent un des types les plus communs de représentations graphiques, on sait relativement peu de choses sur la façon dont sont traitées ou produites les informations contenues dans une carte. Cet article examine des données récentes concernant les processus cognitifs impliqués dans l'utilisation de cartes. Les recherches actuelles sont axées sur deux approches du traitement des cartes; l'approche holistique et l'approche analytique. Dans la stratégie holistique, les cartes sont traitées spatialement, en tant qu'objet concret. Dans la stratégie holistique, les cartes sont traitées plus verbalement et plus abstraitement. Trois recherches se rapportant à cette question sont examinées. On propose que les deux approches, holistique et analytique, soient considérées comme des dimensions du traitement de cartes, et que la stratégie optimale consiste habituellement en l'intégration et l'utilisation souple des stratégies holistiques et analytiques.

Acknowledgement

The research reported in this paper was supported by grants from the Australian Research Grants Committee, the Advisory Research Committee of Queen's University, and the Faculty of Education of Queen's University. The contributions of Margaret Lanca, Phillip Moore, and Neville Schofield are gratefully acknowledged.

References

Boulter, D., & Kirby, J.R. (1991). *Identification of strategies employed by students in solving transformational geometry problems.* Paper presented at the annual conference of the Canadian Society for the Study of Education, June, Kingston, Ontario.

Cooper, L.A. (1976). Individual differences in visual comparison processes. *Perception and Psychophysics, 19*, 433-444.

Cooper, L.A. (1990). Mental representation of three-dimensional objects in visual problem solving and recognition. *Journal of Experimental Psychology: Learning, Memory, and Cognition, 16*, 1097-1106.

Dart, F.E., & Pradhan, P.L. (1967). Cross-cultural teaching of science. *Science, 155*, 649-656.

Galea, L., & Kimura, D. (1991). *Sex differences in route learning. Research Bulletin* #700, Department of Psychology, University of Western Ontario.

Hunt, E. (1974). Quote the Raven? Nevermore! In L. Gregg (Ed.), *Knowledge and Cognition*. Potomac, MD: Erlbaum.

Kirby, J.R. (1985, August). *Map inspection during reading*. Paper presented to the Australian and New Zealand Psychological Societies, Christchurch, NZ.

Kirby, J.R. (1990, July). *Spatial cognition in education*. Paper presented to the International Congress for Applied Psychology, Kyoto, Japan.

Kirby, J.R. (1991, August). *Collaborative and competitive effects of verbal and spatial processes*. Paper presented to the European Association for Research on Learning and Instruction, Turku, Finland.

Kirby, J.R., & Das, J.P. (1978). Skills underlying Colored Progressive Matrices. *Alberta Journal of Educational Research, 24*, 94-99.

Kirby, J.R., & Lanca, M. (submitted). Verbal and spatial processes in map learning.

Kirby, J.R., & Lawson, M.J. (1983). Effects of strategy training upon Progressive Matrices performance. *Contemporary Educational Psychology, 8*, 421-434.

Kirby, J.R., Moore, P.J., & Schofield, N.J. (1988). Verbal and visual learning styles. *Contemporary Educational Psychology, 13*, 169-184.

Kirby, J.R., & Schofield, N.J. (1991). Spatial cognition: The case of map comprehension. In G. Evans (Ed.), *Learning and teaching cognitive skills* (pp. 109-125). Melbourne, Australia: Australian Council for Educational Research.

Lawson, M.J., & Kirby, J.R. (1981). Training in information processing algorithms. *British Journal of Educational Psychology, 51*, 321-335.

Monmonier, M. (1991). *How to lie with maps*. Chicago, IL: University of Chicago Press.

Paivio, A. (1986). *Mental representations: A dual-coding approach*. New York: Oxford University Press.

Schofield, N.J., & Kirby, J.R. (in press). Position location on a topographical map: Effects of abilities, preferences, and instruction. *Cognition and Instruction*.

Comprehension of Graphics
W. Schnotz and R. W. Kulhavy (Editors)

Chapter 5

Identifying and Simulating Cognitive Strategies for the Description of Spatial Networks

Michel Denis, Frédérique Robin, Michael Zock & Abdellatif Laroui

Université de Paris-Sud, Orsay, France

ABSTRACT

When subjects are required to describe spatial networks with a constraint on the starting point of their description, dominant linearization strategies can be evidenced in discourse. These strategies consist in producing descriptive sequences which minimize the number of elements stored in working memory and/or the duration of the storage. Analysis of description latencies reveals the effect of the cognitive load associated with network complexity and suggests that the implementation of optimal strategies depends on a more extensive analysis of networks by the subjects. Lastly, we report the first steps in the design of a text generator that simulates different kinds of natural descriptive strategies.

Most of the chapters in this volume present ways in which cognitive psychology has approached graphics comprehension processes through descriptions of studies where individuals are asked to extract the relevant features from a visual pattern and build up a meaningful representation of it. People, in fact, often operate on multimodal inputs. For example, instructional texts typically combine graphics and verbal material, and readers need to integrate both into a unified, meaningful representation (e.g., Kulhavy, Lee, & Caterino, 1985).

The research reported in this chapter extends this approach to the comprehension of graphics by studying the processes involved in their description. Rather than simply interpreting visual patterns, people must sometimes satisfy the additional requirement of describing them to other people. For instance, a speaker may be asked to describe a given graphic pattern to a listener in such a way that this person can build a corresponding representation (and later produce a drawing of the pattern) without having ever seen it. This kind of task is common in everyday life and occurs when people try to explain to others how to get from one place to another, or when they try to describe complex objects (such as geographical maps) or visual scenes.

Cognitive approaches to description

The processes involved in the description of visual patterns lie at the crossroads of several disciplines, and primarily linguistics, cognitive psychology, and artificial intelligence (cf. Denis, Carité, & Robin, 1991). One of the goals of text linguistics is to identify the markers and structures of descriptive discourse. Another goal is to determine whether the building of coherent text structures is rule-governed. If so, the issue is to identify these rules which specifically apply in the generation of descriptive discourse, in contrast to other kinds of texts and in particular narratives. Cognitive psychology is concerned with descriptive strategies and the cognitive factors likely to place constraints on the production of linguistic outputs. A distinction is usually made between conceptualization operations (how speakers build a representation of the entity to describe) and formulation operations (how speakers implement procedures which will correctly express this representation in the form of a linear discourse). The structures and operations involved in the production of descriptions can then be implemented by researchers in artificial intelligence and computer-assisted teaching, who can put them to practical use by constructing automatic text generators, and test them in instructional contexts.

In the example situation of a person inspecting a visual pattern to generate a description for another person, the two representations - the one built by the speaker, and the other one built by the listener - are assumed to be visuo-spatial; that is, they incorporate some form of the spatial extension of the original visual pattern. Whether qualified as "visual images" or "mental models", they are assumed to be analog representations, in the sense that they preserve the topological relations between the constituent parts of the visual pattern (cf. Denis, 1991; Johnson-Laird, 1989; Paivio, 1991).

Natural language is the interface between the speaker's and the listener's mental representations. Although a verbal description can also be termed a "representation" of visual input, this representation has considerably different properties. In addition to the fact that it is generated by a representational system which relies on arbitrary symbols, its main distinctive feature is that it is structured in a linear, sequential fashion. This is inherent to the properties of the system which produces discourse, in which information can only be transmitted in a sequential manner, such that no more than one statement can be produced at the same time. Verbal outputs are thus sequential structures by nature.

Imposing linearization onto multidimensional representations is not a trivial operation. The operation in particular requires the speaker to make a decision as to whether the object should be first described at some macrostructural level. Then, when starting the enumeration of component elements, the speaker has to make a decision regarding which element in the configuration should be mentioned first, then which elements should be introduced, and in which order. Making these kinds of decisions is not problematical at all when the object or the situation to be described has an explicit or easily derivable temporal structure (cf. Linde & Labov, 1975). The problem is far more complex when the object or the situation is structured in such a way that its components are of comparable prominence and are distributed over a multidimensional space without any identifiable underlying linear structure.

Planning descriptive discourse

As for any other type of discourse, the planning of descriptive discourse is generally assumed to involve at least two kinds of processes: conceptual (or prelinguistic) processes, which are responsible for the construction of a representation of the object to be described, and formulating processes, which provide a linguistic surface form for this representational content. To use the distinction introduced by Levelt (1989), macroplanning (as opposed to microplanning) for the speaker first consists in selecting the information to be transmitted. This operation requires the elaboration of the goal of the communicative act and, if necessary, its segmentation into subgoals. As mentioned before, if the object to be described is linear (such as a route), the hierarchy of goals and subgoals is entirely determined by the structure of the object.

If the object is multidimensional (such as a geographical map), then the question arises of how to order the information in the most appropriate way.

It is well established that improper discourse organization results in an increase of the processing load for readers or listeners, and a decrease in ability to memorize (cf. Denis & Denhière, 1990; Ehrlich & Johnson-Laird, 1982; Foos, 1980). Quality of discourse organization usually correlates with the speaker's skills to communicate efficiently. How understandable or "friendly" a discourse is for a listener depends on the speaker's selection of a particular sequence from among a finite, but usually very large set of possible sequences. This sequence should first of all be such that the speaker is able to exert efficient control on its generation. The speaker should monitor his or her output and keep track of what has already been said and what still remains to be mentioned. The sequence should also be adapted to the cognitive expectations and processing capabilities of the addressee. Some of the most important control mechanisms are those used to guarantee discourse coherence (by avoiding referential discontinuities) and to maintain indeterminacy at its minimum (for instance, by stating that "A is to the right of B", rather than "A is beside B").

Microplanning refers to the set of operations by which the speaker attributes a propositional structure to the set of informations selected. These operations are intended to translate a conceptual structure into its corresponding linguistic form. The message is linguistically coded, which implies access to a mental lexicon as well as to a grammar, in order to compute an appropriate syntactic structure. Then, phonological coding consists in elaborating an articulatory program for the planned discourse. One of the most significant constraints on human discourse in this respect is that it is incremental; that is, the generation of an output is initiated before the message to be expressed is completely planned.

To summarize, the core issue in description is that the speaker has to make a series of decisions, in particular regarding the order in which the different parts of the to-be-described object should be mentioned. These decisions are especially important when the structure of the object places minimal constraints on the structure of the discourse. In this respect, one of Levelt's major findings is that specific requirements (e.g., starting the description of a spatial configuration from a particular point) elicit specific processing strategies on the part of speakers. Levelt suggested that these strategies are regulated by cognitive factors. In particular, he showed that cognitive factors related to the limited size of both speakers' and listeners' working memory determine the order in which the different parts of an object are described.

The description of spatial networks in a constrained context

The material used in Levelt's experiments consisted of networks in which colored circles are connected to each other by horizontal and vertical lines. Subjects were presented with the networks, and asked to describe them so that another person could build an accurate representation of them. The speakers had only one constraint: to start their description from a specific circle from which two branches headed in opposite directions. Subjects had to make a choice on which branch to describe first.

One of the main outcomes of these experiments was to demonstrate speakers' natural tendency to produce descriptions that minimize either the number of elements to be stored in working memory or the duration of the storage. Levelt identified three main types of regularities for three classes of networks. An example of the first class of networks is shown in Figure 1a. Two branches, a short one and a longer one, lead off from the green circle. The duration of maintenance of the starting point in working memory (during the description of the first branch) will vary as a function of which branch is described first. Duration of storage before returning to the green circle to describe the other branch is longer if the longer branch is described first. Thus, it should be more economical to describe the shorter branch first, since duration of storage will be shorter. The data collected by Levelt (1982) confirm that when subjects are required to start their description from the green circle, the probability is higher than 50% that they will describe the shorter branch before the longer one.

Figure 1b presents an example of the second class of networks. Here, subjects are required to start their descriptions from the red circle. From there, two branches head in opposite directions. A linear branch extends to one side, and a more complex T-shaped branch (which leads to a further intersection) is on the other side. The linear branch and the T-shaped branch have the same number of circles, and they only differ with regard to their structural complexity. As a consequence, less information has to be held in working memory during the description

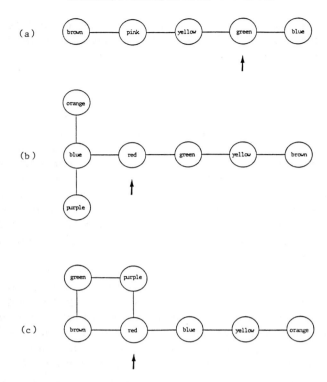

Figure 1. Three types of spatial networks.

of the first branch when this is the linear branch. As a matter of fact, in this latter case, subjects only have to keep track of one circle, the red one, which is the backtrack point before describing the other branch. If subjects start their description with the complex branch, they have to store both the red and the blue circle. In fact, results show that when subjects start their descriptions from the red circle, the probability is higher than 50% that they will describe the branch without any embedded choice points before the branch with one or several embedded choice points.

The third class of networks is illustrated in Figure 1c. Three branches lead off from the red circle. One branch is linear, and the other two branches form a square-shaped loop. The adequate strategy, here, consists in describing the loop first, then the linear branch. Using this strategy, subjects avoid storing any backtrack point at all times, and simply follow a linear path. Note that when subjects start their descriptions from the red circle, they have to choose from three possible directions. Thus, the probability for them to describe the loop before the linear branch should be greater than 67%. This tendency, in fact, was only observed for a subset of subjects (Levelt, 1982).

Further experiments on the description of spatial networks

Our experiments used the same kind of materials, but new variants on the network structures were introduced in order to explore several factors more systematically (cf. Robin & Denis, 1991). The first operation consisted in varying the differential informational load between the two branches of a network. For instance, in the first type of networks, one branch was only made up of one circle, but the other branch could have one, two, or three circles. Adding circles to one side of the network was expected to increase the cognitive load involved in the processing of the longer branch. Hence, the probability for subjects to describe the shorter branch first should be higher. The second variant consisted in altering the visual presentation of some branches by making them visually more complex. For instance, instead of being a straight line, the linear branch in the second and third class of networks was distorted. This was expected to affect the probability of occurrence of typical descriptive strategies. We assumed in particular that subjects would tend to describe the other branch first, since it might appear to be comparatively less complex. Finally, in addition to recording subjects' responses in order to identify the strategy used in each case, we measured description latencies, with the hope that differences in these times would reflect the load associated with the implementation of strategies.

Fifty adult subjects (half male, half female) participated in the experiment. They were recruited on the Orsay campus and were paid for their participation. In addition to one network which was symmetrical (network 1.1.0), the material was constructed from a set of 15 asymmetrical patterns, which were complemented with the set of their 15 mirror image patterns. In all, subjects were presented with a total of 31 networks. Each trial consisted in the presentation of a network to the subject on a sheet of standard-sized A4 paper. Two seconds later, the experimenter named one circle of the network as the starting point for the description. The time elapsing between experimenter's naming of the starting circle and subject's beginning of the description was recorded for each network.

First class of networks (shorter vs. longer linear branch)

Figure 2 shows the set of networks in the first class, where the occurrence of descriptive strategies was manipulated by varying the number of circles on one of two linear branches.

Not surprisingly, in the case of control network 1.1.0, no clear preference emerged for either direction: 54% of the subjects first described the branch on the left, and 46% first described the branch on the right. It was expected that adding circles to one side of the network would increase the cognitive load associated with the processing of the longer branch, and that subjects would exhibit a tendency to describe the shorter branch first. The data confirmed these expectations, since in the case of network 1.1.1, 68% of the subjects preferred to describe the shorter branch before the longer one. This probability rose to 78% when the difference between the two branches was further increased (network 1.1.2). Thus, variations designed to affect cognitive load during the description of the longer branch consistently increased the probability of using the expected strategy.

Similar outcomes were obtained for variants of the above networks, where the two branches were connected to each other orthogonally. Network 1.2.0 elicited 57% of responses favoring the vertical branch, while 43% of subjects first described the horizontal branch (without any differences for the two symmetrical versions of this network). For networks 1.2.1 and 1.2.2, the probability of describing the shorter branch first was 75% and 78%, respectively. Probability was 71% and 68% in the case of networks 1.2.3 and 1.2.4.

One highly interesting pattern of results emerged from the analysis of response latencies. From network 1.1.0, to network 1.1.1, and finally to network 1.1.2, the time to start describing steadily increased. Thus, as networks were more demanding in terms of the amount of cognitive resources which would be required if subjects implemented non-optimal strategies, response latencies were longer. The same pattern emerged for the other sets of networks. Apparently, when subjects were engaged in the process of deciding whether to start their description in one direction or another, processing times varied as a function of the quantity of information to be processed. Larger amounts of information were reflected in greater amounts of time.

Probably the most relevant finding in the analysis of latencies is what differentiates subjects who eventually used the optimal descriptive

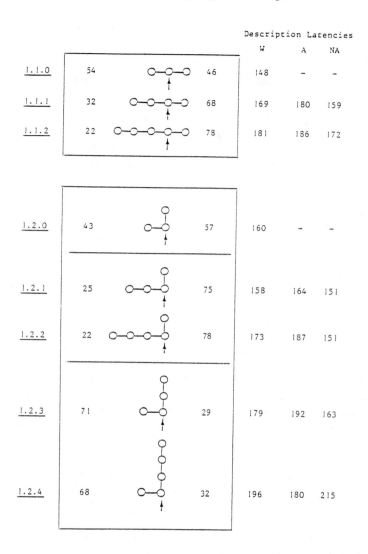

Figure 2. The set of networks in the first class (shorter vs. longer linear branch). In this and the two following figures, arrows indicate starting points for descriptions. The proportions of subjects exhibiting each directional choice are given for each network (average proportion for each network and its mirror version). Mean description latencies (cs) for the whole sample of subjects (W), and for consistent strategy appliers (A) and non-consistent appliers (NA), appear to the right of each figure.

strategy (shorter branch first). For each network, we selected the group of subjects who consistently chose the optimal strategy for both versions (that is, the version shown in Figure 2 and its mirror counterpart). These subjects were considered as consistent strategy appliers. The remaining subjects were qualified as non-consistent appliers. What emerges is that the consistent strategy appliers had overall significantly longer description latencies than non-appliers for all the networks of this class (with the single exception of network 1.2.4). A likely explanation of these time patterns is that application of the optimal strategy is dependent on more extensive analysis of the network before responding.

Second class of networks (linear vs. embedded branch)

On the second class of networks, where the differential branch load was manipulated by the presence of an embedding point on one of the two branches, the expectation was that subjects would tend to describe the linear branch first, then the more complex branch with the embedding point. The results in Figure 3 show that this was the case, since the majority of the subjects (63%) preferred to describe the linear branch first (network 2.1). One variant consisted in adding one circle to each branch (network 2.2). The number of circles on both sides remained the same but since the relative complexity of the complex branch was increased, it was expected that the probability for subjects to describe the linear branch first would be greater. This was indeed the case, although the effect was relatively weak (probability increased from 63% to 69%).

Another variant was introduced for this class of networks. The presentation of the linear branch of networks 2.1 and 2.2 was altered to make it visually more complex. Instead of a straight line, the linear branch appeared distorted. We expected that the complexity of the supposedly complex branch (with an embedded point) would be relatively attenuated, and that the visual "appeal" of this branch would tend to increase. This variant should thus lower the probability of using the expected strategy, and even favor the branch with an embedded point as the first branch to describe. The results confirmed expectations in that the probability of describing the linear branch first decreased to 52% for network 2.3, and further decreased to 43% for network 2.4, thus yielding the reverse of the theoretically optimal strategy. In the case of networks 2.3 and 2.4, not only the relative (perceived)

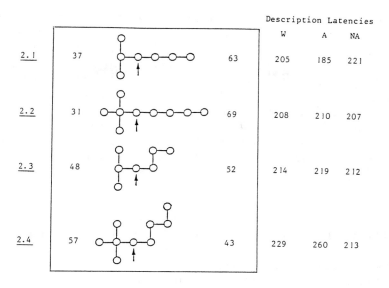

Figure 3. The set of networks in the second class (linear vs. embedded branch).

complexity of the complex branch is lower than before, but in addition the fact that its structure is an appealing Gestalt increases the probability that it will be described first. Subjects, thus, apparently do not only judge branch complexity in terms of the number of embedded points, but also in terms of structural complexity (or amount of distortion) of the linear branch.

The first type of variation (adding one circle to each branch of network 2.1) did not produce any substantial effect on response latencies. Latencies were of similar magnitudes for networks 2.1 and 2.2. On the other hand, the second type of variation (distorting the linear branch) increased response latencies, which suggests that greater visual complexity of the pattern tended to delay the onset of description. Finally, for this class of networks, no reliable difference emerged from the comparison of appliers and non-appliers. The only exception was for network 2.4, where the subjects who consistently applied the dominant strategy (in this case, describing the embedded branch first) had longer onset delays before starting their descriptions. This result is in line with the data collected for the first class of networks.

Third class of networks (loop vs. linear branch)

According to Levelt, the strategy expected to be dominant for this class of networks consists of describing the loop first, then the linear branch. In fact, the occurrence of this strategy is dependent on the length of the linear branch. For network 3.1, where this branch contains only one circle, only 43% of subjects described the loop first (see Figure 4). The probability of describing the loop first substantially increased for network 3.2, where the addition of further circles to the linear branch was intended to increase its load. However, the proportion of subjects who chose the loop-first strategy still remained moderate (56%).

The manipulation of the linear branch in network 3.3 (from straight to broken line) further increased the probability that subjects would first engage themselves in the description of the loop. In fact, 69% of the subjects used the predicted loop-first strategy. The occurrence of this strategy further increased when both visual complexity and load of the linear branch (in terms of number of circles) were increased. In the case of network 3.4, the loop-first strategy was produced by 74% of the subjects.

Response latencies were similar for networks 3.1 and 3.2, and they clearly increased when the linear branch of network 3.3 was a broken line, then again when one further circle was added in network 3.4. Thus, as patterns made the optimal strategy more useful, the time required for elaborating the response was longer. In addition, latencies were longer for subjects who used the loop-first strategy.

The implementation of descriptive strategies thus appears to be governed by cognitive factors. The occurrence of specific descriptive strategies can be predicted on the basis of an analysis of the cognitive load associated with the processing of different parts of the to-be-described object. Certain factors have been pointed out in earlier research. The present study examined modifications in the structure of branches, and shows that there is an increase in cognitive load associated with the processing of these branches. These changes in structure systematically modify the likelihood of implementing some specific strategies. Furthermore, the analysis of response latencies provides converging evidence in that more demanding networks involve longer onset delays before starting descriptions. The data also provide clear indications that more processing time is involved before producing a response which is in accordance with the optimal (dominant) strategy. The response latency findings may reflect the fact that subjects perform

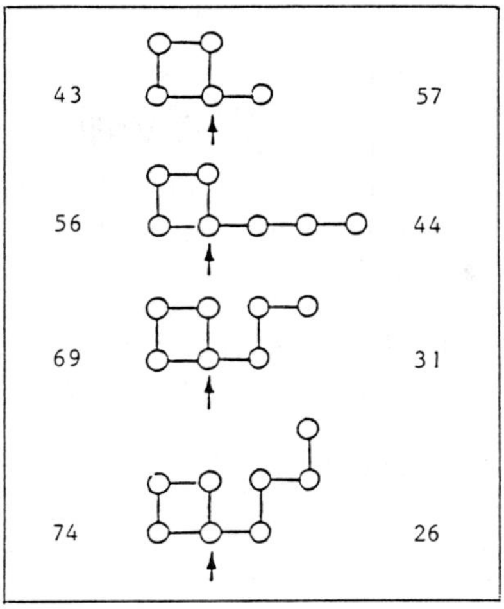

	Description Latencies W	A	NA
3.1	210	206	213
3.2	202	206	199
3.3	222	244	194
3.4	240	256	222

Figure 4. The set of networks in the third class (loop vs. linear branch).

some implicit computation before responding, and that the more computation, the better adapted the outputs. Apparently, the subjects who will tend to be consistent strategy appliers also probably engage in deeper analysis of the networks before describing them.

The simulation of descriptive strategies

The specification of discourse operations involved in description is obviously a relevant task when cognitive scientists aim at having these operations performed by automatic generation systems, and when adequate text structures need to be defined (cf. Dale, Mellish, & Zock, 1990; Kempen, 1987). For instance, a system intended to describe complex objects will benefit from directives on how to search the data base with a variety of strategies. A specific strategy (for instance, describing the structure of the object either before or after describing its functions) may be selected as a function of user characteristics (user's expertise or the type of task he or she has to perform) (cf. Paris & McKeown, 1987).

Once the descriptive procedures most likely to yield felicitous communication have been identified, this analysis can be used to elaborate an automatic system for text generation. Current advances in artificial intelligence make these automatized procedures feasible on the basis of principles drawn from the analysis of natural language strategies (cf. Novak, 1988; Paris & McKeown, 1987). In addition, there is general consensus that text generation systems can be enhanced by more explicit cognitive modelling. For instance, the incremental nature of generation, as well as the interactions between different knowledge bases (conceptual and linguistic), are increasingly being integrated into the design of systems (cf. Zock, 1988). These approaches, in return, are likely to favor the development of hypotheses on the interactions between conceptual processes and formulation processes in text generation.

For all these reasons, we felt that it would be useful to develop a text generator to simulate different kinds of descriptive strategies. Starting from a visual scene (for instance, a geographical configuration, or a spatial network such as those used in the experiments above), and incorporating a constraint specified by the user of the system (for instance, starting the description from a given point), the system should be capable of generating different types of texts, through the application of principles identified in the analysis of natural strategies.

The generator we built is an extension of SWIM, a prototype system (cf. Zock, 1991). It operates at two levels: (a) construction of a representation of the to-be-described object in terms of a conceptual graph; (b) expression of the description in natural language. A graphic module first generates networks similar to those used in the above-mentioned experiments. Once a network is displayed on the screen, the system generates an internal representation which encodes the locations of each node and its neighbors. The representational format used at this level considers each circle as a frame. Each circle explores its vicinity, and when a circle is detected in this space, its code is recorded in the appropriate field.

Once this internal representation has been built, the system decides on a strategy which will guide the description. The strategy is based on a set of heuristics and weightings derived from the model, based on previously collected cognitive data. Running of the strategy is based on the application of production rules which are used by an inference engine. The analysis is done by forward chaining. The system uses the

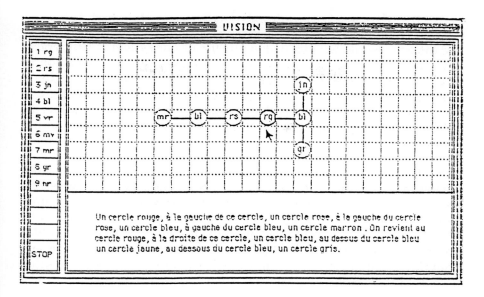

*Figure 5. Output produced by the text generator for network 2.1.
English translation: "A red circle. To the left of this circle, a pink
circle. To the left of the pink circle, a blue circle. To the left of the blue
circle, a brown circle. Let's go back to the red circle. To the right of
this circle, a blue circle. Above the blue circle, a yellow circle. Below
the blue circle, a grey circle."*

same kinds of rules as most people do. In particular, branches that
involve the lowest cognitive load are processed first.

After the strategy is selected, the system produces an output similar to
natural language. This operation takes place in two steps: (a)
construction of an internal representation of the output; (b) translation
of this representation into natural language. The internal representation
is built in the form of a conceptual graph. Then, the formal expression
is translated into a verbal expression. At this level, the system attaches a
color adjective to each circle and, according to the location where the
circle is to be mentioned in the sentence, a definite or an indefinite
article. If the article is repeated later, a demonstrative pronoun is used.
The system specifies whether the circle is above, below, at the right or
at the left of another circle. Figure 5 presents an example of a network
(network 2.1) and the verbal output produced by the system.

Conclusion

For the time being, the production module of our system is still largely deterministic. In particular, it does not allow for pronominalization or factorization. However, it is a first step in the direction of our long-term goal of joint collaboration between cognitive psychology and artificial intelligence in elucidating the factors which determine the choice of particular strategies in the description of spatial configurations.

The simulation is the first step in building new kinds of networks and testing the behavior of the system. The texts produced by the system should match the kinds of texts people are likely to produce. In other words, if our model incorporates relevant kinds of knowledge and strategies, it could predict human performance in the description of new spatial configurations, including more realistic ones, such as maps and routes.

RÉSUMÉ

Lorsque des sujets doivent décrire des réseaux spatiaux avec une contrainte sur le point d'initialisation de leur description, des stratégies dominantes de linéarisation discursive sont mises en évidence. Ces stratégies consistent à produire des séquences descriptives qui minimisent le nombre d'éléments conservés en mémoire de travail ou bien la durée de ce maintien en mémoire. L'analyse des latences de description révèle l'effet de la charge cognitive associée à la complexité des réseaux à décrire et suggère que l'application des stratégies optimales dépend d'une analyse plus approfondie des réseaux. Enfin, nous rapportons les premières étapes de la construction d'un générateur de textes capable de simuler différentes stratégies descriptives.

Acknowledgements

The work reported in this chapter was supported by two CNRS research grants, one from the Programme de Recherche sur les Sciences de la Communication, ASP "Communication multimédias: Interactions texte et image" (1990), and the other from the Programme Cognisciences, Réseau Régional Paris-Sud (1991). The authors are grateful to Maryvonne Carfantan and Connie Greenbaum for their assistance in the preparation of this paper.

References

Dale, R., Mellish, C., & Zock, M. (1990). *Recent advances in natural language generation.* New York: Academic Press.

Denis, M. (1991). *Image and cognition.* New York: Harvester Wheatsheaf.

Denis, M., Carité, L., & Robin, F. (1991). Cognitive approaches to the processing of descriptions. *Zeitschrift für Psychologie,* Supplement 11, 148-154.

Denis, M., & Denhière, G. (1990). Comprehension and recall of spatial descriptions. *European Bulletin of Cognitive Psychology, 10,* 115-143.

Ehrlich, K., & Johnson-Laird, P.N. (1982). Spatial descriptions and referential continuity. *Journal of Verbal Learning and Verbal Behavior, 21,* 296-306.

Foos, P.W. (1980). Constructing cognitive maps from sentences. *Journal of Experimental Psychology: Human Learning and Memory, 6,* 25-38.

Johnson-Laird, P.N. (1989). Mental models. In M.I. Posner (Ed.), *Foundations of cognitive science* (pp. 469-499). Cambridge, MA: The MIT Press.

Kempen, G. (1987). *Natural language generation: New results in artificial intelligence, psychology and linguistics.* Dordrecht, The Netherlands: Martinus Nijhoff.

Kulhavy, R.W., Lee, J.B., & Caterino, L.C. (1985). Conjoint retention of maps and related discourse. *Contemporary Educational Psychology, 10,* 28-37.

Levelt, W.J.M. (1982). Linearization in describing spatial networks. In S. Peters & E. Saarinen (Eds.), *Processes, beliefs, and questions* (pp. 199-220). Dordrecht, The Netherlands: Reidel.

Levelt, W.J.M. (1989). *Speaking: From intention to articulation.* Cambridge, MA: The MIT Press.

Linde, C., & Labov, W. (1975). Spatial networks as a site for the study of language and thought. *Language, 51,* 924-939.

Novak, H.-J. (1988). Generating referring phrases in a dynamic environment. In M. Zock & G. Sabah (Eds.), *Advances in natural language generation: An interdisciplinary perspective* (Vol. 2, pp. 76-85). London: Pinter Publishers.

Paivio, A. (1991). *Images in mind: The evolution of a theory.* New York: Harvester Wheatsheaf.

Paris, C.L., & McKeown, K. (1987). Discourse strategies for describing complex physical objects. In G. Kempen (Ed.), *Natural language generation: New results in artificial intelligence, psychology and linguistics* (pp. 97-115). Dordrecht, The Netherlands: Martinus Nijhoff.

Robin, F., & Denis, M. (1991). Description of perceived or imagined spatial networks. In R.H. Logie & M. Denis (Eds.), *Mental images in human cognition* (pp. 141-152). Amsterdam: North-Holland.

Zock, M. (1988). Natural languages are flexible tools: That's what makes them hard to explain, to learn and to use. In M. Zock & G. Sabah (Eds.), *Advances in natural language generation: An interdisciplinary perspective* (Vol. 1, pp. 181-196). London: Pinter Publishers.

Zock, M. (1991). SWIM or sink: The problem of communicating thought. In M. Swartz & M. Yazdani (Eds.), *The bridge for international communication: ITS and foreign language learning.* New York: Springer-Verlag.

PART II

GRAPHICS AND MENTAL REPRESENTATIONS

Comprehension of Graphics
W. Schnotz and R. W. Kulhavy (Editors)

Chapter 6

Representation and Processing of the Spatial Layout of Objects with Verbal and Nonverbal Input

Hubert D. Zimmer

Universität des Saarlandes, Saarbrücken, FRG

ABSTRACT

Memory for the spatial relations between pictures of objects or their names was tested in three series of experiments. In the first set, triplets of items had to be recalled or recognized. No effect of the triplet structure was observed in recall and in recognition of words, but recognition of pictures was faster if the target was primed by an item from the same triplet. In the second set, a map with 16 distinct locations of objects was learned from visual or verbal input and subjects were tested by an old/new recognition. Both groups yielded comparable spatial priming effects. In the third set, subjects learned the arrangement of pictures by placing the pictures themselves on specified positions in an empty map or by watching the experimenter doing that. At test, they had to relocate the items on the same or a rotated map. Neither enactment nor rotating the frame of reference influenced memory. The results are discussed as supporting the assumption of multiple memory systems that store different information and that are independently used in different tasks.

It is frequently assumed that different cognitive systems exist, each specialized to process a specific type of information, and each following its own rules. Language, for example, should be processed in other modules or subsystems than visual information, which includes processing of pictures, maps and diagrams (cf. Ellis & Young, 1989). In the following, I will briefly discuss this assumption in its relevance for spatial processing, then I will report some findings on spatial memory after different encoding operations. In the closing section I will mention some consequences of the modular assumption for memory and information processing.

If (modality) specific systems are assumed, at least one subsystem is considered to process spatial information, and this subsystem is more strongly associated with pictorial than with verbal processing. Kosslyn's buffer, for example, is a spatial system (e.g., Kosslyn, 1990), as is the 'visual sketch pad' (Baddeley & Lieberman, 1980; Logie, 1989), and also the 'picture-node-system' of Engelkamp and Zimmer (e.g., Engelkamp & Zimmer, forthcoming). Even if no specific subsystem is assumed to store spatial information, a specific representational type besides propositions and temporal strings is introduced (Anderson, 1983).

The following two assumptions, therefore, can be repeatedly found in the literature. First, spatial information is more likely to be encoded with pictures than with words (e.g., Park & Mason, 1982; Pezdek, Roman & Sobolik, 1986). Second, the visuo-spatial subsystem is used independently of the input modality, if it is necessary to process configural or shape information (e.g., Farah, Hammond, Levine & Calvanio, 1988; Zimmer, 1988). From these assumptions, we have to expect that spatial relations are differently processed with verbal or pictorial input, if subjects have to attend only to the identity of items, and that subjects rely on the spatial processing system if they have to encode items plus location.

These assumptions are also held in the Multi Modal model (e. g. Engelkamp & Zimmer, forthcoming). However, in this model a motor subsystem is additionally assumed to be, involved in overt actions, and a conceptual system is suggested that functions as a general purpose system with explicit predicates and that guide retrieval in verbal tasks (e.g., free recall). In the following, these subsystems are discussed in terms oftheir role for spatial processing. First, it is shown that which spatial effects occur depend on the task and the modality of the stimulus. Even with pictures, sometimes no spatial effects are observable, whereas with words spatial effects sometimes occur that are comparable to those observed with pictures. Afterwards, some findings about spatial memory in overt actions are reported. Voluntary movements processed by the motor system have to be coordinated in space and time. Therefore, the visual and the motor system may join a common spatial representation. Yet, this assumption is not compelling. It is equally likely that we have different spatial representations, that is, an exocentric spatial system representing location in absolute spatial coordinates and primarily used in vision, and an egocentric spatial representation used to direct movements (e.g., Phillips, 1983). If two different spatial representations exist, enactment does not necessarily influence spatial processing.

Triplets of pictures or words in recall and recognition

The first set of experiments should show to what extent spatial relations are automatically encoded with pictorial or verbal input, and to what extent these relations are used in two different memory tasks, recall and recognition. Spatial relations could be encoded at different levels, at a sensory level that is near to the data entry or at at an abstract conceptual level. At the same time, free recall is assumed to be conceptually driven, whereas recognition is assumed to be data-driven. Therefore, the same or different systems may be used at encoding and retrieval, and as a consequence spatial relations may sometimes cause memory effects and sometimes not. To test these assumptions, we conducted two experiments.

The first experiment was a free recall task (Zimmer, 1989). Subjects saw a series of slides, each depicting a triplet of objects or their names. The items on each slide were spatially arranged in form of a triangle. In the case where the three elements were pictures, these relations should be encoded and retained to some extent, even if subjects only paid attention to the identity of the items and did not focus on spatial relations (cf. Santa, 1977). In the case where words were presented in the same way, the elements of a triplet should be less strongly interconnected. If subjects in a free recall task use these triplet structures for retrieval, access to one element of a triplet should prime the other elements of the same triplet. Therefore, items from the same triplet should be recalled more often together than separated by elements from other triplets (cf. also Kulhavy, Stock & Caterino, this volume).

In this experiment twenty subjects saw ten triplets, half of them saw objects, half saw object names. Each slide was presented for seven seconds, and subjects were instructed to learn the objects or words for recall. Nothing was said about a possible importance of the triplet structure. Two minutes after the presentation, subjects did a free recall test and wrote down items in their preferred order. For more details see Zimmer (1989, Exp. 3). Proportion recalled and clustering were measured. Clustering was calculated as ARC scores (adjusted ratio of clustering; Roecker, Thompson & Brown, 1971) which in the case of no clustering has a value of 0 and in the case of perfect clustering a value of 1. Scenes were treated as "catgeories" and the adjacent recall of two members from the same scene was counted as a "repetiton". The results are given in Figure 1 (left panel). As can be seen, pictures were, as usual, better recalled than words. However, clustering was generally low; for words it was only slight, and for pictures it was nearly absent.

Does that mean that the three elements of the triplets were encoded separately and that no spatial relations were represented? To test this, we ran a second experiment, this time to test recognition. In this experiment, 32 subjects saw 15 triplets; half of them saw pictures, the other half words. Each slide was presented for eight seconds in two trials. Instructions were the same as in the recall group. For recognition, the items were intermixed with the same number of new items. In the test, two presentation conditions for old items were used. In the related condition, two items from the same triplet were presented consecutively; in the unrelated condition, the two items were from different triplets. Across subjects, the item-to-relatedness relations were counterbalanced. Subjects had to react to each item, i.e., prime and target item were treated the same, and they were not informed about the relatedness structure of the list. The subject's decision terminated the presentation of the target, and the next item immediately followed.

The mean recognition times for hits - recognition was nearly perfect - dependent on prime-target relations are also depicted in Figure 1 (right panel). In contrast to recall in recognition, the triplet-structure was effective with pictures but not with words, as is to be expected from a modality-specific encoding of spatial relations. For pictures the reactions were clearly faster if the prime was from the same triplet than if it was from another triplet. With words, the relatedness was not effective.

To summarize, in recognition of pictures we observed an influence of triplets, but not with words, whereas we generally have no triplet effects in free recall. Because the instructions were the same, we assume that the configural or spatial information was similarly encoded in the two experiments, but that this information was differently used. The automatically encoded spatial information is represented within the visual subsystem. However, except for specific strategies (see below), free recall is conceptually driven. Thus, location information does not

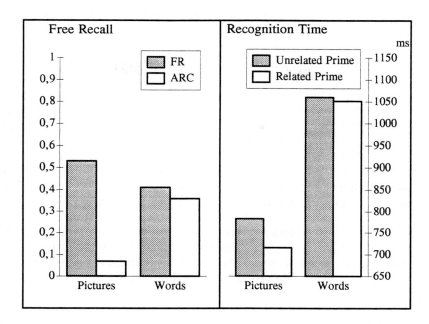

Figure 1. Left panel: Free recall performance and clustering by triplets as a function of encoding condition, pictures or words were presented in sets of three items. Right panel: Recognition times dependent on encoding condition and prime-target relation.

influence recall, even though the information would be available. This is different in recognition, which is a data-driven process. Now the to-be-recognized item taps its specific subsystem during stimulus processing. Therefore, priming effects occur with pictures for which spatial information was encoded, but not with words, which should usually be encoded individually. However, as the experiments of Kulhavy, Stock & Caterino (this volume) have shown, the influence of maps on recall may be different, if subjects are forced to intentionally encode and to use the spatial relations to retrieve items. In this case, a map can be used as an additional retrieval path and this also enhances text recall. This may also be the case with the loci method. However, what has yet to be shown, is to what extent and under what conditions spatial relations are present within the sensory and/or within the conceptual system.

Matrices of pictures or words in spatial priming

The previously reported experiments only reflect the automatic encoding and use of configural information, because subjects were not instructed to attend to spatial or triplet information. They were asked to learn individual items, which were given by their identity, but not by their location. The effects, thus, could have been different, if subjects had tried intentionally to learn the location of objects. This was done in the following experiments. Additionally, we looked not only at triplet relations, but also at spatial information proper. For the priming effect, it was sufficient to group items together. Spatial relations of objects within the triplet configuration need not be more closely analysed. To change that, we used a spatial priming task in the following experiment.

In these experiments, subjects were instructed to intentionally learn the location of features on two fictious islands. On these islands, 21 positions were specified, arranged in a 7 by 3 matrix. On 16 of these positions an item was placed. Two conditions were constructed. In the map condition subjects saw a physical map. In the text condition subjects read a text that decribed the map. Subjects were informed about the matrix structure, and then they got a text as, for example, "In the extreme north-western part of the island, there is a bridge. East of the bridge there are skyscrapers. East of the skyscrapers there is a petrol station. South of the petrol station there is a school. ..." In this way all elements were placed on unique positions on a connected path explicitly relating each element to one of its neighbours that was mentioned before.

Memory for location was tested in a free relocation and a recognition task. In free relocation items had to be recalled from memory and placed at their correct positions. We assume that with the explicit instruction to learn locations both groups used the visual system to process spatial information. However, pictorial stimuli have privileged access to this system. Spatial information is directly available, whereas in the text condition the information has to be recoded. Therefore, locational memory should be higher in the picture than in the text condition. In the recognition test each item had to be qualified as an old item, i.e., from one of the two islands, or a new one. Spatial information was tested as spatial priming. In the case of spatial priming a target is recognized faster if the prime was proximal in space than if it was distant (e.g., McNamara, 1986). Comparable spatial priming effects in the text and the physical map conditions would be taken as evidence of comparable spatial representations.

To test spatial priming, four different prime-target relations were constructed. In the unrelated condition ('Different') the prime was an old item, but from a different island as the target. In the 'Far' condition the prime was from the same island but remote, for example, the prime far north and the target in the south. Additionally, two Near conditions were realized, which differed in the text group. In Near_1 cases, prime and target were neighbours on the map, and they were mentioned together in the same sentence of the text. In the Near_2 conditions, they were also neighbours on the map, but they were not mentioned together in any sentence. If a spatial mental model was constructed, stronger priming effects should occur in the spatially proximal prime-target relations than in 'far' or 'different' cases. If the structure is comparable in the two encoding conditions, the priming effects in the two groups should also be comparable. In particular, equal priming effects in the Near_2 condition speak in favour of a spatial encoding. In this condition, prime and target were never explicitly related in the text; their spatial relation was only given in the spatial structure of the filled matrix, and could not be directly infered from the text.

Three experiments were run with a total of 80 subjects (for details cf. Denis & Zimmer, in press). The experiments differed in the sequence of free relocation and recognition, in test expectation (subjects expected a drawing of the map or a free description) and in study time. The priming effects were not affected by these variations, therefore the averaged recognition times over all three experiments are reported (Figure 2). Additionally, the recall performances of the free relocation task in Experiment 1 are given, in which relocation was the first task.

Memory of item identity with physical maps was better than with texts, and memory of positions was better still. The conditional probability to recall the correct position given an item is recalled was .87 in the physical map, but only .61 in the text group. In recognition false alarms were very low, and independent of condition. Hit rates were high, about .95 in the physical map and between .80 and .90 in the text group. In the text group, they varied unsystematically with relatedness. In recognition times, a clear spatial priming effect occured. The two near conditions differed neither in the physical map nor in the text group, but in both groups these reaction times were shorter than those in the Far condition. The Different condition was generally slower than the Far condition, but it was significant in the text group only.

These results clearly confirm our expectations. All subjects showed 'spatial' effects. A common way to explain the results is to assert a

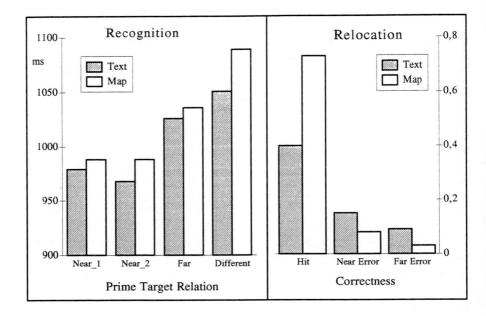

Figure 2. Left panel: Recognition times dependent on encoding condition (the spatial layout was learned from a text or a physical map) and prime target relation (the prime was near to or far from the target, or it was from a second 'map'). Right panel: Relocation performance in the text and the map condition.

spatial mental model, and additionally, that access to that model is tied up with spatial constraints. The effects in the text group were the same as in the map condition, independent of whether the spatial relations were explicitly given in the text or whether they were only stated in the spatial quality of the matrix. Therefore, we assume that the text group constructed and used a model comparable to the physical map group. However, this model is built up faster and more correctly from visual nonverbal input than from texts, but even with verbal input the complete spatial layout is reconstructed at encoding if locations have to be learned. We assume that for spatial tasks the visual spatial subsystem is automatically used.

Memory for spatial positions with actions

In the Multimodal Model we assume a motor as well as a spatial subsystem. The motor system is used if subjects really perfom actions. Does enactment also influence spatial memory? From a large number of experiments we know that enactment enhances memory for the identity of the performed actions (cf. Engelkamp & Zimmer, 1989). However, actions have to be coordinated temporally as well as spatially; thus a contribution of enacting to spatial memory is also possible. Such an assumption is supported, for example, by the interference of enactment with spatial tasks (e.g., Quinn & Ralston, 1986). Therefore, we would not be surprised if putting an object in a definite position would enhance memory for objects' position relative to only watching the object at be placed.

However, people probably have different mental representations of space for different frames of reference (cf. Phillips, 1983). At least two representations have been suggested; an exocentric map, representing objects' location from a birds-eye view in a 'map-like' manner, and an egocentric map, representing spatial information relative to the actor's position. In the exocentric spatial map, positions of objects are not changed if the observer moves, but in the egocentric map, which is used to reach or to grasp objects in actions, the spatial information is changed during movement. Locational actions, i.e., placing objects at definite positions, therefore, may add egocentric information to memory of subjects, but leaves exocentric information unchanged. To test this, the following experiment was conducted.

Thirty-six subjects participated in the experiment. Subjects in two enacting conditions held a stack of 16 cards from the game «Memory» in their hands. The two groups had the same encoding condition, but they differed in their testing condition. In front of the subjects, a blank map (about one square meter wide) was placed with 64 possible positions. These positions were, for example, arranged in one of the maps on a 4 by 8 matrix that was placed on top of two concentric circles. The inner circle had 12 positions, the outer circle had 20 positions. Every five seconds the experimenter indicated a position by pointing at it, and the subject then placed the upper card on the stack at that position. This procedure sequentially placed the 16 objects on the map. After subjects finished, they had 30 seconds to view the entire map. Then the whole procedure was repeated. A third visual-enactment group was run as a control. Those subjects had the same timing, but they watched the experimenter who filled in the map in the same way as did the subjects in the motor groups.

To test spatial memory a relocation task was done afterwards. All cards were given to the subjects and they had to place each card at its correct position. They were allowed to rearrange the cards. Subjects of the enactment-enactment group and those of the visual-enactment group placed the cards themselves on the empty map. The enactment-verbal group did the test verbally, i.e., subjects told the experimenter where to place a card. For this purpose small numbers were written at each position. The empty maps for relocation were presented in two versions. In the standard condition subjects got the empty map in their original orientation and they had to place the cards. In the second, the rotated condition subjects also got an empty map, but this map was now tilted 90 degrees, so that the original top was moved to left.

These different testing conditions should disclose whether, and if so, which type of spatial information is enhanced by enactment. If enactment enhances location memory, the two enactment groups should have a higher memory performance than the visual group whose performance is taken as baseline. If enactment during learning improves egocentric, but not exocentric information, location memory should be better when the egocentric representation can be better used. In this case, the enactment-enactment group should show better memory performances than the enactment-verbal group, because enactment at test should rely on the egocentric respresentation whereas the verbal description at test should more strongly rely on the exocentric representation. However, this advantage should be restricted to the test with the empty map oriented in its original form, and the effect should disappear with the rotated map. In terms of an 'object-centered' frame of reference, which is given in the exocentric spatial map, the positions of the objects are independent of rotation. However, in terms of the egocentric system, the new positions on the rotated map differ from those at learning, because positions were encoded relative to the actor's position, for example, 'top' is now 'left'. It is, therefore, to be expected that an egocentric representation suffers more from rotation than an exocentric representation.

As can be seen from Figure 3, enactment did not enhance location information. Memory was not impaired by rotation, and testing on rotated maps was as good as testing with the original orientation. Contrary to the expectation, the enactment-enactment group, which from the perspective of encoding specificity should have had the best

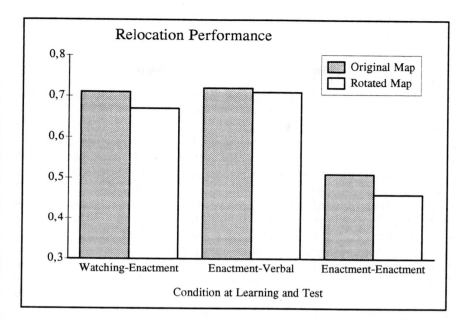

Figure 3. Mean relocation performance dependent on encoding and test condition (encoding/test).

performance, was significantly worse than the enactment-verbal and the visual-enactment group.

Taken together these results speak against the assumption that enactment enhances spatial information of the type that is needed for the task we used. It speaks in favor of the assumption that for learning locations of objects, exocentric representations are used and that enactment does not help in doing so. Therefore, it is for further experiments to demonstrate the influence of an egocentric representation on location memory, and to show that conditions exist in which an egocentric representation is more suitable than the exocentric one for spatial tasks. Such conditions may then also profit from enactment. However, it is also possible that an egocentric representation is generally not very efficient in long term memory, because it is continuously updated, and therefore interfered with by each positional change of the subject during enactment.

General discussion and practical implications

These experiments show once again that a specific encoding condition cannot per se be classified as the most efficient or best way of learning. Even conditions such as enactment, which strongly enhance memory in other tests may be inefficient under specific circumstances. The same is true for some effects of pictures and graphics.

In the first set of experiments, independent of modality, no effects of the spatial arrangement of items were observed in free recall, whereas in recognition 'spatial' effects were observed with picture stimuli, but not with words. However, in the second set of experiments, in which spatial processing was demanded by the task, the same spatial effects occured with words as with pictures, Although, some differences in memory between the two modalities persisted. Remembering location information was easier with pictures than with texts.

We explain these effects as a function of the specific constraints of the visual subsystem. We assume that the visual subsystem necessarily processes spatial information. It is automatically used to encode pictures, and it is used to construct a spatial mental model if requested. However, as we have seen, whether these spatial representations influence memory or not depends on the task. Generally speaking, if a specific type of information is represented and processed within a definite subsystem, the considered information only influences processing if the same subsystem is used again at the time of test. Which subsystem is taped is a matter of datadriven processes, of processes automatically initiated by the given task, or of explicit instructions.

The second subsystem considered, the motor system, is used in enactment and in motor tasks (e.g., Zimmer & Engelkamp, 1985). If subjects overtly enacted, recall and recognition of actions are strongly enhanced as other experiments have shown (cf. Engelkamp & Zimmer, 1989). Contrary to these effects, in the reported third set of experiments the information on the location of objects in 'small' maps was not enhanced. Surprisingly, memory for location was not better if the object was actively placed at its location by the subject than if the experimenter placed it. It may be that enactment in general does not influence spatial memory. However, it could also be that an egocentric spatial representation exists aside from an exocentric one, and that enactment does not enhance the exocentric, but only the egocentric representation. This question needs further research.

These observations have theoretical and practical consequences. In theoretical terms, these results support the assumption of different, independent subsystems of memory. This assumption is also supported by neuropsychological findings (e.g., Shallice, 1988). Each memory system is specialized to process its specific information. It is automatically taped by its specific input, and to use a subsystem enriches memory by the processed modality-specific information. The reported results speak in favor of an independent visual-spatial subsystem that is automatically used in picture processing and in spatial learning, but not in recall. The motor system engaged in overt enactment seems to be independent of that subsystem. If motor encoding embraces spatial information, the information may be different from that encoded in visual spatial processing. Perhaps spatial motor encoding is egocentric, which is different from the exocentric visual spatial representation. Clinical and neurological findings also show that more than one subsystem for spatial processing may exist, each specialized for specific information (e.g., Ellis & Young, 1989; Kosslyn, Flynn, Amsterdam & Wang, 1990).

For practical purposes, the results mean that to evaluate a specific encoding condition or learning strategy, one always has to keep in mind the task memory is used for (cf. the concept of transfer appropriated processing put forward by Morris, Bransford & Franks, 1977). Taking that conclusion seriously implies that each specific way of encoding has to be tested separately in respect of its efficiency for the task of interest. If we want to elude this disappointing consequence, we have to construct a functional model of memory. We have to say which subsystem in memory processes which type of information, and to then relate specific tasks to subsystems and modalities. Different subsystems are not equally suited to process each type of information. The visual system, for example, seems to be good for spatial relations, but not for temporal aspects. Overt enactment strongly enhances memory for the presence of an item, but perhaps not for its location.

In education, these differences become more and more important. The multimedia equipment, for example, that will be available in the near future in computer aided learning easily allows a multimodal and enriched encoding. However, multimodal encoding does not guarantee that memory is enhanced for the information of interest. The different modalities, including the actions performed in using the program, should always influence memory. They should enrich information that was sparsely given in the past, but possiblly at the expense of other information. Even if the same apparent information is transmitted, the use of the information may be qualitatively different. And moreover, even if the 'right' memory trace is enhanced it is not certain, that this information is used. We have thus to take care to enhance metamemory as well as the memory proper, so that subjects intentionally use information that is not used automatically.

RÉSUMÉ

La mémorisation des relations spatiales entre des dessins d'objets ou leurs noms est examinée dans trois séries d'expériences. Dans la première série, des configurations de trois items (dessins ou noms) étaient présentés et les sujets devaient soit réaliser une épreuve de rappel soit une épreuve de reconnaissance. On n'observe pas d'effet de la structure du triplet sur le rappel ou la reconnaissance des mots, mais la reconnaissance des dessins est plus rapide quand la cible était amorcée par un item du même triplet. Dans la deuxième série, les sujets devaient apprendre une carte contenant 16 localisations distinctes d'objets, présentée visuellement ou verbalement. Le test consistait en une épreuve de reconnaissance. Un effet d'amorçage spatial comparable est observé pour les deux groupes. Dans la troisième série, les sujets devaient apprendre la configuration des dessins soit en les plaçant eux-mêmes sur une carte vierge selon les positions qui leur étaient spécifiées, soit en observant l'expérimentateur les placer. Le test consistait à replacer les items sur la carte vierge, ou sur cette même carte à laquelle on avait fait subir une rotation. Ni le mode d'apprentissage, ni la rotation du cadre de référence n'ont d'influence sur la mémorisation. La discussion des résultats nous amène à faire l'hypothèse de multiples systèmes de mémoires stockant des informations différentes et utilisés indépendamment dans des tâches différentes.

References

Anderson, J.R. (1983). *The architecture of cognition*. Cambridge: Harvard University.

Baddeley, A.D., & Lieberman, K. (1980). Spatial working memory. In R. Nickerson (Ed.), *Attention and performance* (Vol. 8). (pp. 521-539). Hillsdale: Lawrence Erlbaum.

Denis, M., & Zimmer, H.D. (in press). Analog properties of cognitive maps constructed from verbal descriptions. *Psychological Research*.

Ellis, A., & Young, A.W. (1989). *Human cognitive neuropsychology*. Hillsdale: Lawrence Erlbaum.

Engelkamp, J. & Zimmer, H.D. (1989). Memory of action events: a new field of research. *Psychological Research, 51*, 153-157.

Engelkamp, J. & Zimmer, H.D. (forthcoming). The multimodal memory: Remembering pictures, actions and language.

Farah, M.J., Hammond, K.M., Levine, D.N., & Calvanio, R. (1988). Visual and spatial mental imagery: Dissociable systems of representations. *Cognitive Psychology, 20*, 439-462.

Kosslyn, S.M. (1990). Mental imagery. In D.N. Osherson, S.M. Kosslyn, & J.M. Hollerbach (Eds.), *Visual cognition and action. An invitation to cognitive science*, Vol 2. (pp. 73-98). Cambridge: MIT Press.

Kosslyn, S.M., Flynn, R.A., Amsterdam, J.B., & Wang, G. (1990). Components of high-level vision: A cognitive neuroscience analyses and accounts of neurological syndromes. *Cognition, 34*, 203-277.

Logie, R.H. (1989). Characteristics of visual short-term memory. *European Journal of Cognitive Psychology, 1*, 275-284.

McNamara, T.P. (1986). Mental representations of spatial relations. *Cognitive Psychology, 18*, 87-121.

Morris, C.D., Bransford, J.D. & Franks, J.J. (1977). Levels of processing versus transfer appropriate processing. *Journal of Verbal Learning and Verbal Behavior, 16*, 519-533.

Park, D.C., & Mason, D.A. (1982). Is there evidence for automatic processing of spatial and color attributes present in pictures and words. *Memory and Cognition, 10*, 76-81.

Pezdek, K., Roman, Z., & Sobolik, K.G. (1986). Spatial memory for objects and words. *Journal of Experimental Psychology, 12*, 530-537.

Phillips, W.A. (1983). Short-term visual memory. *Philosophical Transactions of the Royal Society of London, B 302*, 295-309.

Quinn, J.G., & Ralston, G.E. (1986). Movement and attention in visual working memory. *Quarterly Journal of Experimental Psychology, 38A*, 689-703.

Roecker, D.L., Thompson, C.P., & Brown, S.C. (1971). Comparison of Measures for the Estimation of Clustering in Free Recall. *Psychological Bulletin, 76*, 45-48.

Santa, J.L. (1977). Spatial transformations of words and pictures. *Journal of Experimental Psychology: Human Learning and Memory, 3*, 418-427.

Shallice, T. (1988). *From neuropsychology to mental structure*. New York: Cambridge University.

Zimmer, H.D. (1988). Formkonzepte und Bildmarken: Zwei verschiedene Repräsentationen für visuell-sensorische Merkmale? *Sprache und Kognition, 7*, 40-50.

Zimmer, H.D. (1989). Visuelle und semantische Merkmale im Recall. *Sprache und Kognition, 8*, 115-125.

Zimmer. H.D. & Engelkamp, J. (1985). An attempt to distinguish between kinematic and motor memory components. *Acta Psychologica, 58*, 81-106.

Comprehension of Graphics
W. Schnotz and R. W. Kulhavy (Editors)
© 1994 Elsevier Science B.V. All rights reserved.

Chapter 7

Size in Picture and Text

Johannes Engelkamp & Gilbert Mohr

Universität des Saarlandes, Saarbrücken, FRG

ABSTRACT

Episodic memory for serial order on the size dimension was investigated. Subjects had to study four-term orderings and were tested by a comparative judgement task. The stimuli were either verbal or pictorial. Under both modalities the correlation of spatial and size information was manipulated. Error rates were considered the dependent variable. A clear picture superiority effect was obtained. For verbal material end-term effects and distance effects were found. For pictorial stimuli a flat function for error rates over testpairs was observed, when spatial and size information were perfectly correlated. With incongruent size and spatial information the error pattern approached that for verbal material. The findings support the assumption that pictorial stimuli provide different or additional memory codes that can influence memory under appropriate conditions.

Graphics are often used to convey size information. They seem to be especially suitable for refering to relative differences between measures regardless of the semantics of these measures. To prefer graphical depictions to verbal descriptions only makes sense if one assumes that the former is easier to understand or more efficiently to be stored than the latter. This assumption, however, has never been tested empirically as far as we can see. Our research on size comparisons based on either pictorial or verbal stimuli may contribute to a test of this implicit assumption.

The concrete question addressed in our investigations can be stated in the following way. Do subjects who actually perceived size differences show better memory for these differences than subjects who were told about such differences? The test of this question is straightforward. Subjects can either be presented with pictures showing objects of different sizes or they can be presented with simple texts which provide the sizes of different objects verbally. The verbal stimuli, for instance, could be a list of simple sentences like the following:

> Object X is 5 cm long.
> Object Y is 10 cm long
> Object Z is 15 cm long

There are several possibilities to test memory performance. Subjects could be requested to reproduce the order of objects along the size dimension analogous to a serial recall. Subjects could be required to recall specific positions within this order similar to a cued recall. Or, subjects could be given pairs of objects with the instruction to indicate which element of the pairing had been longer or shorter in the acquisition phase. The latter comparative judgement procedure has often been used in experiments investigating memory for order information, however, without adressing the question of different stimulus modalites. Therefore, it seems sensible to use this procedure for the comparision of the two stimulus modalities as well.

What do we know about memory for pictorial and verbal stimuli in general and what do we know in particular about memory for relative sizes stored under both presentation modes? First of all, there is a robust picture superiority effect (PSE) in free recall as well as in recognition (e.g., Engelkamp, 1991, and Madigan, 1983 for reviews). This PSE is sometimes attributed to the excellent conceptual encoding of pictures (e.g., Anderson, 1980) and sometimes to the particular efficiency of a visual system that is supposed to be involved in the encoding and storage, when pictorial information is processed (Paivio, 1986). Some authors assume that verbal stimuli on the one hand lead to a pure conceptual code, whereas pictorial stimuli, on the other hand, result in pictorial as well as in conceptual codes (Nelson, 1979). Hence, the PSE is explained by the availability of multiple codes in the case of pictorial stimuli in contrast to a single conceptual code in the case of verbal stimuli.

Predictions concerning memory for ordinal size information could be based on the same multiple code hypothesis. One could argue that verbal stimuli lead to a pure conceptual code. Thus, the absolute size of an object might be stored in a proposition like "5 cm(object X)", relative sizes might be stored in propositions like "longer (Y,X)". Pictorial stimuli, on the other hand, provide a second source of information because they afford the direct storage of a visuo-spatial code that preserves the size differences within the stimuli. However, is there any empirical evidence supporting the assumption that pictorial input leads to a visuo-spatial code in a more or less automatic way?

If pictures or words are presented in a spatially distributed manner, for instance, randomly distributed over the cells of a matrix, it turns out that memory for location is extremly good for pictures, but comparatively poor for words (e. g., Anderson, 1976; Naveh-Benjamin, 1987; Pezdek, Roman & Sobolik, 1986). Whereas nearly all items of a picture that can be remembered can also be correctly relocated, memory for words and their locations are strongly dissociated. Only half of the remembered words can be correctly relocated. Thus, it seems as if location is more or less automatically encoded in the case of pictorial material, but widely discarded in the case of verbal input, supporting the assumption that a visuo-spatial code is generated with pictorial but not with verbal acquisition material. However, if we assume that "locus in space" is spontaneously preserved because of a direct storage into a visuo-spatial code system, it seems obvious to assume that size information is retained in this system as well.

There are, however, authors who assume that order information is translated into a spatial code (Huttenlocher, 1968; Trabasso & Riley, 1975); Huttenlocher (1968), for instance, promoted a "rating scale analogy" for the storage of linear orders. According to this proposition, ordinal information as size relations are encoded and stored into a spatial array. If this holds true, we have to consider two levels of spatial information in the case of pictorial acquisition stimuli presented for the generation of a linear order: the directly stored spatial layout of the pictorial display and the spatial code generated by the encoding of, for instance, the size relations. These two levels can be compatible or incompatible. Size information could be presented in a way that it is consistently correlated with positional information within the acquisition stimulus. The smaller objects could always be projected to the right and the larger objects could always be projected to the left on a screen. Objects could, however, also be presented in a way that there is no perfect correlation of position and size. Assume that there is a set of four objects A, B, C, D. The subject perceives pairs of the elements of such a set that allow the encoding of the order $A < B < C < D$. Now, some of these pairs could be presented so that the smaller element is given on the right and some pairs could be presented so that the smaller element is on the left. If spatial configurations are automatically encoded with pictures and if size relations are translated into spatial positions such partial reversals should clearly result in interference. Error rates should distinctively increase if the two levels of spatial codes are inconsistent. With verbal material such reversal should have no effects, because we do not have these two levels of spatial information. Spatial information within verbal acquisition material, as argued above, is supposed to be quickly discarded.

A further question that arises concerns the error pattern over the different testpairs and the influence of input modality on this pattern. Let us again assume that subjects are to encode a linear order of four objects. What is the typical error pattern over the six possible testpairs for such an ordering? For verbal material such studies have been conducted (Potts, 1972, 1974). In these studies subjects are usually presented with verbal material such as "A is larger than B, B is larger than C, and C is larger than D". They are then tested for all possible size relations among these objects. It is assumed that subjects try to form an integrated structure of the whole set such as "A < B < C < D" (Potts, 1972, 1974; Trabasso & Riley, 1975). There is evidence that subjects first try to identify the end-terms, e.g., the largest and smallest elements, and then try to correctly fill the slots in between. Consequently, end-term effects or anchor effects are to be expected. That is, in the case of four-term sets the most errors are to be expected for the test pair that includes no anchor element (BC). The lowest error rate, on the other hand, is to be expected for the pair that contains both anchor elements (AD).

From studies focussing on reaction times as the dependent variable we know that the anchor effects are modulated by distance effects. That is, the adjacent pairs AB and CD, for instance, need more processing time than the pairs AC and BD. Both effects -- the anchor effect as well as the distance effect -- have been repeatedly observed in reaction time data when verbally presented linear orderings were to be learned (Potts, 1972, 1974). It seems reasonable to expect a similar pattern for the error rates when the task is difficult enough to avoid ceiling effects (cf. Trabasso & Riley, 1975).

Shall we expect similar error patterns for verbal and pictorial stimuli? Two reasons suggest the expectation of a different pattern for pictorial input. First, subjects who are presented with pictorial stimuli might use

 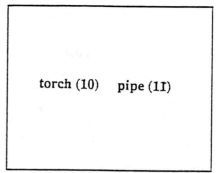

torch (10)   pipe (1I)

Figure 1.   Examples of the pictorial and the verbal studied stimuli

the visuo-spatial code to make their decisions and the error rate pattern might depend on the code accessed. Secondly, if pictorial input enables storage and access to both propositional and visuo-spatial code this might help to considerably reduce the overall error rate, which in turn might result in ceiling effects.

Thus, the experiment was set up to test three hypotheses. First, there should be less errors under pictorial than under verbal stimulus conditions. Secondly, the error rate pattern over the testpairs should resemble end-term as well as distance effects for verbal material, but a relatively flat function for pictorial material. Thirdly, the variation of the relationship between positional and size information is expected to affect the pictorial condition, but not the verbal condition.

Method

The general procedure of the experiment was as follows: Subjects were presented with a set of four objects or their labels. In the following, we refer to the four objects of a set by the terms A, B, C, D (A denotes the smallest element). The items were presented pairwise as illustrated in Figure 1.

The three adjacent pairs (AB, BC, CD) were presented for study in a fixed sequence starting with AB followed by BC followed by CD. All six possible pairings of a four-term set were tested. The test stimuli did not provide any size information. The subjects were presented with same-sized object or name pairs and had to indicate on which side the formerly larger object was presented by pressing the left or right button of a keyboard.

Material

Ten sets of four objects were constructed. The pictorial items were black-and-white line drawings of everyday objects. The verbal items were the labels of these objects. The size difference between two adjacent objects in pictorial study simuli was constantly 10% for all sets. This difference was easy to perceive. The verbal study stimuli were structured as follows. The labels were projected to the same locations as its pictorial counterparts. The size information was provided by numbers -- symbolizing length in cm -- in brackets immediately behind the respective label.

The objects of each set were chosen, so that the comparative judgement could not be based upon pre-experimental knowledge about size relations.

Two versions of the CD pair of each set were prepared. In one version the D element was depicted on the right in the other version it was depicted on the left of the screen. The CD reversal was realized for pictorial as well as for verbal stimuli.

All pictorial test-stimuli were same-sized. The verbal test-stimuli were identical to the study stimuli except that the brackets and the size information had been deleted. Each of the six possible testpairs was tested twice: Once with the formerly larger element on the left, once with the formerly larger element on the right.

One set was used as the practice trial. The remaining nine sets were given to all subjects in a fixed order.

Design

A 2 x 2 x (6) split-plot design was set up with the factors Modality (pictures/words), Presentation Form (CD/DC) and Testpair (AB, BC, CD, AC, BD, AD). The first two factors were measured between-subjects. The factor Testpair was measured within-subjects.

Subjects

Seventy-two subjects participated in the experiment, eighteen subjects in each of the four groups. All subjects were students of the University of the Saarland. They were paid for their participation.

Procedure

Subjects were instructed that they had to learn the relative sizes of four different objects which were presented pairwise and successively at a rate of eight seconds per pair. They were informed that they would receive study and test trials alternately. They were also exactly informed about the test procedure. After having received the instructions, subjects were presented with the practice trial in order to familiarize them with the procedure. Then the nine experimental trials followed.

The test-trials were structured in the following way. Each testpair was announced by an acoustic stimulus 500 ms before the presentation of the test stimulus began. With testpair stimulus onset, a millisecond timer was started which was stopped by the subject's keypress. Subjects had 3000 ms to indicate their decision. If they did not react within this intervall, the next trial started automatically. Each test-pair presentation was separated by a pause of 1000 ms. This pause started either with the keypress or after the 3000 ms maximum presentation time. The pause ended with the acoustic signal announcing the next trial. Between the last testpair of a study-test block and the first studypair of the next study-test block, the procedure was stopped and could be reactivated by the subject her-/himself. Study phase and test phase were separated by a fixed, blank 5 s retention interval.

Results

There were less than 1% no-reactions. No-reactions were scored as errors. Table 1 shows the mean error rates in an overview.

A 2x2x(6) ANOVA with the factors Modality, Presentation Form and Testpair over subjects as the random variable was conducted. There was a reliable effect for the factor Modality ($F(1,68)=12.26$; $MSe=0.03$; $p<.001$). Subjects produced more errors with words (10.8%) than with

Table 1. Mean error rates (percentages) for verbal and pictorial stimuli as a function of presentation form (CD vs. DC) and testpair.

testpair		AB	BC	CD	AC	BD	AD
pictorial							
	CD	8 (7.2)	7 (5.7)	5 (4.8)	7 (6.1)	6 (8.1)	6 (8.4)
	DC	7 (6.8)	10 (9.4)	4 (4.5)	3 (3.5)	3 (4.5)	1 (1.9)
verbal							
	CD	11 (7.6)	20 (16.8)	9 (6.3)	9 (7.8)	7 (7.7)	3 (4.0)
	DC	10 (13.0)	20 (16.1)	17 (13.5)	8 (11.1)	10 (12.6)	6 (10.6)

Note. The standard deviations are given in parantheses.

pictures (5.6%). There was no effect for the factor Presentation Form (F<1), but a significant effect for the factor Testpair ($F(5,340)=19.43$; MSe=0.005; p<.001). This effect was, however, qualified by an interaction of the factors Testpair and Modality ($F(5,340)=5.41$; MSe=0.005; p<.001) which was again qualified by a weak threefold interaction ($F(5,340)=1.93$; MSe=0.005; p<.09).

In order to trace this weak threefold interaction two separate 2x(6) ANOVAs were conducted: one over the two groups receiving pictorial input and one over the two groups receiving verbal material.

The analysis for the verbal stimuli yielded only a significant effect for the factor Testpair ($F(5,170)=16.86$; MSe=0.006; p<.001).

The analysis for the pictorial stimuli yielded the following effects. The factor Presentation Form just fell short of the usual significance level ($F(1,34)=3.23$; MSe=0.006; p<.08). Error rates tended to be higher for the CD presentation form (6.5%) than for the DC presentation form (4.7%). There was a clear effect for the factor Testpair ($F(5,170)=4.54$; MSe=0.003; p<.001), and there was a weak interaction of the factors Testpair and Presentation Form ($F(5,170)=2.17$; MSe=0.003, p<.06).

As can be seen in Table 1 and as a Scheffé test revealed (Diffcrit/p=.10=7), the DC presentation form for pictorial stimuli produced the error pattern that we expected for verbal material. The highest error rate was observed for the BC-pair, and the lowest rate was found for the AD-pair. On the other hand, there were no differences between the testpairs under the CD presentation form.

Discussion

There are three main findings. First, there is a picture superiority effect. Verbal stimuli result in less accurate decisions than pictorial stimuli. This effect is in line with the assumption that the processing of pictorial stimuli results in additional codes that can be accessed in the testphase and that provides information which helps to be more accurate.

Secondly, the function of the error rates over the testpairs shows end-term effects and distance effects. Accuracy is increased if one of the two end-terms is included in the testpair. And, accuracy tends to decrease with increasing distance between the two terms of a testpair. This finding supports the idea that integrated propositional codes are constructed. Thus, the error rate pattern mirrors the reaction time pattern repeatedly found with the same paradigm (Potts, 1972, 1974).

Thirdly, the typical error pattern interpreted as indicating the generation of an integrated propositional code, is confined to three of our four conditions. The interactions present in our data set suggest that end-term effects are clearly obtained only with verbal material. The situation with pictures is different. Pictorial input produces a rather flat function in the CD version indicating neither end-term nor distance effects. The error pattern under the DC presentation form, on the other hand, is almost identical to that of the verbal stimuli although on a lower level. The flat function under the CD presentation form is unlikely to be due to a ceiling effect, because the overall error rate for the CD form is higher than the rate for the DC form.

We assume that the finding of the usual end-term and distance function for the DC presentation form indicates that the CD reversal led our subjects to primarily base their judgements on a propositional code resulting in a pattern similar to that of the verbal material. The fact that the overall error level is nevertheless lower than that for the verbal material might indicate that propositional encoding based on pictures is more efficient than that based on verbal material.

Conclusion

The reported experiment demonstrates that graphical depictions can have advantages over verbal descriptions. This holds true in any case when differences on a size dimensions are to be encoded. We attribute this advantage of pictorial over verbal stimuli to the fact that size information contained in pictures is directly stored in a visuo-spatial code from which it can be read off if necessary. In addition, it seems as if the propositional code generated with pictorial stimuli is more reliable than the propositional code generated with verbal input.

In our case, the verbal material is presented in the form of predicates to individual concepts. Subjects are not explicitly given the comparative expressions. Thus, they have to recode the absolute size values into a comparative or relational structure. These recoding operations possibly make the representation of an integrated linear order of all elements in a set more difficult to achieve. As a result the specific error pattern with end-term and distance effects is obtained.

This general conclusion must, however, be specified relative to the background of the observed interaction of the factors Testpair and Presentation Form. This interaction suggests that pictures do not automatically induce an additional recoding. Either the propositional code is not generated or it is generated, but not accessed during test. On the other hand, if the more difficult DC presentation form is presented, the typical error pattern associated with propositional codes shows up again. The DC-presentation form does not only produce the typical error pattern usually observed with verbal material it also decreases the low error level with pictures even more. The conclusion from this finding could therefore be that for an optimal encoding of pictures it is not sufficient to pictorially present size information. To obtain optimal encoding with pictures one should take care to induce dual encoding and to encourage access to both propositional and visuo-spatial code during test.

The paradigm used here was kept as simple as possible. It contained only size variations. Such variations in size or on any other dimension are usually depicted as a function of another variable or several other variables in graphics used to illustrate, for instance, scientific results. More complex graphics lead to additional problems not included in our design (cf. the contributions of Gobbo and of Maichle in this volume). Whether it can be stated that depictions are to be preferred to verbal descriptions in these more complex cases is an open question which needs further research.

RÉSUMÉ

La mémoire épisodique des ordres sériels concernant la taille est examinée dans une expérience. Les sujets devaient étudier des séries de quatre termes de longueur différente. Les performances étaient mesurées à l'aide d'une épreuve de jugement de comparaison. Les stimuli étaient soit verbaux, soit picturaux. La correspondance entre l'information spatiale et l'information sur la taille était manipulée ; dans la moitié des cas, la position des objets formant les paires présentées ne correspondait pas à l'ordre sériel. L'analyse des taux d'erreurs révèle un effet marqué de supériorité de la présentation picturale sur la présentation verbale. Pour le matériel verbal, des effets de distance et d'ancrage sur les extrêmes sont observés. Pour les stimuli picturaux, il n'y a pas d'effet quand les informations de taille et de position sont congruentes. Par contre, quand les deux informations étaient incongruentes, le pattern d'erreurs est proche du pattern observé pour le matériel verbal. Les résultats suggèrent que les stimuli picturaux permettent des formes de codage différentes ou supplémentaires pouvant influencer la rétention dans des conditions appropriées.

Acknowledgements

The experiment reported in this paper was supported by a grant form by the Deutsche Forschungsgemeinschaft (En 124/9-1).

References

Anderson, J.R. (1980). *Cognitive psychology and its implications*. New York: Freeman.

Anderson, R.E. (1976). Short-term retention of the where and when of pictures and words. *Journal of Experimental Psychology: General, 105*, 378-402.

Engelkamp, J. (1991). *Das menschliche Gedächtnis*. Göttingen: Hogrefe.

Huttenlocher, J. (1968). Constructing spatial images: A strategy in reasoning. *Psychological Review, 75*, 550-560.

Madigan, S. (1983). Picture Memory. In J.C. Yuille (Ed.), *Imagery, memory and cognition* (pp. 65-89). Hillsdale: Lawrence Erlbaum.

Naveh-Benjamin, M. (1987). Coding of spatial information: An automatic process? *Journal of Experimental Psychology: Learning, Memory, and Cognition, 13*, 595-605.

Nelson, D.L. (1979). Remembering pictures and words: Appearence, significance and name. In L.S. Cermak & F.I.M. Craik (Eds.), *Levels of processing in human memory*. Hillsdale, New Jersey: Erlbaum.

Paivio, A. (1986). *Mental representations*. New York: Oxford University Press.

Pezdek, K., Roman, Z., & Sobolik, K.G. (1986). Spatial memory for objects and words. *Journal of Experimental Psychology: Learning, Memory, and Cognition, 12*, 530-537.

Potts, G.R. (1972). Information processing strategies used in the encoding of linear orderings. *Journal of Verbal Learning and Verbal Behavior, 11*, 727-740.

Potts, G.R. (1974). Storing and retrieving information about ordered relationships. *Journal of Experimental Psychology, 103*, 431-439.

Trabasso, T., & Riley, C.A. (1975). The construction and use of representations involving linear order. In R. L. Solso (Ed.) *Information processing and cognition* (pp. 381-410). New York: Lawrence Erlbaum.

Chapter 8

Visual Aids to Knowledge Construction:
Building Mental Representations from Pictures and Words

Richard E. Mayer

University of California, Santa Barbara, USA

ABSTRACT

When do illustrations and pictures help students to understand verbal descriptions of how a simple device works? Based on a dual-coding theory of learning from words and pictures, four conditions are proposed: (a) the material is explanative, that is, it presents a cause-and-effect chain of how something works rather than a list of arbitrary facts; (b) the illustration or animation is explanative, that is, it presents several frames depicting changes in the system and is coordinated with a verbal description of the changes, rather than a single frame uncoordinated with a verbal description; (c) the learner lacks prior knowledge about the system; and (d) the test evaluates understanding, such as problem-solving transfer, rather than retention of specific details. The predictions were confirmed in a series of 28 experimental tests.

The goal of this chapter is to examine how visual aids presented during instruction can influence the process of knowledge construction in learners. By knowledge construction, I refer to the idea that learning involves building a mental representation rather than simply absorbing or receiving knowledge (Resnick, 1989). In science learning, which is the focus of my research work, building mental representations involves constructing mental models of scientific systems (Bobrow, 1985; Kieras & Bovair, 1984; Gentner & Stevens, 1983; Johnson-Laird, 1983; Mayer, 1989a; White & Frederiksen, 1987). A mental model is a mental representation consisting of parts and causal relations among the parts in which a change in the state in one part is related to a change in the state of another part. By visual aids, I refer to illustrations in textbook-based instruction or animations in computer-based instruction. Although approximately half the space in science textbooks is devoted to illustrations, little is known concerning the characteristics of effective text illustrations (Mayer, in press), and although computer-based instructional systems are capable of providing dazzling animations, little is known concerning the characteristics of effective animations (Reiber, 1990).

For example, consider the following scenario: a student goes to an encyclopedia and reads the entry for "pumps" in order to learn how a bicycle tire pump works. The student reads the material thoroughly, and is able to recall approximately 25% of it. However, when you ask the student to use that information to answer problem-solving questions, such as "If a pump doesn't work what could be wrong?", the student is not able to produce any more creative solutions than a student who did not read the material. For this student, the verbal knowledge acquired from the encyclopedia is inert--it cannot be used to solve new problems. Apparently, the student--while memorizing some of the words--has failed to produce a useful mental model of the pump; that is, the student has failed to identify the key parts--such as the handle, piston, cylinder, inlet valve, outlet valve, and hose--and has failed to understand causal relations such as when the piston moves up the inlet valve opens and the outlet valve closes.

Pointing to the role of knowledge construction in learning, Resnick (1989, p. 4) recently observed that "to learn something, to come to understand it is, in the current cognitive science parlance, to construct a mental model." Pointing to the need to develop instructional aids to knowledge construction, Resnick (1989, p. 4) asked, "How can we best assist learners in their process of constructing powerful and accurate mental representations of situations?" In this paper, I focus on the construction of mental models in science learning. How can we help students to understand how various scientific systems and devices work? How can we insure that science students will construct mental representations that support creative problem solving performance? This brief review examines the role of certain types of visual aids in achieving these instructional goals.

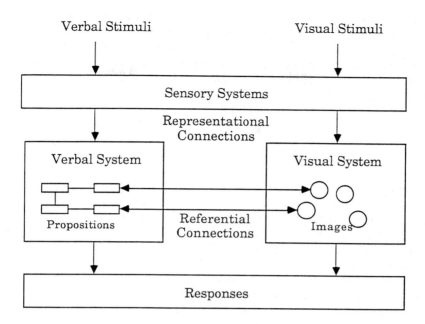

Figure 1. A Dual-Coding Model of Learning From Words and Pictures. Adapted from Figure 2 in Mayer & Anderson (1991). Copyright by American Psychological Association. Reprinted by permission.

A dual-coding theory of learning from words and pictures

My interest in visual aids is stimulated by a version of Paivio's (1971, 1986; Clark & Paivio, 1991) dual-coding theory, as summarized in Figure 1. The theory proposes that three types of connections can be constructed by learners when they are presented with verbal and visual material: (a) representational connections between verbal material and mental representations of verbal material, such as remembering "when the piston moves up, the inlet valve opens"; (b) representational connections between visual stimuli and mental representations of visual material such as visualizing the piston moving up within the cylinder as the inlet valve opens; and (c) referential connections between visual and verbal representations, such as mapping the verbal description of the piston moving up onto the visual image of the piston moving up. In a previous paper (Mayer & Anderson, 1991), we have argued that while retention of verbal information requires the building of only one kind of connection (i.e., verbal representational connections), improvements in creative problem solving performance require that the learner build all three kinds of connections. It follows that when creative problem solving is an instructional goal successful visual aids must enable the learner to build useful visual representations and connect them with relevant verbal representations.

Illustrations as aids to knowledge construction

Learning how a system works via text and illustrations

As an example of a visual aid to knowledge construction, consider how the illustration in Figure 2 and the text given below interact to help a learner construct a mental representation of how a pump works.

> *Bicycle tire pumps vary in the number and location of the valves they have and in the way air enters the cylinder. Some simple bicycle tire pumps have the inlet valve on the piston and the outlet valve at the closed end of the cylinder. A bicycle tire pump has a piston that moves up and down. Air enters the pump near a point where the connecting rod passes through the cylinder. As the rod is pulled out, air passes through the piston and fills the areas between the piston and the outlet valve. As the rod is pushed in, the inlet valve closes and the piston forces air through the outlet valve. (World Book Encyclopedia, Volume 15, 1987, p. 794).*

In this case, the mental model constructed by a successful learner includes the following parts: a handle that can move up or down, a piston that can move up or down, an inlet valve that can be open or closed, a cylinder that can can contain high or low pressure air, and an outlet valve that can be open or closed. The causal relations constructed by a successful learner include the following chain of events: if the handle is pulled up, then the piston moves up, the inlet valve opens, the outlet valve closes, and air enters the cylinder; if the handle is pushed down, then the inlet valve closes, the outlet valve opens, and air exits through the hose. The learner's model can be enhanced by incorporating a physical principle underlying the chain of events, such as the idea that air moves from areas of higher pressure to areas of lower pressure.

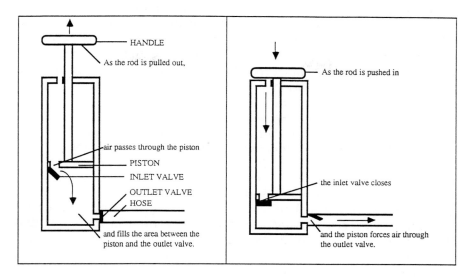

Figure 2. Illustration to Accompany Pump Text. Adapted from Figure 2 in Mayer & Gallini (1990). Copyright by American Psychological Association. Reprinted by permission.

To assess learning we can ask retention and transfer questions. For retention we can ask the learner to "write down all you can remember from the passage you have just read" as if "you are writing an encyclopedia for beginners." For transfer, we can ask students to generate answers to questions such as, "What could be done to make a pump more reliable, that is, to make sure it would not fail?" or "Suppose you push down and pull up on the handle of a pump several times but nothing comes out. What could have gone wrong?"

As another example, consider the following passage on brakes in conjunction with the illustration of a braking system in Figure 3:

> *Hydraulic brakes use various fluids instead of levers and cables. In automobiles, the brake fluid is in the chambers called cylinders. Metal tubes connect the master cylinder with wheel cylinders located near the wheels. When the driver steps on the car's brake pedal, a piston moves forward inside the master cylinder and through the tubes to the wheel cylinders. In the wheel cylinders, the increase in fluid pressure makes a set of smaller pistons move. These*

*smaller pistons activate either drum brakes or disk brakes,
the two types of hydraulic brakes. Most automobiles have
drum brakes on the rear wheels and disk brakes on the
front wheels. Drum brakes consist of a cast-iron drum and
a pair of semicircular brake drums. The drum is bolted to
the center of the wheel on the inside. The drum rotates with
the wheel, but the shoes do not. The shoes are lined with
asbestos or some other material that can withstand heat
generated by friction. When the brake shoes press against
the drum, both the drum and the wheel stop or slow down.
(World Book Encyclopedia, Volume 2, 1987, p. 571).*

A potentially useful mental model for a drum braking system includes:
a brake pedal that moves forward and back, a piston inside a master
cylinder that moves forward and back, brake fluid in the tubes that
increases or decreases in pressure, smaller pistons inside the wheel
cylinder that move forward or back, brake shoes that move out or in,
and a drum attached to a wheel that rotates or stops. The causal
relations constructed by a successful learner include the following chain
of events: if the pedal is pushed, the piston moves forward, brake fluid
increases in pressure, the smaller pistons move forward, the brake shoes
move forward, and the drum and wheel stop. As with the pump system,
the learner's model can be enhanced by incorporating a physical
principle underling the chain of events, such as the idea that fluid moves
from areas of higher pressure to areas of lower pressure and the idea
that friction slows a moving object.

As with the pump material, we can assess retention by asking the
learner "write down all you can remember from the passage you have
just read" as if "you are writing an encyclopedia for beginners" and we
can ask assess transfer by asking questions such as, "What could be done
to make a car's brakes more reliable, that is, to make sure it would not
fail?" or "Suppose you push down on the brake pedal but nothing
happens. What could have gone wrong?" We refer to the pump and
brakes passages as explanative material because they seek to explain a
cause-and-effect chain, rather than to describe or enumerate facts.

The cognitive conditions for effective illustrations

In a series of experiments carried out in our lab at Santa Barbara, we
compared the test performance of students who read explanative

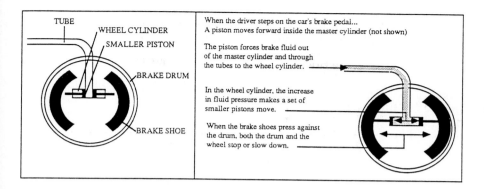

Figure 3. Illustration to Accompany Brakes Text. Adapted from Figure 1 in Mayer (1989b). Copyright by American Psychological Association. Reprinted by permission.

passages containing illustrations with the performance of students who read the same passages without illustrations (Mayer, 1989b; Mayer & Gallini, 1990). This work has allowed us to tentatively identify four conditions under which visual aids, such as the illustrations in Figures 2 and 3, have a strong effect on learning: (a) when the material is explanative, that is, the material contains a cause-and-effect chain rather than a list of facts, (b) when the illustrations are explanative, that is, the illustrations consist of a series of frames depicting the states of the system along with integrated verbal labels describing the state changes rather than a one-frame static picture, (c) when the students lack domain knowledge, and (d) when the test evaluates problem-solving transfer.

For example, Table 1 summarizes the average percentage of improvement in the performance of learners given explanative illustrations with text (illustrations group) over learners given text only (control group), when all or some of these conditions were met. In five separate experiments involving material such as brakes and pumps, inserting illustrations in text in accord with all four conditions increased the number of creative problem-solving solutions an average of 91% (Mayer, 1989b, Experiments 1 and 2; Mayer & Gallini, 1990, Experiments 1, 2, and 3). In contrast, when condition b was not met such as when the illustrations did not contain verbal labels corresponding to the text (Mayer, 1989b; Experiment 2) or when the illustrations presented only one-frame rather than a series of frames averaged 10%; when the sub-

Table 1. Median improvement in test performance for illustration group versus control group for four conditions.

Conditions met	Mean improvement	Number of tests	Description of deficiency
abcd	+91%	5	[None]
acd	+10%	4	Illustrations lack verbal labels or have one frame
abd	+8%	3	Learners lack domain knowledge
abc	-10%	5	Test cover verbatim retention or recall of details

jects possessed high levels of domain-knowledge (in violation of condition c), the increase averaged 8% (Mayer & Gallini, 1990; Experiments 1, 2, and 3); and when the test evaluated verbatim retention or recall of extraneous details (in violation of condition d), performance averaged 10% less in the illustrations group than the control group (Mayer, 1989b, Experiments 1 and 2; Mayer & Gallini, 1990; Experiments 1, 2, and 3). This pattern of results is consistent with the proposal that powerful effects on meaningful learning occur when visual aids provide opportunities that otherwise would not be available for constructing a visual model of the system and connecting that visual model to corresponding verbal representations.

Animations as aids to knowledge construction

Learning how a system works via narrations and animations

The next step in our program of research was to extend our investigation of graphics from learning via textbook-based instruction to learning via computer-based instruction. For example, consider the situation in which a student has access to a computerized encyclopedia; the student clicks on "pumps" and hears the following narration presented while at the same time viewing an animation based on the illustration in Figure 2: "When the handle is pulled up, the piston moves up, the inlet valve opens, the outlet valve closes, and air enters the lower part of the cylinder. When the handle is pushed down, the piston moves down, the inlet valve closes, the outlet valve opens, and air moves out through the hose." If a student clicks on "brakes", the computer presents the following narration concurrently with an animation based on the illustration in Figure 3: "When the driver steps on the car's brake pedal, a piston moves forward inside the master cylinder. The piston forces brake fluid out of the master cylinder and through the tubes to the wheel cylinder. In the wheel cylinders, the increase in fluid pressure, makes a set of smaller pistons move. These smaller pistons activate the brake shoes. When the brake shoes press against the drum, both the drum and the wheel stop or slow down." The narration is presented in synchrony with the animation so that, for example, when the narration says "the inlet valve opens" the animation shows the inlet valve moving from the closed to the open position, and so on. In essence, the student receives a distilled explanation of how a system works in words and in pictures.

This concurrent presentation of verbal and visual explanation fosters the conversion of the narration into a coherent verbal representation (i.e., building verbal representational connections), the conversion of the animation into a coherent visual representation (i.e., building visual representational connections), and, most importantly, the linking of visual and verbal representations (i.e., building referential connections). As with illustrations-in-text, we propose that the animations will be most effective in eliciting these three cognitive processes when (a) the material is explanative; (b) the animation is explanative, that is, it depicts the changes in the system and simultaneously presents a corresponding auditory description of the changes; (c) the subjects are inexperienced; and (d) the tests evaluate meaningful understanding.

The cognitive conditions for effective animations

In order to test some of these predictions we asked students to view animations and/or listen to narrations of how pumps or brakes work for a total of three presentations, and then answer retention and transfer questions. Table 2 summarizes the improvement in test performance of students who received both animation and narration (animation group) versus students who received narration only (control group), based on a

Table 2. Improvement in test performance for animation group versus control group under three conditions

Conditions met	Mean improvement	Number of tests	Description of deficiency
abcd	+100%	4	[None]
acd	+23%	4	Animations not concurrent with narration
abd	n/a	0	Learners lack domain knowledge
abc	-3%	3	Tests cover verbatim recall

series of four experiments (Mayer & Anderson, 1991, in press). The first row of Table 2 shows that when all four conditions were met--the material is explanative, the narration is synchronous with the animation, the students are inexperienced, and the test covers problem-solving transfer--then students given animation and narration performed twice as well on the test as students who received only narration (Mayer & Anderson, 1991; Experiments 1 and 2; Mayer & Anderson, in press, Experiments 1 and 2). However, the second row shows that when the identical animation was presented either after or before the narration (rather than concurrently), the effect of the narration on problem-solving performance was minimal (Mayer & Anderson, 1991; Experiments 1 and 2; Mayer & Anderson, in press, Experiments 1 and 2); similarly, the fourth row shows that when we compare students who received concurrent narration and animation to those receiving narration only on tests of verbatim recall, the animations produced no positive effects (Mayer & Anderson, 1991; Experiment 2; Mayer & Anderson, in press, Experiments 1 and 2). We did not test high prior-knowledge students, but if we had we would have expected the effects of animations to be minimal.

Conclusion

Theoretical implications

The pattern of results over a series of nine experiments is consistent with the dual-coding model summarized in Figure 1. According to the model, coherent verbal material--presented in printed or oral form-- allows the learner to construct verbal representations; well-designed visual material--presented as multi-frame illustrations or animations-- allows the learner to construct visual representations. However, an additional process--the constructional of referential connections between verbal and visual representations--is needed to support creative problem solving performance. A key to opening this third process is contiguity of presentation of visual and verbal material. Our research suggests a contiguity principle in which referential connections are more likely to be constructed when words and pictures are presented near one another in space (as in visual illustrations that include verbal labels) or in time (as in concurrent presentation of narration synchronized with animation).

Instructional implications

Although the potential advantages of visuals have been extolled by instructional designers, research on illustrations and animations is far from complete (Houghton & Willows, 1987; Mandl & Levin, 1989; Reiber, 1990; Willows & Houghton,1987). Our program of research provides some modest support for the idea that visual devices such as illustrations or animations can have powerful effects on learning under certain circumstances. Over a series of experiments (Mayer, 1989b, Mayer & Anderson, 1991, in press; Mayer & Gallini, 1990) a consistent pattern is emerging concerning the characteristics of effective visual aids for helping students to construct mental models for simple devices and systems.

First, illustrations and animations can be effective only when the material itself is potentially understandable as a system in which a change in one part causes a change in another part. This kind of material corresponds to one of the text structures commonly used in science textbooks called sequence--a description of the cause-and-effect chain of events in a process (Cook & Mayer, 1988). The brakes and pumps systems described in this paper meet this condition, whereas a factual description of the history of their invention or an enumeration of the types of pumping or braking systems would not.

Second, illustrations or animations are effective when they allow the student to build a coherent mental model of the system, consisting of the main parts and causal connections among changes in state of the parts. In our research we have found that this goal can be accomplished by presenting multi-frame illustrations or animations that allow the learner to infer state changes, but not by a single static picture that shows only one state of the system. In addition to helping the student build a visual representation, the illustrations or animations must help the learner connect the visual representation with a verbal one. In our research this is accomplished by embedding verbal labels within illustrations and by temporally coordinating narration with animation.

Third, illustrations and animations are most effective when the learner would not naturally engage the cognitive processes of building referential connections between visual and verbal representations. Consistent with this condition, in our research, visual aids have been more effective for students who lack prior knowledge of technical domains than for students who possess high levels of prior knowledge.

Finally, illustrations and animations are most effective when the goal of instruction is meaningful learning as measured by problem-solving transfer. In our research, visual aids tended to double the number of creative solutions produced by learners but not to have strong effects on verbal retention of details.

RÉSUMÉ

Quand les illustrations et les dessins aident-ils les étudiants à comprendre des descriptions verbales du fonctionnement d'appareils simples? Basées sur une théorie du double codage de l'apprentissage à partir de mots et d'images, quatre conditions sont proposées: (a) le matériel est explicatif, c'est à dire, il présente la chaîne des causes à effets du fonctionnement, plutôt qu'une liste arbitraire de faits; (b) l'illustration ou l'animation est explicative, autrement dit, plusieurs cadres figurant des changements dans le système sont présentés et sont combinés à une description verbale des changements, plutôt qu'un cadre unique non combiné avec une description verbale; (c) l'apprenant ne dispose pas de connaissances antérieures concernant le système; et (d) le test évalue la compréhension, comme dans les tâches de résolution de problème, plutôt que la rétention de détails spécifiques. Les prédictions sont confirmées dans une série de 28 tests expérimentaux.

Acknowledgement

I wish to thank Raymond Kulhavy and Wolfgang Schnotz for their encouragement and helpful comments.

References

Bobrow, D.G. (Ed.). (1985). *Qualitative reasoning about physical systems.* Cambridge, MA: MIT Press.

Clark, J.M., & Paivio, A. (1991). Dual coding theory and education. *Educational Psychology Review, 3*, 149-210.

Cook, L.K., & Mayer, R.E. (1988). Teaching readers about the structure of scientific text. *Journal of Educational Psychology, 80*, 448-456.

Gentner, D., & Stevens, A.L. (Eds.). (1983). *Mental models.* Hillsdale, NJ: Erlbaum.

Houghton, H.A., & Willows, D.M. (Eds.). (1987). *The psychology of illustration: Volume 2. Instructional issues.* New York: Springer-Verlag.

Johnson-Laird, P.N. (Ed.). (1983). *Mental models: Towards a cognitive science of language, inference, and consciousness.* Cambridge, MA: Harvard University Press.

Kieras, D.E., & Bovair, S. (1984). The role of a mental model in learning to operate a device. *Cognitive Science, 8,* 255-274.

Mandl, H., & Levin, J.R. (Eds.). (1989). *Knowledge acquisition from text and pictures.* Amsterdam: North-Holland.

Mayer, R.E. (1989a). Models for understanding. *Review of Educational Research, 59,* 43-64.

Mayer, R.E. (1989b). Systematic thinking fostered by illustrations in science text. *Journal of Educational Psychology, 81,* 240-246.

Mayer, R.E. (in press). Illustrations that instruct. In R. Glaser (Ed.), *Advances in instructional psychology.* Hillsdale, NJ: Erlbaum.

Mayer, R.E., & Anderson, R.B. (1991). Animations need narrations: An experimental test of a dual-coding hypothesis. *Journal of Educational Psychology, 83,* 484-490.

Mayer, R.E., & Anderson, R.B. (in press). The instructive animation: Helping students build connections between words and pictures in multimedia learning. *Journal of Educational Psychology, 84.*

Mayer, R.E., & Gallini, J.K. (1990). When is an illustration worth ten thousand words? *Journal of Educational Psychology, 82,* 715-726.

Paivio, A. (1971). *Imagery and cognitive processes.* New York: Holt, Rinehart & Winston.

Paivio, A. (1986). *Mental representations: A dual coding approach.* New York: Oxford University Press.

Reiber, L.P. (1990). Animation and computer-based instruction. *Educational Technology Research and Development, 38,* 77-86.

Resnick, L.B. (1989). Introduction. In L.B. Resnick (Ed.), *Knowing, learning, and instruction: Essays in honor of Robert Glaser* (pp. 1-24). Hillsdale, NJ: Erlbaum.

White, B.Y., & Frederiksen, J.R. (1987). Qualitative models and intelligent learning environments. In R. W. Lawler & M. Yazdani (Eds.), *Artificial intelligence and education: Vol. 1. Learning environments and tutoring systems* (pp. 281-305). Norwood, NJ: ABLEX.

Willows, D.M., & Houghton, H.A. (Eds.). (1987). *The psychology of illustration: Volume 1. Basic research.* New York: Springer-Verlag.

World Book Encyclopedia. (1987). Chicago: Author.

Chapter 9

Illustrations, Mental Models, and Comprehension of Instructional Text

Valérie Gyselinck & Hubert Tardieu

EPHE et Université René Descartes, Paris, France

ABSTRACT

Considering that an illustration can be regarded as one possible external expression of a part of a mental model, we investigated the role of illustrations in the strengthening of a mental model built from an instructional text. In a first phase, two groups of subjects read a text dealing with the cellular division process. In a second phase, a group saw drawings alone which illustrated the process, whereas the other group read the text again. In each phase, two comprehension tests were used to evaluate the representation built by subjects. The course of reading was interrupted by questions assumed to reflect either a linguistic representation (paraphrases) or a mental model (inferences), and subjects had to verify inference statements at the end of the presentation. Results showed that gain in performance between the two phases was the same whether the subjects had seen the illustrations or the text again. This absence of difference was observed during as well as at the end of the presentation, and for paraphrases as well as for inferences. It therefore appears that the mental model has to reach a sufficient level of elaboration, in order that illustrations alone can reinforce it.

There is general consensus about the fact that to understand a text is to go beyond a representation of its linguistic features, in order to build a mental representation of the meaning of the text and the world denoted by it. There is less consensus on the nature of this representation and the processes through which it is constructed.

To account for language comprehension, Johnson-Laird (1980; 1983) proposed the notion of mental model to conceptualize the idea of a mental representation which would take cover both the text and the world denoted by this text. Van Dijk & Kintsch (1983) developed the notion of situation model which is considered to be similar to that of mental model (Ehrlich, in press). Johnson-Laird defines a mental model as an internal model of the world: "A model represents a state of affairs (...) its structure mirrors the relevant aspects of the corresponding state of affairs in the world" (Johnson-Laird, 1980, p. 98). The construction of a model, which is optional, depends on the text characteristics, and in particular, on referential continuity and plausibility, but it also involves inferences based on the subject's specific and general knowledge.

Two kinds of investigations have been conducted in an attempt to validate the notion of mental model in text comprehension. First, several experiments have been designed to validate the relevance of a representation of the situation portrayed by a text (e.g. Garnham, 1981; Ehrlich & Johnson-Laird, 1982). Second, some researchers have tried to determine the content of the models. Most of them have focused on spatial mental models (Glenberg, Meyer & Lindem, 1987; Morrow, Greenspan & Bower, 1987; Perrig & Kintsch, 1985; Taylor & Tversky, 1992). What emerges from these studies is that a mental model can be regarded as a network of relations between representational elements (tokens). These tokens represent characters, objects or events, and their relations can be causal, spatial or temporal. For example, objectives and intentions of a main character play a major role to organize relations between tokens in narratives (see Bower & Morrow, 1990).

The studies on spatial mental models bring up the question of the relationship between mental models and images. Besides propositional representations and mental models, Johnson-Laird (1983) considers mental images as a special class of mental models: "(...) mental models (...) are the structural analogues of the world and images (...) are the perceptual correlates of models from a particular point of view" (p. 165). In other words, an image can be considered as an instantiation of some aspects of a mental model.

Our purpose is to investigate whether an image can be a device to strengthen a model elaborated from an instructional text. Text illustrations, which are external images, can be considered as particular graphics representing some aspects of the world denoted by the sentences, i.e. non linguistic equivalents of the world. Whereas several researchers have studied the impact of illustrated instructional texts on comprehension (e.g. Waddill, McDaniel & Einstein, 1988; Mayer, 1989), few of them have considered illustrations as a mean to investigate mental models (see Mandl & Levin, 1989). Illustration provided during reading in the form of a picture (Glenberg & Langston, 1992) or provided before reading in the form of a layout (Morrow et al., 1987), seems to be a device for mental model building. However, the respective role of text and illustration are not clearly distinguishable in these experiments. Hence, we propose to study the role of illustrations provided alone after a mental model has been built from a text. This requires assessment of the effect of illustrations on a previously constructed mental model.

The trickiest problem in this type of investigation is to define adequate dependent variables to evaluate the level of elaboration of the mental model. Since a mental model is an episodic representation resulting from a constructive activity implying the use of world knowledge, a mental model is both a by-product and the source for inferences. So, the subjects' ability to draw inferences should reflect the elaboration of the model (Perrig & Kintsch, 1985; Tardieu, Ehrlich & Gyselinck, 1992; Taylor & Tversky, 1992).

Thus, the experiment consisted in two phases: the first phase aimed to allow subjects to build a mental model from a text, and the second phase aimed to study the impact of illustrations on the strentghening of the model. Two comprehension tests were designed to evaluate the representation built by subjects in each phase. One was on-line, and consisted of questions which interrupted the presentation of the material. One type of question was based on an elaborative inference, and was meant to address the course of building of the mental model. The other type of question was based on a paraphrase and aimed to address the linguistic representation. The second test was off-line and consisted in verifying inferred statements aimed at testing the mental model at the end of the presentation.

Our main assumption was that in the second phase, the presentation of illustrations would improve the mental model elaborated from the text more than the second presentation of the text. More specifically, as response speed to on-line inference questions was assumed to reflect the quality of mental model (Tardieu et al., 1992), greater improvement was expected for the response speed of on-line inferences. This improvement was also predicted for off-line inferences, because a good model should involve efficient retrieval structures (Fincher-Kiefer, Post, Greene & Voss, 1988).

Method

Subjects. Subjects were undergraduates enrolled in Psychology who had studied the mitosis process two years before. Out of the 75 subjects who participated to the experiment, those who failed to answer to any of the on-line inference questions accurately were excluded. Final data analysis included 64 subjects, half in each group.

Apparatus. The experiment was run in the Experimental Psychology laboratory of Paris V University. Subjects were seated facing a display with their hands resting on a three-button box. A computer controlled stimulus presentation and response data collection.

Material. The text was an instructional text dealing with the cellular division process. Mitosis is characterized by a series of state changes in the cell.These changes can be described by words or illustrated by drawings. The text was twenty two sentences long. Twenty two drawings corresponding to the sentences of the text were made. These drawings translated the linguistic text information into graphical information, and have, according to Levin's (1981) classification, a representational function. Each drawing included captions which only denoted the elements mentioned in the sentence. For example, Figure 1 presents the corresponding drawing of the fourth sentence: These filaments of chromatine get thicker and shorter: they become more distinct and then turn into chromosomes.

The on-line comprehension test consisted of six three-choice questions based on elaborative inferences generated from the text and two three-choice questions based on paraphrases of the text sentences. From the sentences: "The nuclear membrane disintegrates progressively while the two centrioles move apart and migrate to opposite poles of the cell. Fibers appear around each of the centrioles. Fibers radiate from the opposite poles until they meet and the nucleus starts to disappear", the inference question drawn was: "Fibers connect between: (a) the centrioles (b) the chromosomes (c) the filaments".

From the fourth sentence (see above), the paraphrase question used was: "Chromosomes are made up from: (a) filaments of chromatine (b) thickened centrioles (c) network of cytoplasm."

For the off-line comprehension test, two categories of inferred statements were designed. Four 'temporal' statements reordered various transitory states of the mitosis process (example: "The migration of

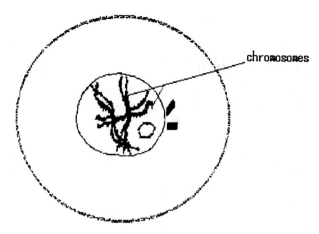

Figure 1. An example of drawing.

chromosoms toward a pole of the cell takes place after their split.") and four 'causal' statements were based on an 'if-then' reasoning (example: "The injection of colchicine which stops the spindle from forming, prevents chromosomes from individualizing"). Of the four statements of each category, half were true and half were false.

Procedure. The experiment lasted about half an hour and subjects were run individually. Subjects were randomly assigned to one of the presentation types (text or drawings) for the second phase.

In the first phase, after a short practice text, subjects of the text group had to read the text on mitosis and take the on-line and off-line tests. Subjects were invited to read the sentences appearing in the center of the display at their own pace. They were instructed to read to understand the phenomena and to be able to answer questions as accurately and as quickly as possible. The presentation of a new item deleted the previous one. At a specific time, which subjects could not predict, a question was presented below the display. After reading the question, the subjects pressed a key which caused the display of the three-choice response. They answered by pressing the appropriate button and then the following items were presented until a new question appeared. Three questions based on an elaborative inference and one question based on a paraphrase interrupted presentation. Response accuracy and response time once the three choices had appeared were recorded. At the end of the presentation, subjects had to verify each of the eight statements presented one by one, by pressing the True or the False button. Response accuracy and response time were recorded.

In the second phase, subjects were presented the practice text again, and procedure and instruction were the same as in phase one. Three new inference questions and a new paraphrase question interrupted the presentation. At the end of the presentation, subjects had to verify the same statements as in phase one.

For subjects assigned to the drawings group, procedure, material and instruction in the first phase were exactly the same as the ones used for the text group. In the second phase, subjects began with drawings illustrating the practice text. They then were presented drawings of the mitosis process which they were invited to study carefully in order to understand the phenomena. Self paced presentation of drawings was interrupted by three new inference questions and a new paraphrase question presented below the display in a linguistic form. At the end of the presentation, subjects had to verify the eight statements of the first phase.

At the end of the experiment, all the subjects were administered the French version of Vividness of Visual Imagery Questionnaire (VVIQ) (Denis, 1982), to make the two groups of subjects homogeneous as regards their imagery ability.

Design. The independent variable, type of presentation in the second phase (text or drawings) was between-subjects and defined two independent groups of subjects (text in the first and in the second phase (TT) or text in the first and drawings in the second phase (TD)). The other variables, Phase (one, two), type of Questions (inference, paraphrase) and category of Statements (temporal, causal) were within-subjects. The assignment of questions to the phases was counterbalanced across subjects. In addition, the eight statements were presented in a new random order for each subject and each phase, as well as the correct response position in the multiple-choice questions.

Results

The percentage of correct responses and the correct response times on the two tests were analyzed. Data were submitted to 2 X 2 X 2 ANOVAs (Presentation X Phase X Question (or Statement)). For all the

Table 1. Percentage of Correct Responses and Correct Response Time in s (with Standard Deviations in Parentheses) on the on-line Test as a Function of Question and Phase for Text-Text (TT) and Text-Drawings (TD) Groups.

	Paraphrase			Inference		
	phase1	phase2	(p2-p1)	phase1	phase2	(p2-p1)
Correct Responses						
TT	81.2 (39.6)	93.7 (24.5)	12.5	56.8 (21.1)	61.0 (25.6)	4.2
TD	87.5 (33.6)	87.5 (33.6)	0	54.8 (24.8)	61.0 (25.6)	6.2
Times						
TT	9.51 (11.06)	6.77 (4.99)	-2.74	10.18 (6.47)	10.51 (6.98)	0.33
TD	8.16 (5.10)	5.80 (4.29)	-2.36	12.16 (6.98)	11.33 (8.29)	-0.83

dependent variables, the ANOVAs showed no significant differences between groups of subjects in phase one. Relevant analysis concerned differences in performance between phase one and phase two, and the Phase by Presentation interaction.

Response accuracy on the on-line test. Accuracy improved on the paraphrases between the two phases (6.25%), but this effect did not reach signifiance (F < 1). As can be seen on Table 1, no improvement was observed when the subjects were presented drawings, whereas subjects tended to benefit from a second text presentation (12.5%), but the Phase by Presentation interaction was not significant (F < 1). Similarly, subjects improved on inferences (5.25%) but this effect did not reach signifiance (F(1,62) = 2.31). This lack of effect was observed whatever the type of Presentation in phase 2.

Correct response times on the on-line test. There was a significant speed up of 2.5 s for paraphrases (F(1,62) = 4.04; P < .05; MSe = 3863). This effect was observed whatever the Presentation, the interaction was not significant (F < 1). No improvement was observed between the two phases for inferences (see Table 1) and neither the effect of Phase, nor the interaction were significant (Fs < 1).

Response accuracy on the off-line test. Temporal statements led to better performance than causal statements in phase 1 (respectively 71.4% and 29.9%).The Statement effect was highly reliable (F(1,62) = 77.58; P <.0005; MSe = .699). So each category of statement was analyzed separately. The second presentation led to a better performance than the first one for temporal statements (increment of 5.85%) but the effect did not reach signifiance (F(1,62) = 2.65). Although the TD group tended to improve more than the TT group (respectively 9.4% and 2.3%, see Table 2), the interaction was not significant (F(1,62) <1). Performance improved on causal statements between the two phases (14.5%). The effect of Phase was significant (F(1,62) = 10.25; P < .005; MSe = .699). The TD group tended to improve more than TT group, but the interaction was not significant (F < 1).

Correct response times on the off-line test. Similarly to accuracy, temporal statements led to faster responses than reasoning statements in phase 1 (respectively 10.28 s and 13.47 s), and the difference was significant (F(1,62) = 8.68; P < .001; MSe = 274). A very slight increase was observed for temporal statements between the two phases (-O.3 s) but the effect was not significant (F < 1). Moreover, the Phase by Presentation interaction was not significant (F <1). On causal statements, subjects answered faster after the second presentation than after the first (- 4.1 s), and the effect of Phase was significant (F(1,62) = 13.92; P <.0005; MSe = 274). But, as is shown on Table 2improvement was similar whatever the type of presentation, and the interaction was not significant (F < 1).

Table 2. Percentage of Correct Responses and Correct Response Time in s (with Standard Deviations in Parentheses) on the off-line Test as a Function of Statement and Phase for Text-Text (TT) and Text-Drawings (TD) Groups.

	Temporal			Causal		
	phase1	phase2	(p2-p1)	phase1	phase2	(p2-p1)
Correct Responses						
TT	75.0	77.3	2.3	38.2	44.5	6.3
	(17.9)	(24.0)		(29.0)	(22.6)	
TD	67.9	77.3	9.4	21.7	44.5	22.8
	(26.3)	(26.4)		(27.9)	(23.5)	
Times						
TT	10.76	10.95	0.19	13.96	9.64	-4.32
	(4.51)	(7.15)		(5.34)	(4.14)	
TD	9.79	9.05	-0.741	2.98	9.03	-3.95
	(4.05)	(2.78)		(10.6)	(3.72)	

Discussion

This experiment was designed to test the hypothesis that illustrations strengthen the mental model elaborated from a text. All subjects read the text in the first phase, then one group was presented drawings and the other group re-read the text in the second phase. The major result was that differences in performance between the two phases were similar for the two groups. More precisely, the presentation of drawings led to performance improvement comparable to the second presentation of the text. This result suggests that graphic information and linguistic information allow for the construction of mental representations with very similar properties, a finding in line with Denis and Cocude (1989). Why did illustrations not strengthen the model more than the text, as was hypothesized?

One explanation is that the text used in this experiment could easily elicit imagery activity. In each group, the subjects may have formed mental images of the mitosis process right from the start of text presentation. Thus presenting drawings next would either have interfered with the previously constructed model or would have not provided anything more. However, the complexity of the mitosis process makes this explanation unlikely. The level of performance after two presentations (accuracy for inferences was about 55%) suggests that the text was actually difficult. Perrig and Kintsch (1985) showed that subjects were unable to draw inferences when text was difficult to understand even after three presentations, although subjects were successful when the text was simplified. As the quality of mental model was evaluated from performance on the inference questions, it is likely that our subjects in both groups only had a sketchy model of the text. So, the weakness of the model elaborated in the first phase could be an important reason why illustration could not strengthen it in the second phase. Hence, so that illustrations presented after reading could reinforce a mental model, the already constructed model might need to be almost fully developed and not just sketched.

Another explanation which could explain the difficulty of building a mental model of the text is that illustrations were presented alone, unassociated with the sentences in the text. This might have prevented subjects from relating information provided by the drawings and information from the previously presented text, and hence may not have allowed subjects to integrate them into a single representation.

This study did not show evidence that illustration was a good device for the enrichment of a mental model. To clarify the status of illustration in the mental model constructed from a text, researches should move in the following directions. First, the properties of illustrations and those of instructional texts as well should be characterized to determine what in the text needs to be illustrated (e.g. objects or relations between objects) and what kind of graphics must be used (e.g. realistic or schematic illustration). Second, the attempt to point out the relationship between mental model and mental images should be carried on (see

Denis & de Vega, in press), as well as the relationship between illustrations and mental images. For example, it is unclear whether an illustration is directly represented in the mental model. Are illustrations turned into mental images during processing? Do mental images create new representational elements in the model, or do they establish additional relations between tokens already contained in the mental model? Such questions argue for the necessity of strengthening ties between studies on imagery and those centered on mental modeling in text comprehension.

RÉSUMÉ

Considérant qu'une illustration peut être vue comme une expression possible d'une partie d'un modèle mental, nous avons étudié le rôle d'illustrations dans l'enrichissement d'un modèle mental construit à partir d'un texte à visée didactique. Dans une première phase, deux groupes de sujets lisaient un texte traitant du processus de la division cellulaire. Dans une deuxième phase, un groupe voyait des dessins seuls qui illustraient le processus, alors que l'autre groupe relisait le texte. Dans chaque phase, deux tests de compréhension ont été utilisés pour évaluer les représentations construites. Le cours de la lecture a été interrompu par des questions supposées refléter soit une représentation linguistique (paraphrases) soit un modèle mental (inférences), et les sujets devaient vérifier des énoncés inférés en fin de présentation. Les résultats ont montré que le gain de performances entre les deux phases était le même que les sujets aient vu les illustrations ou relu le texte. Cette absence de différence a été observée aussi bien en cours qu'en fin de présentation et pour les paraphrases comme pour les inférences. Il semble donc que le modèle mental doive atteindre un niveau d'élaboration suffisant pour que des illustrations présentées seules puissent le renforcer.

References

Bower, G.H., & Morrow, D.G. (1990). Mental models in narrative comprehension. *Science*, *247*, 44-48.

Denis, M. (1982). Imaging while reading text: a study of individual differences, *Memory and Cognition*, *10*, 540-545.

Denis, M., & Cocude, M. (1989). Scanning visual images generated from verbal descriptions. *European Journal of Cognitive Psychology*, *1*, 293-307.

Denis, M., & de Vega, M. (in press). Modèles mentaux et imagerie mentale. In M.F. Ehrlich, H. Tardieu, et M. Cavazza (Eds.), *Les Modèles mentaux: approche cognitive des représentations*. Paris: Masson.

Ehrlich, K. & Johnson-Laird, P.N. (1982). Spatial descriptions and referential continuity. *Journal of Verbal Learning and Verbal Behavior*, *21*, 296-306.

Ehrlich, M.F. (in press). *Mémoire et compréhension du langage*. Lille: Presses Universitaires de Lille.

Fincher-Kiefer, R., Post, T.A., Greene, T.R., & Voss, J.F. (1988). On the role of prior knowledge and task demands in the processing of text. *Journal of Memory and Language*, *27*, 416-428.

Garnham, A. (1981). Mental models as representations of text. *Memory and Cognition*, *9*, 560-565.

Glenberg, A.M., & Langston, W.E. (1992). Comprehension of illustrated text: Pictures help to build mental models. *Journal of Memory and Language*, *31*, 129-151.

Glenberg, A.M., Meyer, M., & Lindem, K. (1987). Mental models contribute to foregrounding during text comprehension. *Journal of Memory and Language*, *26*, 69-83.

Johnson-Laird, P.N. (1980). Mental models in cognitive science. *Cognitive Science*, *4*, 71-115.

Johnson-Laird, P.N. (1983). *Mental models: Towards a cognitive science of language, inference, and consciousness*. Cambridge: Cambridge University Press.

Levin, J.R. (1981). On functions of pictures in prose. In F. Pirozzolo & M.C. Wittrick (Eds.), *Neuropsychological and cognitive processes in reading*. New York: Academic Press.

Mandl, H., & Levin, J.R. (1989). *Knowledge acquisition from text and pictures*. Amsterdam: North-Holland.

Mayer, R.E. (1989). Systematic thinking fostering by illustrations in scientific text. *Journal of Educational Psychology*, *81*, 240-246.

Morrow, D.G., Greenspan, S.L., & Bower, G.H. (1987). Accessibility and situation models in narrative comprehension. *Journal of Memory and Language, 76,* 165-187.

Perrig, W., & Kintsch, W. (1985). Propositional and situational representations of text. *Journal of Memory and Language, 24,* 503-518.

Tardieu, H., Ehrlich, M.F., & Gyselinck, V. (1992). Levels of representation and domain-specific knowledge in comprehension of scientific texts. *Language and Cognitive Processes, 7,* 335-352.

Taylor, H.A., & Tversky, B. (1992). Spatial mental models derived from survey and route descriptions. *Journal of Memory and Language, 31,* 261-292.

van Dijk, T.A., & Kintsch, W. (1983). *Strategies of discourse comprehension.* New York: Academic Press.

Waddill, P.J., McDaniel, M.A., & Einstein, G.O. (1988). Illustrations as adjuncts to prose: A text-appropriate processing approach. *Journal of Educational Psychology, 80,* 457-464.

Comprehension of Graphics
W. Schnotz and R. W. Kulhavy (Editors)
© 1994 Elsevier Science B.V. All rights reserved.

Chapter 10

Reference Maps as a Framework for Remembering Text

Raymond W. Kulhavy & William A. Stock

Arizona State University, Tempe, USA

Linda C. Caterino

Walker Research Institute, Tempe, USA

ABSTRACT

This paper develops a theory based in dual coding, that explains why learning a map improves memory for associated text information. The basic premise is that visual displays such as maps are encoded as intact images which retain the spatial properties of the objective stimulus. Such images possess a computational advantage in working memory because the information within them is simultaneousy available to cue retrieval of related text. The paper describes eight experiments all of which support both the image coding and working memory assumptions.

There is evidence that reference maps improve memory for related text content (Dean & Kulhavy, 1981). Abel and Kulhavy (1986) suggested that maps improve memory for text by serving either an instantiation or mnemonic function. Maps perform an instantiation function when they help learners assign unique meaning to portions of a related text. This position derives from a schema-theoretic point of view, where maps "activate" a relevant schema that can be used to interpret a text (Anderson & Pearson, 1984; Royer & Cable, 1976). Schema explanations are based on the premise that instantiating stimuli (here maps) can be directly related to the prior knowledge base of the learner, and that the activation of prior knowledge facilitates learning of associated stimuli (here text).

On the surface, instantiation is an attractive candidate for explaining map-text facilitation. However, an inspection of relevant research is at odds with this position. Virtually all of the research has used maps that are fictitious, or unfamiliar to the subject population. Such maps have doubtful value in terms of activating prior knowledge. Further, the texts used in such research are typically concrete, easily understandable, and normed to insure comprehensibility. These conditions are distinctly different from those in research where pictures are used to instantiate convoluted prose [see Bransford and Johnson (1972) for the classic example]. Hence, we conclude that the instantiation explanation does not apply to the research available with maps and text.

The second possible explanation advanced by Abel and Kulhavy (1986) is that maps serve a mnemonic function for text recall. In this case, map information is used to directly cue retrieval of associated text events. There is no requirement that the map serve any purpose other than furnishing information that facilitates text memory. Most map-text research appears to fall within the mnemonic category, and we have framed the remainder of our discussion in terms of this function.

Three reliable outcomes appear in map-text research. First, maps increase text recall only when the maps are presented as organized stimulus units. When map features are presented as lists, or in a fragmented manner, memory for associated text decreases (e.g., Reynolds, 1968; Schwartz & Kulhavy, 1981). Second, maps improve memory for text only when learners expend considerable effort to encode the map as an organized or intact unit. Virtually every study demonstrating map-text facilitation has used specific techniques to insure that the map is learned as an organized entity (Dean & Kulhavy, 1981). Third, maps increase text recall only when the information in the text is directly related to map content. When text information is not specifi cally associated with features on the map, recall is about the same for map-present and map-absent groups (e.g., Mastropieri & Peters, 1987).

Our explanation of map-text facilitation is based on a version of dual coding theory (e.g., Paivio, 1986). In this case, maps are coded as images in a non-verbal memory store, while text is coded sequentially as propositions into verbal memory. Also, there exist associative connections between non-verbal and verbal stores, so that information in one code can be used to activate information in the other code. Maps improve text memory simply because the information in the map image can be used to cue retrieval of related events in the verbal store (Kulhavy, Lee, & Caterino, 1985). Further, we believe that maps can be encoded as intact representations in memory. Intact map images retain the spatial characteristics of the objective stimuli, and the information within them becomes simultaneously available when they are brought into working memory. Such images have an advantage as far as the cuing of text retrieval is concerned. The advantage derives from the fact that attention can be shifted from location to location across the map image, without exceeding the limits of working memory. This same computational advantage has been discussed by Larkin and Simon (1987) with respect to how people use the information in diagrams for problem solving. Hence, the more intact the representation of the map, the more likely that information in it can be located efficiently and used for retrieving associated text.

If maps facilitate text recall in the manner described above, then an important topic for research is to determine what attributes of maps themselves are responsible for improved text memory. It is our position that maps present two types of information. First, they contain information about individual features, including landmark and point markers such as labels, drawings and topographic symbols. These features may be further differentiated by the addition of what Bertin (1983) calls "retinal variables", such as shape, size and color. We group all visual characteristics of individual map features under the heading "feature information". The second type of information on a map is the spatial relations that exist among features. We group such relations under the heading of "structural information". Structural information denotes the network of direction and distance relations that exist among individual features within a map space, and boundary designations that can be used as reference points for features.

It is an empirical question whether feature or structural information, or both, are responsible for improving text memory. For example, consider the general elaboration position that has developed from research on pictures and prose (e.g., Bradshaw & Anderson, 1982; Willows and Houghton, 1987). When individual visual stimuli, such as pictures or drawings, are studied in association with words, sentences or segments of text, recall of the verbal material is generally facilitated. Elaboration explanations hold that processing the two types of stimuli together increases their accessibility in memory - in other words, "two codes are better than one". When elaboration explanations are applied to map-text research, the focus is on the effects of individual feature information. That is, each feature provides an elaborative context for the specific portion of the text passage with which it is associated. This explanation handily accounts for the consistent result that text event recall increases only when events are directly related to specific map features. However, note that this position does not predict a difference between situations where features are presented alone and where they are distributed in a complex spatial display - such as a map. In fact, there is little in the elaboration explanation to suggest that structural information in maps has any effect on the recall of text. We have explored the implications of such a position in a recent paper (Kulhavy, Stock, Woodard & Haygood, in press).

The dual coding position outlined above emphasizes the structural information that appears in maps. We assume that maps are encoded as intact entities in which structural information provides a framework for individual features. Because structure is included in the image, feature information becomes simultaneously available during working memory operations at retrieval. Such reasoning leads to the straightforward prediction that structural information will improve memory for associated text. This explanation accounts for the remaining two consistent outcomes described earlier. First, encoding structural relations probably requires considerable effort on the part of the learner, which accounts for the attention control procedures previously mentioned. Second, when maps are presented as organized entities, people are able to encode the structural relations (e.g., Schwartz & Kulhavy, 1981). Under these conditions, map images can be scanned efficiently, and structural information used to improve retrieval of text.

We have conducted a series of experiments designed to test the assumptions discussed above. The remainder of this paper is devoted to a discussion of this evidence.

Feature attributes and structure

In three separate experiments we tested the relative contribution of feature and structural information to text recall (Kulhavy, Stock, Woodard, & Haygood, in press; Kulhavy & Stock, 1992). All three studies used undergraduate volunteers, a map of an Italian town, and a text of about 600-words that contained events associated with features on the map. In Experiments 1 and 2 features were presented as labels on the map, or as labels-plus-icons, where the icons were line drawings of the feature in question (e.g., temple). In Experiment 1, structure was defined as the number of times subjects placed map features in the correct location prior to hearing the text. In Experiment 2, structure was calculated using a goodness of fit statistic based on the accuracy with which feature interrelations were reproduced during recall of the text. Presenting feature information at retrieval (labels or icons) had no effect on recall of text. In both experiments, memory for map structure was a significant predictor of associated text recall. Embellishing individual features with icons had no effect on text memory in Experiment 1, but did produce facilitation in Experiment 2, where icon drawings were treated as a within-subjects variable.

In Experiment 3, undergraduates again saw the Italian town map and heard the text (Werner-Bellman, Klein, Brooks, Kulhavy & Stock 1992). In this study all features were represented by both labels and icon drawings, but half of the icons in each group were colored and half were not colored. Subjects received instruction either to pay attention to properties of individual features, or to encode the map as an intact image. Structural encoding was measured by the goodness of fit index based on the reconstructed feature interrelations. Again, goodness of structural encoding directly predicted memory for text events. Neither icon color nor encoding instructions were related to text recall in an important manner. Proportion event recall for the low and high structure groups for each of the three experiments is depicted in Figure 1.

Map structure and retrieval

In a two experiment series, we investigated the effects of disrupting the organization structure of the map itself during text retrieval (Kulhavy, Stock, Peterson, Pridemore, & Klein, 1992). Undergraduates studied a city map while hearing a text containing both feature names and related events. In the first study, subjects retrieved text events while viewing a second map that, (a) was a duplicate of the original (intact map), (b) had the features rearranged within the map space (changed map), or (c) displayed only the land border of the original map with no feature information (border only). Event retrieval was highest for the intact map group, with the groups ranked: intact map > border-only > changed map. In the second experiment, subjects again studied the map

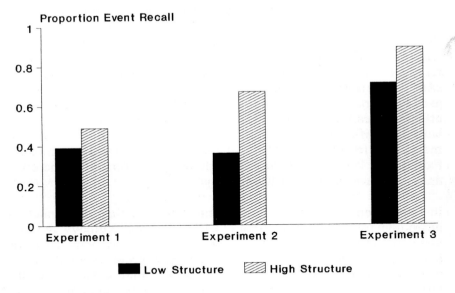

Figure 1. Mean proportion of text events recalled as a function of low and high encoded map structure for each of three experiments.

and text, and received either the intact map or individual features as retrieval cues. The intact map yielded significantly higher text recall.

Because we used a retrieval methodology in the two experiments just described, several colleagues suggested that the results could be best explained by the Principle of Encoding Specificity (Tulving & Thomson, 1972). To test this possibility, we conducted a third experiment in which subjects learned either an intact map or a page of map features, with the same stimuli factorially varied at retrieval (Brooks, Werner-Bellman, Peterson, Stock, & Kulhavy, 1992). For text fact recall, the encoding-retrieval conditions ranked themselves: Intact Map-Intact Map > Intact Map-Feature Page = Feature Page-Intact Map > Feature Page-Feature Page ($p < .05$). These data are difficult for encoding specificity to explain, since the group seeing the page of features at both encoding and retrieval should have out performed the different stimulus conditions. We conclude that a strong version of encoding specificity does not account for the retrieval differences in the initial two studies.

Stimulus order effects

We have just completed two additional unpublished experiments in which we varied the order in which the map and text were studied. We reasoned that order of presentation should influence how effectively subjects can form associations between map and text information. Our assumptions regarding working memory activities suggest an asymmetry in recall, depending on which stimulus is learned first. We have already discussed the events that occur when maps are presented before text, encoded as intact images, and used to cue associated text recall. However, when the text is presented before the map and encoded as a sequence of propositions the demands on working memory are different. When the map is presented second, subjects retrieve text propositions into memory in an attempt to associate them with the information on the map (especially when they have been specifically instructed to use the first stimulus to help learn the second). However, keeping propositions in working memory requires considerable resources, and subjects are faced with the choice of using their processing capacity to, (a) learn the map, or (b) make as many map-text associations as possible. Whatever course subjects take, the number of possible map-text associations is reduced, simply because the computational advantage of the intact map representation is lost. This argument leads us to predict that subjects seeing the map first will recall more text information that those seeing it after the text.

In both experiments the maps and text were ecologically valid (Ceylon and the city of Rome) and instructions given to both map-text and text-map subjects were identical. In the first study the subjects recalled about 30% more associated facts from the text when the map was the stimulus first seen. The map-first condition also remembered more map features, and the joint probability of recalling a text fact, given that the related feature was correctly located on a map reconstruction, was significantly higher. In the second experiment we crossed stimulus order with intact versus individual feature presentation. The results were identical for stimulus order, with the map-first group remembering more text facts and map features, and producing higher values of P(text fact | correctly located feature). In addition, the intact map condition outperformed the group seeing individual features across each of the same independent measures.

Conclusions

Taken together, the results of eight experiments indicate that structural information from a map is important for the recall of associated text. These results support the dual coding model developed earlier, and suggest that the organizational properties of the map image are important for cuing retrieval of related information in the verbal store. Encoding the structural information present in complex visual displays, such as maps, increases the efficiency of working memory operations, and allows access to more map image information that can be used to cue retrieval of associated text.

RÉSUMÉ

Cet article développe une théorie fondée sur le double codage qui explique pourquoi l'étude d'une carte améliore la rétention des informations textuelles qui y sont associées. L'hypothèse de base est que les représentations visuelles telles que les cartes sont encodées sous forme d'images intactes qui conservent les propriétés spatiales du stimulus. Ces images ont un avantage computationnel en mémoire de travail car les informations qu'elles contiennent sont simultanément disponibles pour indicer la récupération du texte associé. L'article décrit huit expériences qui toutes sont en faveur à la fois des hypothèses de codage imagé et de mémoire de travail.

References

Abel, R.R., & Kulhavy, R.W. (1986). Maps, mode of text presentation, and children's prose learning. *American Educational Research Journal, 23*, 263-274.

Anderson, R.C., & Pearson, P.D. (1984). A schema-theoretic view of basic processes in reading comprehension. In P. D. Pearson (Ed.), *Handbook of Reading Research* (pp. 255-291). New York: Longman.

Bertin, J. (1983). *Semiology of graphics: Diagrams, networks, maps.* Madison, WI: University of Wisconsin Press (Translated by William J. Berg).

Bradshaw, G.L., & Anderson, J.R. (1982). Elaborative encoding as an explanation of levels of processing. *Journal of Verbal Learning and Verbal Behavior, 21*, 165-174.

Bransford, J.D., & Johnson, M.K. (1972). Contextual prerequisites for understanding: Some investigations of comprehension and recall. *Journal of Verbal Learning and Verbal Behavior, 11*, 717-726.

Brooks, R.B., Werner-Bellman, L., Peterson, S.E., Stock, W.A., & Kulhavy, R.W. (April, 1992). *Retrieving text events associated with maps: Examining the encoding specificity hypothesis.* Paper at American Educational Research Association, San Francisco, California.

Dean, R.S., & Kulhavy, R.W. (1981). Influence of spatial organization in prose learning. *Journal of Educational Psychology, 73*, 57-64.

Kulhavy, R.W., Lee, J.B., & Caterino, L.C. (1985). Conjoint retention of maps and related discourse. *Contemporary Educational Psychology, 10*, 28-37.

Kulhavy, R.W., & Stock, W.A. (April, 1992). *Feature and structural information in the recall of text.* Research Colloquium, Victoria University of Wellington, New Zealand.

Kulhavy, R.W., Stock, W.A., Peterson, S.E., Pridemore, D.R., & Klein, J.D. (1992). Using maps to retrieve text: A test of conjoint retention. *Contemporary Educational Psychology, 17*, 56-70.

Kulhavy, R.W., Stock, W.A., Woodard, K.A., & Haygood, R.C. (in press). Comparing elaboration and dual coding theories: The case of maps and text. *American Journal of Psychology, 106*, 483-498.

Larkin, J.H., & Simon, H.A. (1987). Why a diagram is (sometimes) worth ten thousand words. *Cognitive Science, 11*, 65-99.

Mastropieri, M.A., & Peters, E.E. (1987). Increasing prose recall of learning disabled and reading disabled students via spatial organizers. *Journal of Educational Research, 80*, 272-276.

Paivio, A. (1986). *Mental representations: A dual coding approach.* New York: Oxford University Press.

Reynolds, J.H. (1968). Cognitive transfer in verbal learning: Transfer effects after prefamiliarization with integrated versus partially integrated verbal-perceptual structures. *Journal of Educational Psychology, 59,* 133-138.

Royer, J.M. & Cable, G.W. (1976). Illustrations, analogies, and facilitative transfer in prose learning. *Journal of Educational Psychology, 68,* 205-209.

Schwartz, N.H., & Kulhavy, R.W. (1981). Map features and the recall of discourse. *Contemporary Educational Psychology, 6,* 151-158.

Tulving, E. & Thomson, D.M. (1973). Encoding specificity and retrieval processes in episodic memory. *Psychological Review, 80,* 352-373.

Werner-Bellman, L., Klein, J.D., Brooks, R.B., Kulhavy, R.W., & Stock, W.A. (June, 1992). *Remembering maps and text: Effects of color and organization.* Paper at American Psychological Society, San Diego, California.

Willows, D.M., & Houghton, H.A. (1987). *The psychology of illustration (Vol. 1).* New York: Springer-Verlag.

PART III

DIFFERENTIAL AND
DEVELOPMENTAL ASPECTS

Comprehension of Graphics
W. Schnotz and R. W. Kulhavy (Editors)

Chapter 11

The Mnemonic Benefit of Pictures in Text: Selective Enrichment for Differentially Skilled Readers

Mark A. McDaniel

Purdue University, West Lafayette, USA

Paula J. Waddill

University of Scranton, USA

ABSTRACT

Our research has focused on the extent to which pictures can enhance recall of textually presented information, particularly item-specific (detailed) information and relational information. Two sets of pictures were constructed, one set depicting individual details conveyed in the text and one depicting the relationship among several propositions. Initial findings showed that information targeted by a particular picture set was better recalled when the pictures were included in the text. Several theoretical orientations suggest, however, that this general pattern might vary depending on reading ability. A second experiment confirmed that the just-mentioned pattern emerged only for high- and average-reading ability readers. Low-ability readers benefited very selectively from pictures, with the benefit restricted to recall of illustrated details. These results are interpreted from the view that pictures enable the extraction and retention of information that readers under ordinary circumstances do not encode effectively, providing the readers have the requisite comprehension abilities to begin with.

The work presented in this paper is concerned with what kinds of information described in a prose passage can be better remembered as a consequence of embedding depictive illustrations in the passage. More specifically, drawing on a general approach to text processing and memory that we have been developing (in collaboration with Gilles Einstein) over the past seven years (Einstein, McDaniel, Bowers, & Stevens, 1984; Einstein, McDaniel, Owen, & Cote, 1990), we focus on the extent to which pictures might enhance processing and subsequent recall for two kinds of information in a text: relational information and detailed item-specific information. Relational information represents the integration or organization of individual propositions in the text. It might for example encompass causal relations that bind ideas together or contrastive information that provides an organizational framework for different ideas presented in the text. Detailed or item-specific information refers to information that precisely or more specifically describes individual concepts or propositions in the text. In a text about avalanches in the Himalayas, an example of such information would be the statement: "Two million tons of ice cascade down."

As background we will first describe our general paradigm and some findings on the degree to which pictures depicting relational versus detail information affect text recall. Then we will present several hypotheses suggesting that reading skill might be a critical factor in determining the mnemonic benefits of our different picture types, and we will report the results of an experiment that informs these hypotheses.

The General Paradigm

Thus far we have developed pictures for two "real-world" texts containing 14-17 sentences, one text a Russian fairy tale and the other an exposition about avalanches in the Kanchenjunga Mountains of the Himalayas. Our initial work demonstrated that the effects of pictures depended in part on the particular kind of text used (Waddill, McDaniel, & Einstein, 1988; see also Mayer & Gallini, 1990, for a similar orientation). The thrust of the present work was to investigate the possibility that the mnemonic effects of pictures might further be modulated by individual differences in reading ability, and for this work we have concentrated on the expository (Kanchenjunga) text.

Typically, we present the text in one of three formats. In the detail-picture condition, the passage is accompanied by six black and white line drawings. Each drawing depicts a detail conveyed by one proposition in the story, and each picture is placed on the same page as the sentence containing the illustrated detail (see Appendix for examples). In the relational-picture condition, the passage is accompanied by four line drawings. Each drawing depicts the relationship among four or five propositions in the story, and each relational picture is placed on the same page as the sentences containing the illustrated propositions (see Appendix for examples). The third format is a control condition in which no pictures accompany the passage, with the sentences grouped on pages as in the picture conditions.

Subjects are told that the purpose of the study is to investigate text comprehension and that they later will be asked to rate how easy the story was to understand. No mention is made of a subsequent memory task. Subjects in the picture conditions are told to pay attention to the pictures in order to aid their comprehension. When subjects finish reading the passage, their reading times are recorded, they are asked to rate their comprehension on a scale ranging from 1 (didn't comprehend at all) to 5 (comprehended very well). After completing the rating task, they solve math problems for 5 minutes. Next, they are asked to write down as much of the passage as they can remember and are given as much time as they needed to do so.

Several studies provided the groundwork for the primary investigation of the mnemonic benefit of relational and detail pictures for readers of differing ability. We briefly describe that work before detailing the experiment focusing on individual differences. One concern with the pictures of interest here is the degree to which the pictures target the intended information. Waddill et al. (1988) reported inconsistent benefits of relational pictures for recall of an expository text, and we thought that perhaps those pictures could be more effectively designed. Accordingly, we revised three of the original relational pictures and replaced one other. To gauge whether or not the relational pictures had been improved, we provided subjects with a randomly ordered set of both detail and relational pictures; some subjects received the original set (from Waddill et al.) and others received the revised set. Accompanying the set of pictures was an ordered set of propositions from the text (presented in a separate booklet). After reading the text (presented intact without pictures inserted), subjects were asked to list the particular propositions depicted by each picture. Subjects given the revised picture set were more likely to identify the information we intended to target than those given the original set, and this was most marked for the several revised relational pictures.

Table 1. Experiment 1: Free Recall of Target Detail, Target Relational and Nontarget Information.

	Picture Condition		
Information Type	Control	Detail Pictures	Relational Pictures
Target Detail	.29 (.15)[a]	.45 (.17)	.28 (.14)
Target Relational	.15 (.12)	.15 (.10)	.23 (.11)
Nontarget	.14 (.10)	.14 (.09)	.17 (.11)

[a] Standard deviations in brackets.

We tested the mnemonic effectiveness of the new picture set, using the general paradigm just described. In scoring the recall protocols we assigned each recalled proposition a rating of 2 (entirely correct), 1 (partially correct), or 0 (incorrect). An entirely correct proposition veridically conveyed the gist of the target proposition. A partially correct proposition did not precisely capture the target proposition, but closely related to it. This was a reliable scoring scheme as the correlation between two raters who scored a subset of the protocols was .98. Table 1 presents the proportions of the total possible scores for propositions that were depicted in the detail and relational pictures (target propositions) and propositions that were not depicted in the illustrations (nontarget propositions).

Note first that pictures did not significantly enhance the recall of information not targeted by the picture. Even the relational pictures did not produce a significant benefit in recall for information not depicted in the picture. Both types of pictures, however, produced significant benefits relative to the no-picture control when recall of information illustrated in the pictures was considered. Recall of targeted relational information was significantly greater in the relational picture condition than in the control condition (F(1,90) = 4.95, p < .05, MSe = .01), and recall of detail information was significantly greater in the detail picture condition than the control (F(1, 90) = 20.40, p < .0001, MSe = .01).

The main finding established in this first experiment is that both relational and detail pictures seem to enhance memory for relational and detail information, respectively. The finding that recall of relational information in an expository text can be enhanced by relational pictures extends the findings of Waddill et al. (1988), and suggests that design of effective relational pictures, while not always straightforward, is possible.

The finding that recall of details can be enhanced by appropriate pictures may be somewhat unexpected, in light of previous conclusions that "educators might look to adjunct aids other than pictures (e.g., postquestions) if they wish to enhance students' recall of less essential detail from written text" (Haring & Fry, 1979, p 189). This suggestion is based on Haring and Fry's finding that pictures that included both top-level and low-level (detail) information enhanced recall relative to a no-picture group for the high-level but not the low-level information. At this juncture, it is difficult to identify the factor(s) that might be critical in determining whether including detail information in a picture will provide a mnemonic benefit. Not only did Haring and Fry include both detail and high-level information within the same picture, their pictures were designed to convey all of the idea units expressed in the text, they used a narrative passage, and tested children. Any or all of these factors might have contributed to their failure to find enhancing effects of pictures for recall of details.

At any rate, from the vantage point of many general theoretical orientations (e.g., elaborative network models, Anderson, 1983; sensory-semantic models, Nelson, 1979; dual coding, Paivio, 1986) the present finding is not particularly surprising-provided that different types of information can be depicted pictorially, then presenting the information in both pictorial and text form will enhance memory for that information. One interesting issue from our view, however, is the extent to which this straightforward pattern accurately reflects the impact of pictures on text processing and memory for readers of differing ability. There are at least four different lines of reasoning suggesting that reading ability will be an important determinant of the degree to which pictures will aid memory for text.

Reading ability and the benefits of pictures in text

A general compensatory model suggests that high ability readers are already skilled at extracting and remembering information presented in text, consequently representational aids such as pictures will be superfluous for high-ability readers. The pictures will add little to the representation that the high-ability readers are able to construct from the text alone (cf., Mayer & Gallini, 1990), with the result being that pictures, regardless of what type of information they convey, will not benefit recall for these readers. In contrast, low ability readers need compensatory aids to help them adequately encode textually presented information. Pictures especially might be expected to be useful for low ability readers because they avoid the written format with which these learners have difficulty. Thus, the mnemonic benefit of pictures for targeted information will be limited to, or at least especially pronounced for, lower ability readers.

A selective compensatory model offers a more complex variation on the theme that pictures serve to compensate for skills or tendencies not naturally engaged by the reader. One might assume that better readers are those who focus on the relational information in the text and attempt to form an organized, well-structured memory representation of the text. In doing so, however, they become less focused or attentive to particular details (e.g., the exact amount of ice that cascades down the mountain). On this view, relational pictures will be superfluous for able readers but detail pictures will not be. The opposite would be the case for less able readers. These readers presumably are not proficient at extracting the relational information in the text; instead they focus on the individual details. Accordingly, for these readers relational pictures might be very helpful in converging information not well encoded from the text, but detail pictures would be redundant with the kind of information these readers are already encoding. By this view, relational pictures benefit primarily lower-ability readers and detail pictures are beneficial primarily for better readers.

Though intuitively appealing, the idea that pictures serve a compensatory role for reading deficits has not been supported by the limited research conducted (e.g., Harber, 1980; Rose, 1986). It may be, then, that pictures incorporated into text allow the rich to get richer. On this enrichment view, the skilled readers are able to exploit the pictures to construct even better and more entailed representations of the information than they can with the text alone. Less-able readers, on the other hand, struggle to encode the information regardless of whether or not it is presented in text and/or pictorial format. This view predicts that pictures will enhance text recall for better readers but not for less-able readers.

Finally, a selective enrichment approach is possible. Perhaps, as outlined in the development of the selective compensatory view, good readers focus on relational processing more so than processing of details, and less-able readers do the opposite (cf., Brown & Smiley, 1978). If so, and if pictures serve an enriching function for information that already receives primary consideration, then relational pictures would enhance recall (of relational information) primarily for good readers, but detail pictures would enhance recall (of detail information) primarily for less-able readers.

We conducted a second experiment to test the predictions of these different models.

Method

To ensure that the particular wording of the passage was not critical in obtaining whatever picture effects emerged, two versions of the Kanchenjunga passage were constructed. The two versions were basically paraphrases of one another. Detail-picture, relational-picture, and no-picture control booklets were constructed for each version of the passage. The booklets were constructed in a manner similar to that described earlier except that sentences containing unillustrated propositions were not placed on separate pages. Thus, each booklet consisted of four pages and each page (except for the control condition) contained at least one picture illustrating information on that page.

The design was a 2 (passage version) x 3 (picture type) x 3 (skill level) between-subjects factorial. Subjects were undergraduate college students from introductory psychology courses. They were assigned to one of three skill levels based on their scores on the comprehension subtest of the Nelson-Denny Reading Test, Form D. Subjects whose subtest scores fell at or below the 34th percentile (based on Nelson-Denny college norms) were designated less skilled comprehenders. This group consisted of 60 subjects with the average score of the group (M = 34) falling at the 19th percentile. Subjects whose subtest scores fell between the 41st and 69th percentiles were designated moderately skilled comprehenders. This group consisted of 60 subjects with the average score (M = 46) falling at the 54th percentile. Subjects whose subtest scores fell between the 74th and 99th percentiles were designated highly skilled comprehenders. This group consisted of 60 subjects with the average score (M = 56) falling at the 86th percentile. Within each comprehension-level group, an equal number of subjects was assigned to each cell formed by the factorial combination of passage version and picture type.

The experimental procedure was identical to that described earlier except that subjects completed a postexperimental questionnaire and then took the Nelson-Denny comprehension subtest. The post experimental questionnaire included asking subjects to rate the amount of information discussed in the passage for which they had some prior knowledge (using a scale from 1 - "none of it" - to 7 - "all of it"). Subjects were also asked if they had anticipated a memory test and, if so, if they had done anyting extra while reading to prepare for the expected test. Eighty-one subjects indicated that they had expected and prepared for a memory test. These subjects were replaced with 81 naive subjects at the appropriate skill levels. Two other subjects who did not follow instructions were also replaced, as was one subject who had to be replaced due to an experimenter error.

Results

Initial analyses for all dependent measures indicated no main effect of passage version (except for reading time) and no interactions; therefore, all analyses reported are collapsed across passage version.

Comprehension. Table 2 contains the means for reading time, comprehension rating, and rating of prior knowledge. There were no significant differences in prior knowledge ratings (all Fs < 1). For the comprehension ratings, there was no main effect of skill level ($F(2,179) = 1.80$, $p > .16$, MSe = .60), but there was a significant effect of picture type ($F(2,179) = 3.43$, $p < .05$, MSe = .60) that was modified by a significant interaction ($F(4,179) = 3.24$, $p < .05$, MSe = .60). A Newman-Keuls analysis indicated that for highly skilled comprehenders, a text accompanied by relational pictures was rated as more comprehensible than a text accompanied by detail pictures, but neither detail nor relational pictures significantly affected comprehension ratings relative to no pictures. Moderately skilled comprehenders rated a text accompanied by relational pictures as more comprehensible than

Table 2. Experiment 2: Reading Times, Comprehension Ratings, and Prior Knowledge Ratings.

| Dependent Measure | Picture Condition | | |
	Control	Detail Pictures	Relational Pictures
Reading Time[a]			
High Ability	1.77 (.47)[b]	2.44 (.43)	2.48 (.36)
Moderate Ability	1.91 (.51)	2.87 (.64)	2.75 (.54)
Lower Ability	1.99 (.50)	2.65 (.58)	2.77 (.66)
Comprehension Rating[c]			
High Ability	4.00 (.56)	4.05 (.61)	4.55 (.61)
Moderate Ability	3.75 (.97)	3.65 (.81)	4.40 (.82)
Lower Ability	4.00 (.92)	4.25 (.64)	3.85 (.93)
Prior Knowledge Rating[d]			
High Ability	1.45 (.69)	1.85 (1.09)	1.60 (.94)
Moderate Ability	1.80 (1.24)	1.55 (1.00)	1.85 (1.09)
Lower Ability	1.55 (1.00)	1.55 (.76)	1.45 (.76)

[a] Measured in minutes.

[b] Standard deviations in brackets.

[c] Larger numbers indicate higher comprehension rating.

[d] Larger numbers indicate higher prior knowledge rating.

both a text accompanied by detail pictures and a text without pictures. The addition of detail pictures did not significantly affect their comprehension ratings relative to no pictures. For less skilled comprehenders, pictures had no significant effect on comprehension ratings.

Reading time differed significantly by skill level ($F(2,179) = 4.98$, p < .01, MSe = .28). There was also a significant main effect of picture type ($F(2,179) = 42.59$, p < .0001, MSe = .28) but no interaction (F < 1). Newman-Keuls analyses indicated that the no-picture version was read faster than either of the picture versions (which did not differ from each other), and highly skilled comprehenders read faster than moderately skilled and less skilled comprehenders (whose reading times did not significantly differ from each other).

Recall. Table 3 shows the mean proportion recalled of the target propositions (information depicted in the pictures) and nontarget propositions as a function of picture condition and reading ability (the proportions are based on recall scores, with each recalled proposition receiving a score of 1 or 2 as described earlier). First, planned comparisons collapsing over reading ability confirmed the reliability of the results obtained in our initial first experiment. Recall of targeted relational information was significantly greater in the relational picture condition than in the no-picture condition ($F(1,114) = 28.24$, p .0001, MSe = .01), but detail recall was not significantly enhanced by relational pictures ($F(1,114) = 2.69$, p > .10, MSe = 03). Similarly, recall of detail information was significantly greater in the detail picture condition than in the no-picture condition ($F(1,114) = 31.17$, p < .0001, MSe = .03), but recall of relational information was not significantly enhanced ($F(1,114) = 2.81$ p > .09, MSe = .01). Recall of nontargeted information was not affected by the addition of either picture type (F's < 1).

Next, the above comparisons were computed separately for each reading ability level. The general mnemonic benefit of relational pictures was limited to certain reading levels, with relational information being significantly better recalled (relative to the no-picture control) for high ability and moderate ability readers ($F(1,114) = 15.67$, p < .0005, MSe = .01 and $F(1,114) = 13.49$, p < .0005, MSe = .01, respectively) but not for low ability readers. Moreover, for high-ability readers the mnemonic benefit of relational pictures extended to recall of target details. That is, for high-ability readers only, specific details (that were encompassed by but were not explicitly depicted in the relational pictures) were better recalled in the relational picture condition than in the no-picture control ($F(1,114) = 5.61$, p < .05, MSe = .03). Recall of nontarget information was not enhanced for any reading-ability level (largest F = 1.29).

Table 3. Experiment 2: Free Recall of Target Detail, Target Relational, and Nontarget Information.

Comprehension Skill and Information Type	Picture Condition		
	Control	Detail Pictures	Relational Pictures
High Ability			
Target Detail	.22 (.16)[a]	.35 (.22)	.35 (.18)
Target Relational	.16 (.08)	.19 (.10)	.26 (.11)
Nontarget	.12 (.06)	.13 (.10)	.11 (.05)
Moderate Ability			
Target Detail	.20 (.16)	.40 (.14)	.27 (.20)
Target Relational	.13 (.08)	.15 (.07)	.22 (.08)
Nontarget	.08 (.06)	.11 (.05)	.10 (.06)
Lower Ability			
Target Detail	.20 (.14)	.42 (.23)	.16 (.16)
Target Relational	.13 (.09)	.16 (.12)	.17 (.06)
Nontarget	.09 (.08)	.09 (.08)	.07 (.05)

[a]Standard deviations in brackets

The mnemonic benefit of detail pictures also appeared to be modulated somewhat by reading-ability level, with low and moderate ability readers appearing to benefit more in recall of details than high ability readers. Comparisons of the detail picture conditions with the no-picture conditions at each reading level, however, showed that low, moderate and high ability readers significantly increased their recall of details when presented with detail pictures (F's $(1,114) = 14.56$, $p < .0005$, $MSe = .03$; 12.65, $p < .001$, $MSe = .03$; and 5.28, $p < .05$, $MSe = .03$, respectively). Recall of relational information was not increased by detail pictures for any reading level (largest $F = 1.47$, $p > .22$, $MSe =$

.01), nor was recall of nontarget information enhanced by detail pictures at any reading level (largest F = 1.52, p > .22, MSe = .01).

Finally, to assess how reading-ability level per se impacted text recall, we performed separate one-factor analyses of variance (with reading ability as the independent factor) for recall of each type of information for those subjects in the standard (no-picture) text condition. There was no significant effect of reading ability in any of these analyses.

Discussion

The recall patterns are contrary to the predictions derived from the compensatory models, and as such, are an important exception to findings that text adjuncts and learning strategies primarily serve a compensatory role. In some studies (e.g., McDaniel & Pressley, 1984; see also, Mayer & Gallini, 1990, using illustrated text with subjects differing in prior knowledge), instructed learning strategies and text adjuncts have been found to effectively increase memory performance of lower ability subjects but to have no or limited benefit for higher ability subjects (but see Kirby & Cantwell, 1985, for an opposite pattern).

In contrast, in the present experiment, illustrations embedded in text enhanced recall relative to an unillustrated text condition most generally for high ability readers. Average ability readers benefited from pictures but not as extensively as did high ability readers. Low ability readers benefited only very selectively from pictures, with the benefit restricted to recall of illustrated details. The finding that low ability readers benefited from pictures, however selectively, also contradicted the simple enrichment hypothesis that assumed that only the more able readers would profit from pictures.

To some extent, the results are consistent with the selective enrichment view sketched at the outset. Low-ability readers seem to be inefficient at building coherent mental representations during comprehension, an inefficiency that past research suggests is general across written, spoken, and pictorial presentations (Gernsbacher, Varner, & Faust, 1990). The present results are compatible with these past findings in that pictures designed to depict the relationships among several ideas did not aid the less able readers in recalling such information; indeed for these readers, recall of this information when pictured was nominally lower than when it was not pictured. High-ability readers, on the other hand, seem able to withstand distraction from potentially competing and divergent alternative interpretations of linguistic input, thereby maintaining a coherent representation (Gernsbacher et al.). This process of effectively relating various ideas was bolstered for high ability readers when relational pictures were added to the text.

Apparently, representational pictures of the type used in the present study do not provide the kind of support that less skilled readers need to enhance coherence of related ideas in a text. Because our less skilled readers were university students, however, they read well enough to encode simple details, and it was for this type of information that pictures were beneficial for these readers. Overall then, the results might be captured with the generalization that representational pictures enriched or enhanced the encoding of information that the reader could ordinarily extract.

There are several findings, however, that suggest a refinement of the selective enrichment framework. One finding not anticipated from the selective enrichment hypothesis was that pictures enhanced memory for details for high ability readers. The assumption had been (as outlined in the introduction) that for high-ability readers, pictures focusing on details would not enrich their encoding because high ability readers tend to concentrate on the essential information and disregard the trivial details anyway (cf., Brown & Smiley, 1978). The absence of differences in the no-picture control condition between the different reading-ability groups for recall of both detail and relational information also questions the idea that the high-ability readers focused more on relational information at the expense of details, whereas low-ability readers focused more on individual details.

One way to view the entire pattern of results is that pictures enable the extraction and retention of information that readers under ordinary circumstances do not encode effectively, though they have the requisite abilities to do so.[1] The idea here is that lower-ability readers may generally not selectively focus on details any more so than other readers. Lower-ability readers have the skills to effectively encode details, though, and these skills are more efficiently engaged with picture adjuncts. Lower-ability readers appear to have limitations, however, in terms of encoding relational information (cf. Gernsbacher et al., 1990). Consequently, for these readers, enablement through pictures is not possible because the requisite skills (for extracting well-articulated relations) are not there to begin with. For these readers, enhancement may require an adjunct that actually compensates for the deficiency. One interesting possibility in the present context might be the use of dynamic visual adjuncts that more precisely or concretely demonstrate the relations.

Good readers under ordinary circumstances may not efficiently concentrate on all of the information in the text, but they can activate appropriate encoding processes if adjuncts suggest that it is important to do so for certain information and/or enable effective processing of that information. This suggestion is consistent with recent work showing that good readers are not only sensitive to the relative importance of information in a text, but they are also sensitive to signals concerning the relevance of information to subsequent tasks (Schraw & Wade, 1991). That is, good readers will attend to and remember information, even that which is not necessarily of central importance, if the information is signaled as being relevant. In the current context, the pictures may have served to signal particular information (referred to in the picture) as being somehow special (or relevant). This possibility would account for the finding that even relational pictures enhanced recall of target details for high ability readers. Though the exact details were not depicted in the relational pictures (two million tons of ice cascade down), the more general idea was depicted (ice cascading down the mountain), and this would be sufficient to alert high-ability readers to the relevance (vis-a-vis the emphasis of the picture) of the detail presented in the text.

Most generally, the present results underscore the necessity of considering individual differences in understanding the effects of pictures on the comprehension and memory of prose. General statements about the mnemonic efficacy of pictures in prose that ignore individual differences are likely to be misleading. Considerations of the particular pattern obtained herein with other results on individual differences in picture effects suggest that individual differences may interact with pictures in a complex fashion to determine memory performance. For example, Mayer and Gallini (1990) reported that explanative illustrations designed to help readers build runnable mental models served a compensatory function. That is, these illustrations improved recall for low prior-knowledge learners but not for high prior-knowledge learners. Our subjects' self-ratings of their knowledge about the content of the Kanchenjunga text indicated that they had little prior knowledge of the topic. Our findings extend Mayer and Gallini by showing that representational illustrations can generally enhance recall for low prior-knowledge students. Additionally, however, within this group, further differentiation of individual-differences based on reading ability produced effects reflecting an enrichment or enablement function. It appears that layers of individual differences exist, with pictures exerting compensatory or enabling influences depending on the particular constellation of abilities sampled. Thus, in characterizing the modulating effects of individual differences on the mnemonic effects of text illustrations, one must also be sensitive to not one, but several dimensions on which learners can differ.

RÉSUMÉ

Notre recherche vise à préciser dans quelle mesure les dessins peuvent améliorer le rappel d'informations présentées textuellement, et plus particulièrement, les informations de détail et les informations de type relationnel. Deux ensembles de dessins ont été réalisés, l'un représentant des détails individuels évoqués dans le texte, l'autre représentant les relations entre plusieurs propositions. Les premiers résultats montrent que l'information ciblée par un ensemble de dessins particulier est mieux rappelée quand les dessins sont inclus dans le texte. Cependant, plusieurs perspectives théoriques suggèrent que ce pattern général peut varier selon les capacités de lecture et de compréhension. Une deuxième expérience a permis de confirmer que ce pattern n'est retrouvé que chez les lecteurs de niveau élevé ou moyen. Les lecteurs de niveau faible n'ont bénéficié que très sélectivement des dessins. L'amélioration n'a porté que sur le rappel des détails qui étaient illustrés. Ces résultats suggèrent que les dessins permettent l'extraction et la rétention d'informations que les sujets n'encodent pas spécialement dans des conditions habituelles, pour autant que les lecteurs ont les capacités requises minimales de compréhension.

Notes

1 We appreciate discussions at the workshop for stimulating the development of this interpretation.

Acknowledgement

We are grateful to Jean Dumas for preparing the Abstract in French. Some of the research presented herein was also reported at the Annual Meeting of the Midwestern Psychological Association, May 2-4, 1991, Chicago, Illinois, USA. A complete presentation of this research is reported in Waddill and McDaniel (1992) in *Memory & Cognition, 20,* 472-482.

References

Anderson, J.R. (1983). *The architecture of cognition.* Cambridge, MA: Harvard University Press.

Brown, A.L., & Smiley, S.S. (1978). The development of strategies for studying texts. *Child Development, 49,* 1076-1088.

Einstein, G.O., McDaniel, M.A., Bowers, C.A., & Stevens, D.T. (1984). Memory for prose: The influence of relation and proposition-specific processing. *Journal of Experimental Psychology: Learning, Memory, and Cognition, 10,* 133-143.

Einstein, G.O., McDaniel, M.A., Owen, P.D., & Cote, N.C. (1990). Encoding and recall of texts: The importance of material appropriate processing. *Journal of Memory and Language, 29,* 566-581.

Gernsbacher, M.A., Varner, K.R., & Faust, M. (1990). Investigating differences in general comprehension skill. *Journal of Experimental Psychology: Learning, Memory, and Cognition, 16,* 430-445.

Harber, J.R. (1980). Effects of illustrations on reading performance: Implications for further LD reseach. *Learning Disability Quarterly, 3,* 60-70.

Haring, M.J., & Fry, M.A. (1979). Effect of pictures on children's comprehension of written text. *Educational Communication and Technology, 27,* 185-190.

Kirby, J.R., & Cantwell, R.H. (1985). Use of advance organizers to facilitate higher-level text comprehension. *Human Learning, 4,* 159-168.

Mayer, R.E., & Gallini, J.K. (1990). When is an illustration worth ten thousand words? *Journal of Educational Psychology, 82,* 715-726.

McDaniel, M.A., & Pressley, M. (1984). Putting the keyword method in context. *Journal of Educational Psychology, 76,* 598-609.

Nelson, D.L. (1979). Remembering pictures and words: Appearance, significance, and name. In L.S. Cermak & F.I.M. Craik (Eds.), *Levels of processing in human memory* (pp. 45-76). Hillsdale, NJ: Erlbaum.

Paivio, A. (1986). *Mental representations: A dual coding approach.* New York: Oxford University Press.

Rose, T.L. (1986). Effects of illustrations on reading comprehension of learning disabled students. *Journal of Learning Disabilities, 19,* 542-544.

Schraw, G., & Wade, S. (1991). *Selective learning strategies for relevant and important text information.* Paper presented at the Annual Meeting of the American Educational Research Association, April 6, 1991, Chicago.

Waddill, P.J., McDaniel, M.A., & Einstein, G.O. (1988). Illustrations as adjuncts to prose: A text-appropriate processing approach. *Journal of Educational Psychology, 80,* 457-464.

Appendix I

Detail pictures with text

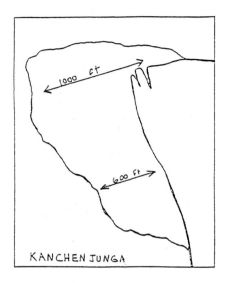

The plasticity of the ice allows Kanchenjunga to develop enormously thick hanging glaciers with walls of ice 600 to 1000 feet wide.

By contrast, the hanging glaciers in the Alps rarely reach 200 feet wide because the ice in the Alpine district is more brittle and breaks away more often.

It's important to note that the size of the hanging glacier determines the size of the avalanche.

Thus, although avalanches are more frequent in the Alps, none approach the magnitude of the Kanchenjunga avalanches.

On kanchenjunga, its not atypical for 2 million tons of ice and snow to cascade down the mountain during the avalanche.

On kanchenjunga the ice walls bend further over the edge of cliffs, and when at last the ice is no longer able to withstand the internal stresses, it cracks, and a huge avalanche occurs.

Appendix II

Relational pictures with text

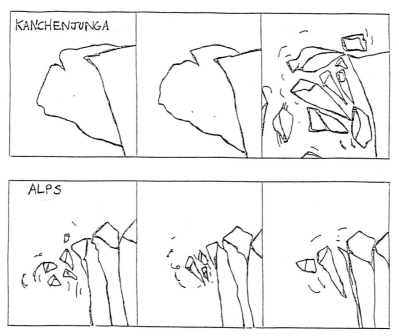

The plasticity of the ice allows Kanchenjunga to develop enormously thick hanging glaciers with walls of ice 600 to 1000 feet wide.

By contrast, the hanging glaciers in the Alps rarely reach 200 feet wide because the ice in the Alpine district is more brittle and breaks away more often.

It's important to note that the size of the hanging glacier determines the size of the avalanche.

Thus, although avalanches are more frequent in the Alps, none approach the magnitude of the Kanchenjunga avalanches.

On kanchenjung, its not atypical for 2 million tons of ice and snow to cascade down the moutain during the avalanche.

On kanchenjunga the ice walls bend further over the edge of cliffs, and when at last the ice is no longer able to withstand the internal stresses, it cracks, and a huge avalanche occurs.

Chapter 12

The Use of Graphics and Texts in Constructing Mental Models

Wolfgang Schnotz[1], Emmanuel Picard[2] & Michael Henninger[3]

[1]University of Jena, FRG
[2]German Institute of Distance Education, Tübingen, FRG
[3]University of Munich, FRG

ABSTRACT

This study investigates differences between deep understanding and superficial understanding of graphics and texts based on the assumption that graphics comprehension is a structure mapping process between visuo-spatial relations in a graphic and semantic relations in a mental model. Adult learners received a time zone map of the earth and a hypertext dealing with time and date, and they had to answer a series of questions about this topic. More successful learners were more likely to access the relevant information at the relevant time than the less successful learners. The more successful learners also interpreted more encompassing sectors of the map, whereas the less successful learners often restricted their interpretation to only small sectors of the map. The mental models of the more successful learners were more elaborated, and these learners were more likely to apply adequate procedures on their mental models. Less successful learners frequently made errors due to a non-application of adequate procedures or an application of inadequate procedures. Based on these results, instructional consequences of how to foster knowledge acquisition from graphics and texts are pointed out.

Instructional materials usually contain both texts and graphics. Whenever an individual comprehends a text, he or she constructs a mental representation of the facts described in the text. Recent cognitive theories assume that this process includes the construction of multiple mental representations: that the reader will construct a mental representation of the text's surface structure, a propositional representation of the semantic content, and a mental model, scenario or situational model (Johnson-Laird, 1983; Sanford & Garrod, 1981; van Dijk & Kintsch, 1983). While, after two decades of intensive research, we have a relatively detailed picture of the cognitive processes involved in text comprehension, we know relatively little about the understanding of graphics. It is only recently that this domain has been dealt with in research on cognition, learning, and instruction (cf. Houghton & Willows, 1987; Kosslyn, 1989; Larkin & Simon, 1987; Mandl & Levin, 1989; Mayer & Gallini, 1990; Willows & Houghton, 1987; Winn, 1989).

From an instructional point of view a frequent complaint is that graphics presented in texts are often processed only superficially: Learners assume that a short scan is sufficient for understanding, and thus refrain from analyzing information in more detail (cf. Weidenmann, 1988, 1989). Thus, the question arises how deeper understanding of graphics in texts could be stimulated, which again requires to know more precisely what deep understanding of graphics really is. The aim of the following study was therefore to analyse how a deep understanding of graphics and texts differs from a superficial understanding. In order to find out the respective differences a group of more successful learners were compared with a group of less successful learners with regard to their integration of graphic and text information during acquisition of knowledge. We first present a theoretical framework for an analysis of graphics and text comprehension. Then we will describe an empirical study where this framework was used to analyse differences between more successful and less successful learners in their use of graphics and texts.

Theoretical Framework

Various researchers have addressed issues relevant to the question of how text understanding interacts with comprehension of graphics. Paivio (1971, 1978) advocated a relatively simple answer. According to his dual encoding theory, cognition includes two separate, functionally independent, but interacting systems of information processing: A verbal system for language information and an image system for visual information. Words and sentences are usually encoded in the verbal system whereas graphics are processed both in the verbal and the image system, which would explain the better retention of graphics information compared with text information. A similar view is held by Kulhavy and his colleagues with their theory of conjoint processing, which assumes that information that has been encoded both verbally and pictorially is recalled better (Kulhavy, Lee & Caterino, 1985; Kulhavy, Stock & Caterino, this volume). Other authors consider the interaction between text and graphic comprehension as an equalizing of a so-called "semantic incline" between both sources of information (Bock & Hörmann, 1974; Bock & Milz, 1977). According to Molitor, Ballstaedt and Mandl (1989), graphics and texts are complementary information sources, if both of them contain specific semantic gaps which can only be filled by the other.

A somewhat different point of view has been adopted by Schnotz and Mikkilä (1991): Text and graphics are considered to be complementary information sources because they represent an object in a symbolic as well as in an analog fashion and, thus, contribute in different ways to the construction of a mental model. Texts trigger the formation of a propositional representation which subsequently serves as a basis for the construction of a corresponding mental model. Graphics convey information by the way in which their components are spatially arranged. They can be considered as an external two-dimensional model allowing for a relatively direct construction of a corresponding mental model, which can subsequently be used to elaborate the propositional representation.

Graphics comprehension as structure mapping on mental models

If one assumes that comprehension implies the construction of mental models and that these models are hypothetical, internal quasi-objects which represent the subject matter by analogy, then the comprehension of graphics could be described as a process of structure mapping. That is, the learner has to find a certain mapping whereby specific visuo-spatial relations between graphic entities correspond to specific semantic relations between entities of the target domain's mental model (cf. Clement & Gentner, 1991; Falkenhainer, Forbus & Gentner, 1989/90; Gentner, 1983; Vosniadou & Ortony, 1989). Such a mapping can proceed in both directions: The learner can construct a mental model on

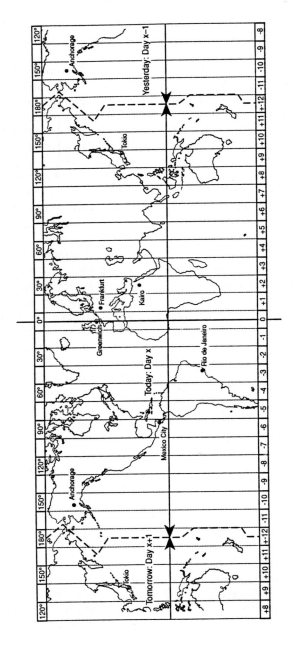

Figure 1. Two dimensional representation of the earth surface with time zones and date zones.

the basis of a graphic, and he/she can evaluate an already existing mental model by means of the respective graphic.

The idea of graphics comprehension as structure mapping on mental models shall be explained in the following with the example shown in figure 1. This figure presents a map with time zones, which often appears in pocket-calendars. From a syntactic point of view, the map consists of an outer frame with a ledge of numbers at its upper and lower margins, of an inner frame with vertical lines drawn in regular intervals, of irregular lines, of areas surrounded by lines, as well as of dots and associated labels. Between these components certain spatial relationships prevail (e.g. left/right, inside/outside). From a semantic point of view, the dots in the map represent certain cities, some lines represent the continental outlines, others represent the meridians or the date line; certain regions represent time zones (without consideration of political borders). In order to understand the graphic, the learner has to map certain visuo-spatial relations within the graphic onto certain relations within the target domain's mental model. If, for example, the dot "Frankfurt" on the map is located four stripes (=4 units) right-hand from the dot "Rio", then this means that Frankfurt is located four units East of Rio in the real world, and thus, a corresponding (quasi-spatial) relation must hold between the respective entitites of the target domain's mental model. (For the sake of simplicity we don't use degrees here, but units of 15 degrees as a measure unit for right-left or East-West distances.)

As the earth rotates in Eastern direction, a sunrise happens earlier in the East and, thus, the clocks there show a later time already. Therefore, the visuo-spatial right/left relations in the graphic can be mapped also on temporal relations in the target domain's mental model: The fact that the dot "Frankfurt" is located 4 units to the right of the dot "Rio" on the map also means that the sun rises 4 hours earlier in Frankfurt and the time there is 4 hours later than in Rio. Such an interpretation corresponds to a deeper comprehension of the map than a mere spatial-geographical interpretation. Which kind of visuo-spatial relations are to be included into the mapping between a graphic and a target domain's mental model depends on the aim of the individual. If a learner is, as in the present example, only interested in the time differences between certain places on the earth, he/she has to focus only on left-right-relations and can disregard above-below-relations (Holyoak & Thagard, 1989).

Application of procedures on mental models

After a mental model has been constructed certain procedures can be applied to it. In the present example, one of these procedures would correspond to a general rule for modifications of the daytime caused by movements towards East or West, which we will refer to as the daytime-correction rule:

IF: crossing a time-zone limit towards East,
THEN: increase current time of the day by one hour.
IF: crossing a time-zone limit towards West,
THEN: decrease current time of the day by one hour.

Since a day ends at midnight 24 o'clock, which is simultaneously the beginning of the next day, the just mentioned general rule for daytime-corrections should not be applied for time corrections beyond midnight. In these cases a more specific rule has to be given priority, which we will refer to as the rule for time corrections at midnight:

IF: crossing a time-zone limit towards East,
           and the previous daytime is 23 o'clock,
THEN: set new daytime to 0 o'clock and
           increase current date by one day.
IF: crossing a time-zone limit towards West,
           and the previous daytime is 0 o'clock,
THEN: set new daytime to 23 o'clock and
           decrease current date by one day.

An application of these two rules, however, would sometimes lead to contradictory results: If one would move, for example, from Tokyo to Anchorage in Eastern direction, the resulting time in Anchorage would be 5 hours later than in Tokyo. If one would move, however, from Tokyo to Anchorage in Western direction, the resulting time in Anchorage would be 19 hours earlier than in Tokyo. In other words: Two different days would prevail in Anchorage. In order to avoid such nonsensical results, the mental model has to be elaborated by the introduction of a further entity representing the so-called date line, and a corresponding rule for the date-corrections at this date line is necessary:

IF: Crossing the date line towards East,
THEN: Decrease the date by 1.

IF: Crossing the date line towards West,
THEN: Increase the date by 1.

By introducing the date line, the problem is tackled that some of the cities like Anchorage and Tokyo exist in several exemplars on the map: By the dotted lines, the map is divided into three areas, which represent different dates, namely "Yesterday: Day x - 1", "Today: Day x", and "Tomorrow: Day x + 1". Therefore, the different dots representing one particular city represent the respective city associated with different dates, and the two dotted lines represent the date line at different points in time: once between Day x - 1 and Day x, and once between Day x and Day x + 1.

Thus, if one wants to represent only the currently valid place-and-time associations, one has to constrain the mapping between the graphic and the mental model to an interval of only 24 hours. One way to introduce such a constraint would be to envisage a type of gliding window as shown in Figure 2, which limits the structure mapping correspondingly. That imaginary window would move along an endlessly repeating "earth-tape" to the left (i.e. in Western direction). Every hour, a time zone would shift out of the windows' right edge with an old date and simultaneously reappear at the left edge with a new date. The gliding window would contain a time scale reaching from 0 to 24 hours. The left edge of the window would represent the place where the time is 0 o'clock and the right edge would represent the place where the time is 24 o'clock. We will refer to this line in the following as the "midnight line".

Complementarity between texts and graphics in mental model construction

If an individual has to answer certain questions or solve certain tasks by means of a mental model, then this model has to have an appropriate structure. It must contain entities, and certain relations must exist among these entities so that the necessary procedures can be applied onto the model and lead to proper results. Both texts and graphics can provide information required for the construction of such a mental model. The relevant entitites within the target domain can be described with more or less specifity in a text, and the corresponding visual entities can be emphasized differently in a graphic (cf. Kosslyn, 1989).

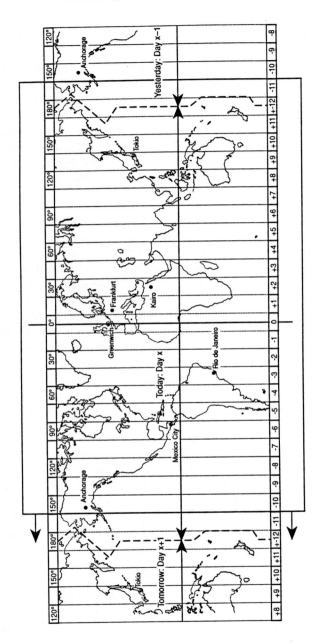

Figure 2. Map of the earth surface with time zones and date zones plus a
gliding window defined by a variable midnight line.

In the map above, for example, the dots representing the different cities and the vertical stripes representing the time zones are easily detectable. Thus, one can also immediately recognize by perception-based inferences that the dot "Rio" is located on the right hand of the dot "Mexico" (cf. Larkin, 1989). These graphical entitites can therefore be used easily in the process of structure mapping between the graphic and a corresponding mental model. However, other entities such as the above-mentioned midnight line and the "gliding window" are not portrayed in the map. Therefore, these entities have to be inferred into the mental model from other information sources, either from prior knowledge or from the accompanying text. Accordingly, texts and graphics can be considered as complementary sources of information with regard to their content, if the entities to be inferred into the mental model receiving only little support by the graphic receive much support by the text, and the entities with little support by the text receive much support by the graphic. Accordingly, a complementarity use of text and graphic would mean that learners use the graphic more intensively if the required information for mental model construction is not available in the text, and that they use the text more intensively if the required information is not available in the graphic. In the following empirical study we used this theoretical framework to investigate differences between more and less successful learners concerning their use of text and graphic for the construction of a mental model.

Method

Subjects and Learning Material. 26 students participated in the study. They received the map shown above in format of DIN A 3 and a text about the topic of "time and date" which was presented as a hypertext. The text information was organized in five thematic blocks ("division of the earth in time zones", "local time and time zone", "day-time diffe-rences", "date differences", and "date zones on the earth"). The individual text sections could be accessed at will by means of a hierarchical menu. The text contained 2750 words.

Procedure. The investigation was performed in individual sessions and contained a phase of intelligence and prior knowledge evaluation, a learning phase and a final test phase. In the first phase, subjects were administered the Intelligenz-Struktur-Test of Amthauer. Furthermore, they received the map shown in figure 1 without additional explanation and, as an evaluation of prior knowledge, were asked to describe what information can be picked up from there. In the learning phase, the subjects were presented step by step the following sequence of questions:

A) *What is the time in Rio de Janeiro and what day is it there, if it is Tuesday 22 o'clock in Mexico City?*

B) *What is the time in Anchorage and what day is it there, if it is Thursday 15 o'clock in Tokyo?*

C) *On a journey towards the East, does one have to put the clock forward by one hour when a new time zone is entered, as long as one does not cross the date line?*

D) *On a journey travelling towards East, does one have to put the clock back by one hour when a new time zone is entered, after crossing the date line?*

E) *An airplane starts in Tokyo on a Thursday evening at 18 o'clock local time and arrives in Anchorage at 9 o'clock local time after flying for a period of 10 hours. What day is it in Anchorage?*

F) *After a stay of two hours, the airplane starts in Anchorage on Thursday at 11 o'clock local time and arrives at Frankfurt at 8 o'clock local time after flying for a period of 10 hours. What day is it in Frankfurt?*

G) *If one crosses the date line on a journey towards the East, does one go from "Today" into "Yesterday" ?*

H) *If one crosses the date line on a journey towards the West, does one go from "Today" into "Tomorrow"?*

I) *Is it possible, as one can choose whether to travel eastwards or westwards, to choose whether to travel from a Thursday into Wednesday or into Friday?*

J) *Is it possible that three days can exist simultaneously on Earth as, for example, Wednesday, Thursday, and Friday?*

K) *When it is Thursday 6 o'clock in Greenwich, is it then Thursday all over the Earth, or are there also any other days? If yes: Which are these other days?*

The subjects were free to use both the map and the text at will. In order to obtain detailed information about the cognitive processes during comprehension, the Thinking Aloud Method was applied: The subjects were asked to verbalize immediately what was going on in their minds. Their verbal statements and observable behavior were tape- and video-recorded. Their access to the hypertext information was recorded automatically. In the final test phase, the subjects were given a comprehension test consisting of 25 relatively complex items which involved concepts such as time shift, date zones, date correction, and the like.

Scoring. Besides the intelligence scores, the verbal protocols from the primary evaluation phase were analysed with regard to how many correct propositions they contained about time zones, time differences, the date line etc. The respective score was considered as an indicator of prior knowledge. The verbal protocols from the learning phase were analysed with regard to how many graphical entities were mentioned by the subject. The respective score was considered as an index for the amount of the subject's mapping activity. Furthermore, the protocols were analysed with regard to the number of incorrect applications of the rules described above. Performance in the final comprehension test was determined as the number of correctly answered items. The group of twelve subjects with the highest scores in the comprehension test (the more successful learners) and the group of twelve subjects with the lowest scores (the less successful learners) were then compared to each other as to their information retrieval and the comprehension processes they had shown in the previous learning phase.

Results

There were no significant differences with regard to intelligence and prior knowledge between the two groups. The mean intelligence was 112.2 (s=7.0) with the more successful and 110.9 (s=9.3) with the less successful learners. The average score of prior knowledge was 4.50 (s=1.68) with the more successful and 4.17 (s=2.25) with the less successful learners. There were, however, considerable differences between the two groups with regard to the use of text information, the use of graphic information, the mental model construction as well as differences with regard to the application of procedures on the mental models.

Differences in the use of text information

The less successful learners read only a slightly greater number of text sections (M=15.2, s=9.5) than did the more successful learners (M=12.1, s=6.4). However, they retrieved text information nearly twice as frequently as the more successful learners (M=26.5, s=21.8 vs.

M=14.6, s=8.4; p=<.10; Mann-Whitney, z=1.27). According to the concept of complementarity, the mental model construction is especially dependent upon retrieval of text information whenever the relevant entities are not supported sufficiently by the graphic. According to the judgement of four experts the concept "time zones" received more support from the map than the concept "date line" and the latter received more support than the concept "midnight line". In the group of the more successful learners 52% of the information retrieval referred to text paragraphs about the date line and the change of the date at midnight, i.e. entities which received little support from the map. In the group of the less successful learners, the respective percentage was only 43%. This difference was significant (Mann-Whitney, z=2.00, p<.05). Obviously, the more successful learners were more selective in accessing text information about entities with little graphical support than the less successful learners.

What refers to the sequential pattern of information retrieval, an increased request for information is to be expected especially, according to the concept of complementarity, if a new entity with little support by the map has to be introduced in the mental model, or if new relations among entities have to be taken into account. This condition was fulfilled with the questions B, E, G and I. In Question B, the date line became relevant for the first time. Question E required for the first time taking into account a time delay, a crossing of the date line and the duration of a flight. In Question G, the concept of date zones (i.e. geographical areas, where the same date is valid at a specific moment) had to be considered the first time. In Task I, the limitation of the interpretable part of the map according to the gliding window mentioned above had to be taken into account for the first time. Figure 3 shows how the text information retrieval about the date line and the date change at midnight is distributed across the 11 questions in both groups. As can be seen from this figure, the more successful learners concentrated their information retrieval more around the above mentioned questions than did the less successful learners. In other words: The more successful learners were more likely to access the relevant text information at the right time than the less successful learners.

Differences in the use of graphic information

On the average the more successful learners mentioned 21.3 graphical entities in their protocols (s=2.5), whereas the respective frequency was

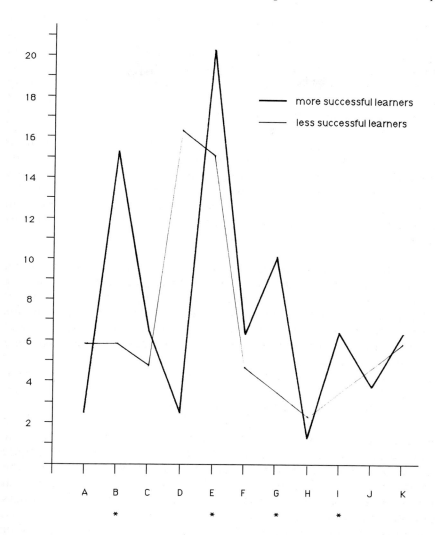

Figure 3. Distributions of requests for information about the date line and the change of date at midnight across questions A to K by more successful and less successful learners.

only 12.5 (s=2.6) with the less successful learners. This difference was highly significant (t(22)=8.38, p<.001). The more successful learners obviously took more entities into account, interpreted more extensive sections of the map and, accordingly, achieved a more coherent mapping (cf. de Kleer & Brown, 1983). Conversely, the less successful learners made fewer references to graphical entities. They often simply chose ad hoc a very limited portion of the map which appeared adequate to them and, thus, came to wrong conclusions. For example, some of those subjects focused only on the two right dots standing for Tokyo and Anchorage in the map and came to the conclusion that the date in Tokyo is always one day later than in Anchorage.

The less successful learners used the map also in a qualitatively different way. They often simply extracted numbers and performed calculations with these numbers without verifying their results by means of the map. Thereby, errors occurred such as that between Tokyo (time zone +9) and Anchorage (time zone -10) a time difference of only one hour prevails ("(9)-(10)= -1"), although one could immediately recognize by inspection of the map that the two cities are 5 (or 19) units apart from each other. Such errors occured five times with the less successful and only one time with the more successful learners. The more successful learners checked the result of calculations more frequently with the help of the map: On the average, they used the map 2.17 times (s=1.03) in order to determine time differences also by measuring (i.e. counting the number time zones between two locations), whereas the respective mean was only 1.42 (s=1.24) with the less successful learners. This difference was marginally significant (Mann-Whitney, z=1.58, p=.06).

Differences in the elaboration of mental models

The less successful learners overlooked the necessary date-correction at the date line significantly more often (M=1.0, s=0.95) than the more successful learners (M=0.25, s=0.45; Mann-Whitney z=2.22, p<.05). Obviously, the entity of the date line was often not inferred by the less successful learners. Furthermore, the midnight line, or the "gliding window" which defines the area of the interpretable section at a specific moment, was not contained in the map and, therefore, had to be inferred into the mental model without graphical support. The less successful learners obviously drew that inference less frequently: When they were asked for the size of the presently valid part of the map (Question I), 75% of them gave a wrong answer, whereas only 17% of the more successful learners answered this question incorrectly (Mann-Whitney, z=2.81, p<.01). One can conclude, that the mental models of the less successful learners were less elaborated than those of the more successful learners.

Differences in the application of procedures on mental models

Erroneous responses seemed to originate not only from inadequately structured mental models, but also from an inadequate application of procedures applied to those models. By means of the thinking aloud protocols, we could distinguish between different types of procedural faults. As mentioned above, the date line (shown as a dotted line on the map) was ignored significantly more often by the less successful learners. We interpreted this to mean that the corresponding mental entity (the 'mental' date line) was frequently missing in their mental models and, thus, the rule for the date-corrections at the date line could not be applied. The less successful learners also created inadequate rules. For example, they often interchanged the condition parts and action parts of the daytime-correction rule:

IF: Crossing a time-zone limit towards East,
THEN: Decrease time of day by 1 hour.
IF: Crossing a time-zone-limit towards West,
THEN: Increase time of day by 1 hour.

While this error appeared, on average, only 0.4 times (s=0.8) with the more successful learners, it happened 2.4 times (s=2.1) with the less successful learners (Mann-Whitney, z=2.63, p < .01). Quite frequently, the subjects concerned argued that time in the East is earlier, because the sun rises earlier there. Obviously, the distinction between the notion of "occurs earlier" and the notion of "is earlier" (i.e., the daytime is less advanced) was lacking for these subjects.

As mentioned above, less successful learners often did not infer a midnight line entity in their mental models. Thus, for these subjects, there was only one place where the date could change: the date line. Therefore, if the date changed for any reason (e.g., due to midnight), then they often interpreted this as a result of crossing the date line. In short: Any place on the earth where the date changes (including the midnight line) was supposed to be the "date line". Accordingly, they used over-generalized date-line rules:

IF: Crossing the (assumed) "date line" towards East,
THEN: Decrease the date by 1.
IF: Crossing the (assumed) "date line" towards West,
THEN: Increase the date by 1.

Which they applied not only to the actual date line, but also to the supposed date line: the midnight line. In the latter case, the subjects performed exactly the opposite of what they should have done: Instead of increasing the date in Eastern direction, they decreased it; and instead of decreasing the date in Western direction, they increased it.

Less successful learners who did not infer the midnight line and, therefore, assumed that the date changes only at one particular place, sometimes also concluded that, in travelling from one place to another, the date changes only once. Therefore, after a first correction of the date, they did not apply any of the respective rules again and argued, that the date change was already settled. Thus, they followed too specific rules which can be applied only if no previous change of the date has taken place:

IF: Crossing the "date line" towards East,
         and the date has not been changed yet,
THEN: Decrease the date by 1.
IF: Crossing the "date lined" towards West,
         and the date has not been changed yet,
THEN: Increase the date by 1.

If these rules, due to the over-specified condition part, are not applied to the real date line, then an error of failing to change the date is made. If the rules are applied also to the midnight line due to the over-generalized notion of the date-line, then the date is changed in the wrong direction. These kind of errors appeared with 50% of the less successful learners, but only with 17% of the more successful learners (Mann-Whitney, $z=1.70$, $p<.05$).

Summary

Summarizing the results one can say that successful and unsuccessful learners did not differ significantly in their intelligence or prior knowledge, but differed considerably in their strategies concerning the use of text information and the use of graphic information. They also seemed to differ in the structure of their mental models and the procedures applied to these models. With regard to the use of the text, the more successful learners were more specific in their information retrieval. They adapted more to the demands of mental model construction in that they accessed relevant information especially at those points in the sequence of questions where new entities had to be inferred into the mental model. These learners were more likely to access the relevant information at the right time than the less successful learners. The more successful learners also used the graphic more intensively: They interpreted more encompassing sectors of the map, included more entities in their structure mapping and, thus, obviously achieved a higher coherence in their mapping than did the less successful learners. The less successful learners often performed only ad-hoc mappings of reduced sectors of the map which included relatively few entities. Sometimes they also used the map only to extract numbers for calculations, without further relating the results to the map. The deficiences in comprehension could be attributed to structural deficits of the mental models on the one hand, and due to procedural deficits in the use of those models on the other hand. The mental models of the more successful learners were obviously more elaborated than those of the less successful learners. The more successful learners were also more likely to apply the procedures required for the questions answering adequately, whereas the less successful learners often made errors due to a non-application of adequate procedures or an application of inadequate procedures.

Instructional consequences

As far as the results of this explorative study can be generalized, the differences revealed between successful and less successful learners give us some indication concerning the design of learning and comprehension aids for fostering knowledge acquisition by means of texts and graphics. If we adopt the view that both comprehension of texts and comprehension of graphics is an adaptive strategic process, then it should be possible to promote comprehension processes by inducing adequate strategies (cf. Brown, 1981; Jenkins, 1979; Jörg & Hörmann, 1978). Since less successful learners use graphics spontaneously in a rather limited way, they should receive guidance on how to use graphics more intensively. Such guidance should help these learners especially to perform a more encompassing mapping between a graphic and the corresponding mental model. This could ensue either directly in that the learner is asked to name the referents of certain graphical entities and to make explicit the meaning of certain spatial relations between graphical entities. The guidance could, however, ensue also indirectly in that the learner is presented certain tasks which cause him/her to systematically establish semantic relations between the entities in the respective mental model. Furthermore, since less successful learners are obviously not well enabled to coordinate graphic and text information adequately, they obviously need also some help concerning the selection of relevant information. It would be possible, for example, to allow only access to such information which is relevant for a concept-driven analysis of the graphic according to the question at the respective moment.

If knowledge acquisition is guided indirectly by specific tasks, the question of how to select and sequence these tasks is of central importance. If one assumes that mental models are constructed progressively in response to emerging demands, then the tasks presented to the learner are not only to be ordered according to increasing difficulty. They are also to be selected and sequenced so that the learner is obliged to operate with his/her mental model in a way that produces cognitive conflicts if the model is not structured adequately (cf. Berlyne, 1960). The issue of which strategies are effective here, how they can be implemented, and how they interact with existing learning techniques will have to be a topic of further research.

RÉSUMÉ

La recherche présentée ici étudie en quoi une compréhension approfondie de graphiques et de textes se différencie d'une compréhension plus superficielle. Le cadre théorique présenté suppose que la compréhension des graphiques est un processus d'organisation structurale entre les relations spatiales présentes dans le graphique et les relations sémantiques du modèle mental correspondant, processus pouvant également être réalisé à partir d'un texte. S'appuyant sur ce cadre théorique, on analyse les différences de performances de traitement de graphiques et de textes entre des "bons" et des "mauvais" compreneurs". On présentait à des adultes une carte des fuseaux horaires de la terre ainsi qu'un hypertexte traitant de l'heure et de la date et ils devaient répondre à une série de questions sur ce thème. Une comparaison des traitements effectués par le groupe des "bons" et des "mauvais" compreneurs indique que les "bons" avaient un comportement plus spécifique dans la récupération d'informations, et qu'ils accédaient plus facilement à l'information pertinente du texte au moment opportun que les "mauvais" compreneurs. Les "bons" ont aussi interprété plus de secteurs environnants de la carte, et, en conséquence, ont atteint une cohérence plus grande dans leur structuration que les "mauvais" compreneurs, qui ont souvent restreint leur interprétation à de petits secteurs de la carte. Les modèles mentaux des "bons" compreneurs" étaient aussi plus élaborés, et ces derniers appliquaient plus facilement des procédures sur leurs modèles mentaux. Les "mauvais" compreneurs ont fait des erreurs provoquées soit par l'absence d'application des procédures adéquates soit par l'application de procédures inadéquates, et ce plus souvent que les "bons" compreneurs. Aux vues de ces résultats, les implications éducatives concernant les moyens de favoriser l'acquisition de connaissances à partir de graphiques et de textes sont envisagées.

Acknowledgements

The authors want to thank R. Lowe, R.E. Mayer, and S. Vosniadou for their comments on an earlier version of this paper.

References

Berlyne, D.E. (1960). Conflict, arousal, and curiosity. New York: McGraw-Hill.

Bock, M., & Hörmann, H. (1974). Der Einfluß von Bildern auf das Behalten von Sätzen. *Psychologische Forschung, 36*, 343-357.

Bock, M., & Milz, B. (1977). Pictorial context and the recall of pronoun sentences. *Psychological Research, 39*, 203-220.

Brown, A.L. (1981). Metacognition: The development of selective attention strategies for learning from texts. In M.L. Kamil (Ed.), *Directions in reading research and instruction* (pp. 21-43). Washington, DC: National Reading Conference.

Clement, C.A., & Gentner, D. (1991). Systematicity as a selection constraint in analogical mapping. *Cognitive Science, 15*, 89-132.

de Kleer, J., & Brown, J.S. (1983). Assumptions and ambiguities in mechanistic mental models. In D. Gentner & A.L. Stevens (Eds.), *Mental models* (pp. 155-190). Hillsdale, N.J.: Erlbaum.

Falkenhainer, B., Forbus, K.D. & Gentner, D. (1989/90). The structure-mapping enginge: algorithm and examples. *Artificial Intelligence, 41,* 1-63.

Genter, D. (1983). Structure-mapping: a theoretical framework for analogy. *Cognitive Science, 7,* 155-170.

Holyoak, K., & Thagard, P.R. (1989). A computational model of analogical problem solving. In S. Vosniadou & A. Ortony (Eds.), *Similarity and analogical reasoning* (pp. 242-266). Cambridge: Cambridge University Press.

Houghton, H.A., & Willows, D.M. (1987). *The Psychology of Illustration. Basic Research. Vol 1.* New York: Springer.

Jenkins, J.J. (1979). Four points to remember: A tetrahedral model and memory experiments. In L.S. Cermak & F.I.M. Craik (Eds.), *Levels of processing in human memory* (pp. 429-446). Hillsdale, N.J.: Erlbaum.

Jörg, S., & Hörmann, H. (1978). The influence of general and specific verbal labels on the recognition of labeled and unlabeled parts of pictures. *Journal of Verbal Learning and Verbal Behavior, 17,* 445-454.

Johnson-Laird, P.N. (1983). *Mental models. Towards a cognitive science of language, inference, and consciousness.* Cambridge: Cambridge University Press.

Kosslyn, S.M. (1989). Understanding charts and graphs. *Journal of applied Cognitive Psychology, 3,* 185-226.

Kulhavy, R.W., Lee, J.B., & Caterino, L.C. (1985). Conjoint retention of maps and related discourse. *Contemporary Educational Psychology, 10,* 28-37.

Larkin, J.H. (1989). Display-based problem solving. In D. Klahr & K. Kotovsky (Eds.), *Complex Information Processing* (pp. 319-341). Hillsdale, NJ: Lawrence Erlbaum Associates.

Larkin, J.H., & Simon, H.A. (1987). Why a diagram is (sometimes) worth ten thousand words. *Cognitive Science, 11,* 65-99.

Mandl, H., & Levin, J.R. (1989). *Knowledge acquisition from text and pictures.* Amsterdam: North-Holland.

Mayer, R.E., & Gallini, J.K. (1990). When an illustration is worth ten thousand words? *Journal of Educational Psychology, 82*(4), 715-726.

Molitor, S., Ballstaedt, S.P., & Mandl, H. (1989). Problems in knowledge acquisition from text and pictures. In H. Mandl & J.R. Levin (Eds.), *Knowledge acquisition from text and pictures* (pp. 3-35). Amsterdam: North-Holland.

Paivio, A. (1971). *Imagery and verbal processes.* New York: Holt, Rinehart & Winston.

Paivio, A. (1978). A dual coding approach to perception and cognition. In H.L. Pick & E. Saltzman (Eds.), *Modes of perceiving and processing information* (pp. 39-52). Hillsdale, NJ: Erlbaum.

Sanford, A.J., & Garrod, S.C. (1981). *Understanding written language: Exploration of comprehension beyond the sentence.* New York: Wiley.

Schnotz, W., & Mikkilä, M. (1991). Symbolische und analoge Repräsentationen beim Verstehen technischer Geräte. *Zeitschrift für Psychologie, Suppl. 11*, 223-235.

van Dijk, T.A., & Kintsch, W. (1983). *Strategies of discourse comprehension.* New York: Academic Press.

Vosniadou, S., & Ortony, A. (1989). *Similarity and analogical reasoning.* New York: Cambridge University Press.

Weidenmann, B. (1988). *Psychische Prozesse beim Verstehen von Bildern.* Bern, Stuttgart, Toronto: Verlag Hans Huber.

Weidenmann, B. (1989). When good pictures fail: An information-processing approach to the effect of illustrations. In H. Mandl & J.R. Levin (Eds.), *Knowledge acquisition from text and pictures* (pp. 157-170). Amsterdam: North-Holland.

Willows, D.M., & Houghton, H.A. (1987). *The Psychology of Illustration. Instructional Issues. Vol 2.* New York: Springer.

Winn, W. (1989). The Design and use of instructional graphics. In H. Mandl & J.R. Levin (Eds.), *Knowledge acquisition from text and pictures* (pp. 125-144). Amsterdam: North-Holland.

Comprehension of Graphics
W. Schnotz and R. W. Kulhavy (Editors)
© 1994 Elsevier Science B.V. All rights reserved.

Chapter 13

Cognitive Processes in Understanding Line Graphs

Ulla Maichle

Institut für Test- und Begabungsforschung, Bonn, FRG

ABSTRACT

This paper describes how good and poor graph readers reason as they interpret line graphs representing multidimensional scientific data. Graph comprehension ability of high school students was assessed with an appropriate, nationally normed test, and high and low scoring subjects were compared with respect, (1) to the amount and type of information extracted spontaneously from line graphs, (2) to the sequence and type of information heeded and vocalized while verifying verbal statements with respect to graphically presented information. Results show that good graph readers extract information of a higher level of complexity than poor graph readers. Analysis of thinking aloud protocols indicate that they use a specific graph schema, directing their attention to typical line graph information, namely quantitative trend information. Results are discussed in terms of a graph comprehension theory. Implications concerning assessment as well as teaching of graph comprehension ability are outlined.

Cartesian line graphs are the preferred method of displaying multidimensional scientific data not only in economics, physics and engineering, but also in particular fields of medical sciences, such as biochemistry, pharmacology and physiology. Hence, a lot of information in educational textbooks at the university level is presented by line graphs.

To what extent are university students in the sciences able to understand line graphs? Bell and Janvier (1981) point out that - although the use of

graphs becomes common in primary school - many secondary pupils
are weak in the ability to interpret global graphical features, and
McDermott et al. (1983) have shown that this is a problem even for
many university students in the sciences. Analysis of the results of the
nationwide testing program for admission to Medical Schools in the
FRG shows that there are remarkable differences among graduates
from high schools in their ability to read graphs (Trost, 1989).
Unfortunately we know relatively little about the nature of these
differences. Learning processes in secondary school may have some
impact: Applicants whose majors have been in mathematics normally
attain the highest graph comprehension scores. But until now we have
not known the specific cognitive operations upon which this transfer
effect is based.

This paper reports an effort to investigate how good and poor graph
readers reason as they interpret line graphs representing scientific
information. The study was inspired by a theory of graph
comprehension outlined by S. Pinker (1990), which is based upon
general perceptual and cognitive assumptions.

Theoretical framework

Some characteristics of line graphs

Generally, line graphs as well as other types of graphs convey
information by the way their parts are spatially arranged. In contrast to
plans, maps or geometrical drawings which use spatial relations to
represent spatial relations, line graphs use spatial relations to represent
non-spatial relations (see Plunkett, 1979). The basic idea is that the
length of a line can be used to represent the value of a variable (even
when the variable itself is not a metric length). Thus, particular values
of variables, such as time, speed or temperature, can be represented as
lengths of line segments. The comprehension of a line graph however
goes beyond a piecemeal understanding of what each individual point on
the graph means. Line graphs represent the correspondence between
changes in variables (e.g. as the time elapsed increases the value of the
dependent variable increases or decreases). The metaphor for an
increase in value is an increase in length, and the graph reader has to
realize that the motion of a point in the graph in two dimensions is used
to represent changes in two variables at once (see Clement, 1988).

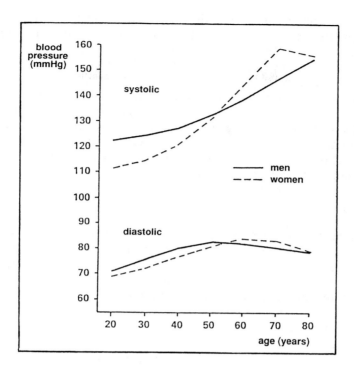

Figure 1. A line graph used in study 1.

A model of graph comprehension

Figure 1 shows a time-plot taken from a physiological textbook, presenting the average systolic and diastolic blood pressure values of men and woman at different ages; this graph plots values on a ratio scale (time) along with values on another ratio scale (blood pressure). The shapes of the lines correspond to the variation of blood pressure values over a period of twenty years.

What does a person know when he or she reads this graph? According to Pinker (1990) there are two types of mental representations that are of importance in the process of graph perception and comprehension: The "visual description" and the "graph schema". The output of the mechanism of visual perception (and the input of the graph comprehension process) is a structural description of the scene, the "visual description". Like a propositional representation a visual description has a clear structure with variables standing for the perceived elements, and with predicates specifying spatial relations among the elements (e.g. "x is above y").

If the reader whishes to extract conceptual information from the graph (e.g. the information that "the average diastolic blood pressure of men increases up to the age of 50" from the graph presented in Figure 1), he or she must know which aspects of the visual constituents of the scene stand for which aspects of the conceptual information. Such knowledge of line graphs is supposed to be represented by a "graph schema". A graph schema can be seen as an active, interrelated knowledge structure, a network of nodes and relations, embodying knowledge of what graphs are for and how they are interpreted in general. A graph schema translates the information found in the visual description into conceptual information, and directs the search for desired pieces of information. According to Pinker a graph schema contains three key pieces of information: The display's pictorial content (i.e. some objects or geometrical figures, such as bars or lines), which are described in terms of visual attributes, the L-shaped framework (coordinate system), specifying the ratio magnitudes of attributes, and the textual material, which specifies the real-world referents.

Beside this general graph schema, an experienced graph reader is supposed to have more specific graph schemata, such as a "bar graph schema" or a "line graph schema". A graph schema embodying knowledge of a subset of bar graphs is presented by Pinker (1990, pp. 97). To my knowledge a description of the structure and elements of a line graph schema has yet to be done. Experiments on the relative ease of extracting information from line graphs may provide some perspectives with respect to this topic; they show that subjects are able to translate line graph information into trend information directly, that is without having to examine local units one by one, whereas absolute value information may not be perceived directly from a line graph (c.f. Culbertson & Powers, 1959; Simcox, 1983; Wainer & Thissen, 1981; Washburne 1927). In this context Pinker points out that the English Language (as well as the German Language) has a lot of words to describe the shapes of lines or pairs of lines (e.g. flat, steep, convex, parallel, intersecting, x-shaped). It is reasonable to assume that this vocabulary reflects a rich "mental vocabulary" of visual predicates for lines. Together with the frequently demonstrated appropriateness of line graphs for conveying trend information, these findings suggest that a line graph schema should enable the reader to translate a variety of line shapes into trend information. Thus, we can assume that when a line graph schema is activated (i.e. when the graph is recognized as being a line graph), the encoding likelihood of trend information should temporarily be "enhanced", whereas the extraction of other types of information, such as absolute value information should be effortful in comparison with trend information.

All studies cited above refer to a single idealized graph reader. Although it is a well known fact that there are great differences among subjects in their ability to read line graphs, we know relatively little about the nature of these individual differences. According to Pinker, there are two factors which allow for individual differences. First, a person may lack a line graph schema at all or a person's line graph schema may lack important components, so that he or she is not able to translate particular visual information into conceptual information (e.g. quantitative trend information). If we assume that good graph readers use a line graph schema and poor graph readers have only a general graph schema at their disposal, we can infer that good graph readers should operate with trend information using less mental effort than poor graph readers whereas the identification or extraction of absolute value information should be more effortful for good graph readers as long as the line graph schema is activated. The two studies presented below will focus on this topic, analyzing (a) what types of information subjects with high and subjects with low degree of graph comprehension ability are attending to when studying line graphs and (b) how subjects in both groups read and interpret line graphs (time plots) representing scientific information.

Study 1

The main purpose of study 1 was to determine what type of information students extract spontaneously (that is, without a particular instruction) from time plots representing multidimensional scientific data. The focus is upon two aspects: Descripton of general results and comparison of good and poor graph readers with respect to the type of extracted information.

Method

Subjects. Thirty-three twelfth-graders from a high school in Bonn, 15 males and 18 females, participated as subjects in this study.

Materials. We applied the test "Diagrams and Tables" (DaT) taken from the "Test for Medical Studies" which is part of the nationwide testing program for admission to Medical Schools in the FRG. The test DaT is designed to measure the ability of reading and interpreting common types of graphs, such as line graphs, bar graphs, and tables in the field of science and medicine. DaT consists of 24 items answerable in a 60-minute time limit. The test is nationally normed, and thus allowed a valid assessment of the subjects general graph comprehension ability. In addition, 6 time plots representing the results of repeated measurements of scientific variables, taken from educational textbooks, were used.

Procedure. Study 1 was performed in a group session. The subjects first took the DaT. After test completion, the time plots were exposed to the students one by one and they were told that they would have ten minutes for each graph to write down as many statements as possible about the information presented in the time plot.

Analysis. DaT: Percentages of correct answers were computed. As a basis for a quantitative analysis of the information extracted from the line graphs, the sentences students had written down were categorized with respect to a coarse, but clear schema as

(a) Point reading; sentences categorized as "point reading" imply the extraction of an absolute point value.
(b) Comparison between two individual point values; these sentences imply the comparison of a pair of absolute values, either qualitatively (e.g. "higher than") or quantitatively (e.g. "10 mmHg lower than").
(c) Trend reading; these sentences imply the descripton of the shape of a line segment in terms of qualitative trend information (e.g. "increasing rapidly").
(d) Comparison between two trends; these sentences imply the comparison between two trends, either qualitatively (e.g. "shows a larger increase than") or quantitatively (e.g. "an increase twice as large").
(e) Visual description; this category contains sentences which describe elements of the visual array pattern in terms of their relative position, specifying elements and the spatial relations among them (e.g. "The systolic blood pressure line is always above the diastolic line").

Table 1. Percentages for different types of information extracted spontaneously from line graphs

Type of information	
Point reading	.08
Comparison between two individual point values	.11
Trend reading	.36
Comparison between two trends	.25
Visual description	.11
Unclear	.09

Note. Percentages are based on 1 176 statements. Number of subjects: 33.

An overall-analysis and a differential analysis of the data for good and poor graph readers were computed. (Eight subjects succeeding in more than 60 percent of the DaT-items were defined as good graph readers, eight subjects succeeding in less than 40 percent were defined as poor graph readers.)

Results

Results of the overall analysis

On the average the students produced 35.6 sentences each (that are about 6 sentences on a time plot). Table 1 provides the relative frequency of the five types of statements.

It is obvious that mainly trend information was extracted from the time plots: More than 60% of the sentences are descriptions of trends or imply a comparison between two trends. Less than 20% of the sentences are concerned with absolute value information, and 11% of the sentences are visual descriptions, referring to elements of the visual array pattern (e.g. lines) and to spatial relations among them (e.g. beside, above).

Results of differential analysis

As to the amount of extracted information, both groups showed similar performance: The mean number of sentences produced by good graph readers was 36.5 (SD = 8.4) and by poor graph readers 34.6 (SD = 14.6). Concerning the type of information however, both groups differed from one another in significant ways. Table 2 presents the results of a differential analysis. Notice that the categories "comparison between two individual point values" and "comparison between two trends" are now subdivided each in comparisons referring to events occurring simultaneously (cross-sectional comparisons) and comparisons referring to events occurring at different times (longitudinal comparisons).

As shown in Table 2, 38% of the poor graph readers' sentences are descriptions of a particular trend or a particular point value (good graph readers: 18%). Good graph readers' sentences on the other hand mainly (53%) imply comparisons between two components (poor graph readers: 32%). About 20% of the comparisons are based on individual point values (poor graph readers: 35%), about 80% are trend comparisons (poor graph readers: 65%). Notice, that 65% of these trend comparisons are "cross-sectional", in that they refer to trends covering the same period of time (e.g. "Between the ages of 50 and 70 the systolic blood pressure values of woman increase more rapidly than the values of men"); 35% are "longitudinal comparisons", in that they refer to trends covering different periods of time (e.g. "The systolic blood pressure values of woman increase more rapidly between the ages of 50 and 70 than between the ages of 20 and 40"). Of particular interest is the finding that poor graph readers generated almost no longitudinal comparisons, neither with respect to individual point values nor with respect to trends. It seems noteworthy that no substantial differencens were found with respect to the category "visual description": 11% and 15% respectively of the sentences were mere descriptions of spatial configurations without reference to conceptual graph information.

Table 2. Percentages for different types of information extracted spontaneously from line graphs by good and poor graph readers

Type of information	Graph readers	
	good	poor
Point reading	.01	.05
Comparison between two individual point values		
- cross-sectional	.02	.08
- longitudinal	.08	.03
Trend reading	.17	.33*
Coparison between two trends		
- cross-sectional	.28	.17
- longitudinal	.15	.04*
Visual description	.11	.15
Unclear	.18	.15

Note. Percentage are based on 292 statements (good graph readers) respectively 277 statements (poor graph readers). *p < .05.

Discussion

The results of the overall analysis are consistent with the findings of experiments cited above on the relative ease of extracting information from line graphs: (1) The most obvious information in line graphs are trends, (2) individual point values are harder to isolate than trend information.

Comparison of the low and high ability group indicates that the groups did not differ significantly in the relative frequency of extracting point value and trend information, but they did differ with respect to the complexity of the extracted information: With reference to larger perceptual units and performing comparisons rather than descriptions of particular components, subjects with high degree of graph comprehension ability extracted information of a higher level of complexity than the low ability subjects. These results are consistent with previous findings in the study of complex cognitive processes, such as problem solving in physics or intellectually demanding games (notably chess). These findings indicate that, compared with beginners, experienced subjects use "chunks" of information rather than isolated items, in order to solve problems. To my knowledge, such research has yet to be done in the field of graph reading. Thus, in order to obtain more detailed information concerning the amount of mental effort, as well as the course of information processing of good and poor graphs readers evaluating information of different levels of complexity with respect to line graphs, a second study was undertaken using the thinking aloud method as an on-line tool for studying cognitive processes.

Study 2

Method

Subjects. Subjects in study 2 were 16 students who participated in study 1, that is 8 subjects with high graph comprehension scores (good graph readers) and 8 subjects with low graph comprehension scores (poor graph readers).

Materials. Four time plots displaying multidimensional scientific data from particular fields of medical sciences. Each graph was presented with a series of five verbal statements, partly true and partly false with respect to the information represented by the graph. The subjects had to evaluate each statement with respect to the time plot. This evaluation asked for a standard set of "interpretive operations" characterized by different levels of complexity

(a) a qualitative, cross-sectional comparison between two trends
(b) a quantitative, cross-sectional comparison between two trends
(c) a quantitative, longitudinal comparison between two trends
(d) a quantitative, cross-sectional comparison between two individual point values.
(e) a quantitative, longitudinal comparison between two individual point values.

A quantitative comparison between two trends requires the calculation of rates of increase or decrease (e.g. "an increase as twice as large"), whereas a qualitative comparison (e.g. "a larger increase") does not ask the subject to perform arithmetic operations.

Procedure. Study 2 was performed in individual sessions. Subjects were asked to think aloud not only while studying the graph but also while reading and evaluating the propositional information. (There was no explicit instruction to "describe" the line graphs.) Thus, the subjects were asked to associate spatial information with propositional information and to judge, whether both types of information were consistent.

Analysis. The verbalizations were tape recorded and the tapes transcribed; additionally the occurence and duration of pauses and hesitations was recorded. The protocols were segmented, which each segment corresponding to a statement about an information unit. Details of this type of protocol analysis are reported elsewhere (Maichle, 1992).

As a basis for quantitative analysis, protocol statements were categorized with respect to the following scheme:

(a) Localizaton of a graph component, (mostly lines, e.g. "This is the systolic blood pressure line.").
(b) Identification of a point value (e.g. "70 years old woman have 80 mm Hg.").
(c) Identification of a trend (e.g. "Between the ages of 20 and 40 the blood pressure increases from 70 to 80.").
(d) Performance of a calculation (e.g. "12 is 2 times 6.").
(e) Rereading/paraphrasing parts of the verbal statements that had to be judged, corresponding to particular information that had to be extracted from the graph:
   - Information concerning time (the independent variable), e.g. "the age of 40", "3 hours after the injection".
   - Relational information (e.g. "5 mmHg higher than", "a larger increase than").
   - Information concerning a level of the dependent variable, such as "the diastolic blood pressure", referring to one of the lines.
(f) Statements indicating the monitoring of the whole evaluation process. This category contains "strategic statements" (e.g. "let me do the calculation now"), as well as "checks" (e.g. "where are the woman?").

(g)   Statements concerning the test situation and the subjects cognitive
      processes and feelings, so called "metacognitive statements", such
      as "its not an easy thing to do while you are talking", "I hate point
      reading!").

The whole evaluation process was subdivided into two phases: (1)
"Orientation phase", referring to first graph checking activities and
containing all verbalizations before the statements were read for the
first time, and (2) "Verification phase", beginning after the first
statement had been vocalized. Because all subjects reading the statements
for the first time, vocalized little more than the text itself, the first
reading was omitted from further protocol analysis. Within each type of
evaluation procedure the relative frequency as well as the total
verbalizations were computed, both for good and poor graph readers.
The total amount of verbalization was taken as an indicator for the
mental effort needed for evaluation.

Results

Individual differences concerning the "Orientation phase"

With only one exception, all good graph readers - before reading the
statements they had to judge - first checked the line graph, naming the
dimensions which the ordinate and the abscissa represent, identifying
the units and most of them checking the range of values. Without
exception they verbalized the labels of the lines, and 4 of the 8 students
even extracted some trend information. On the average, good graph
readers produced 19.3 statements, describing aspects of the line graph
before reading the statements; 17% of the high ability subjects'
verbalizations were dedicated to such initial "graph-checking"-activities.

Poor graph readers showed a less active orientation phase; on the
average they produced 6.7 statements referring to elements of the graph
before reading the statements. Four students named the dimensions and
3 verbalized the labels of the lines. Not a single low ability subject
produced a statement referring to the units and none verbalized trend
information before reading the statements.

Table 3. Mean number of verbalizations produced while thinking aloud performing different types of verifications.

Type of verification	Graph readers	
	good	poor
Comparison between two trends		
- qualitative / cross-sectional	10.8	14.2
- quantitative / cross-sectional	20.1	45.7*
- quantitative / longitudinal	27.4	46.5*
Comparison between two individual point values		
- quantitative / cross-sectional	23.7	39.1
- quantitative / longitudinal	30.4	33.0

Note. Number of good graph readers: 8; number of poor graph readers: 8. *$p < .05$.

Individual differences concerning the "Verification phase"

Amount of verbalization

Table 3 provides the mean number of verbalizations with respect to each of the five types of verification procedures, aggregated over all line graphs. Notice first that while performing qualitative, cross-sectional comparisons between two trends both groups revealed very poor verbalization. Good graph readers produced on an average of 10.8 comparisons, while poor graph readers averaged 14.2 statements while extracting and comparing qualitative trend information.

Good graph readers verbalized most while performing the quantitative, longitudinal comparison between two individual point values: While verifying this type of information they verbalized, on average, three times as much as with qualitative trend comparisons.

As can be seen from Table 3, poor graph readers verbalized most while verifying longitudinal and cross- sectional, quantitative comparisons between two trends; performing this type of verification, low ability subjects verbalized significantly more statements than high ability subjects (p < .05).

If we consider the total amount of verbalization with respect to a task (that is: the verification of 5 different types of statements with respect to one line graph) good graph readers needed less mental effort in order to perform the different tasks than poor graph readers. Despite the more intensive verbalization in the "orientation phase", mean number of verbalizations with respect to the whole procedure (orientation phase in addition to verification phase) is less than for poor graph readers (32.9 as opposed to 45.8). Computation of solution time revealed similar findings, mean solution time of good graph readers being 4.1 minutes for task completion, and for poor graph readers 5.4 minutes.

Type of verbalization
Table 4 presents an overview of the types of verbalizations with respect to three verification procedures which are most interesting for the present purpose: Qualitative, cross-sectional trend comparisons on the one side and quantitative longitudinal comparisons (trends and point values) on the other side.

First, consider the qualitative, cross-sectional trend comparison. Table 4 shows that during the whole procedure only a few such statements were verbalized, most of them concerning parts of the statements that had to be evaluated and the output of the evaluation process. No statements categorized as "identification of a point value" and "calculation" appear in the protocols, and only few statements indicating monitoring processes, such as strategic statements and checks, were verbalized.

Next, consider the "quantitative, longitudinal comparison between two absolute point values", which was the most effortful procedure for good graph readers. Table 4 indicates that in performing this type of comparison high ability subjects produced relatively more statements indicating identification procedures and calculations.

Finally, consider the "quantitative, longitudinal comparison between two trends"; this procedure was significantly more effortful for poor graph readers than for good ones. Table 4 shows that low ability subjects mainly verbalized statements categorized as "graph component

Table 4. Analysis of thinking aloud protocols: Mean number of different types of verbalizations while verifying verbal statements with respect to line graphs.

Type of verbalization	Type of verification					
	trends (qual./cross-sect.)		Comparisons between point values (quant./longitud.) graph readers		trends (quant./longitud.)	
	good	poor	good	poor	good	poor
Localization of a graph component	0.3	0.7	0.7	1.9	-	4.6
Identification of a point value	-	-	6.9	10.8	-	2.8
Identification of a trend	0.7	0.7	2.4	0.7	4.6	2.3
Calculation	-	-	8.6	6.6	4.0	6.9
Evaluation	2.7	2.9	3.0	6.0	3.4	4.6
Rereading / paraphrasing a text segment concerning						
- independ variable (time)	1.0	1.7	0.6	1.1	4.6	6.9
- dependent variable	2.3	2.3	1.3	2.9	2.3	2.9
- relational information	0.3	0.7	0.6	0.9	1.7	4.4
Strategic statement / check	1.0	1.8	3.7	3.5	3.5	5.8
Metacognitive statement	1.0	1.0	1.8	1.1	1.7	2.8
Unclear	1.5	2.4	0.8	0.7	1.6	2.3

Note. Number of good graph readers: 8; number of poor graph readers: 8.

localization", "calculations", and "identification of a point value". In the
protocols of good graph readers no statements indicating the
localization of visual components, such as lines, or the extraction of
particular point values were observed. Instead they produced more
statements implying trend reading and less statements indicating
calculations, than did poor graph readers.

Discussion

The present study was designed to provide evidence for the hypothesis
that good graph readers use a specific graph schema when reading and
interpreting line graphs. With the aid of the thinking aloud method we
expected to gain deeper insight into the cognitive processes of good and
poor graph readers while verifying verbal statements with respect to
line graphs. A first approach to the analysis of protocols concentrated
upon the amount and the type of individual verbalization, the idea
behind being that, (1) the amount of verbalization should reflect the
needed mental effort, and that, (2) certain types of cognitive processes
should be related to the dominance of certain types of verbalizations. A
second approach considered protocols as a whole, distinguishing
between the "orientation phase", implying graph checking and/or graph
description without referring to the verbal statements, and the
"verification phase", implying the verification of propositional
information with respect to graphic information.

Analysis of thinking aloud protocols, suggests that most high ability
subjects, before reading the verbal statements, that had to be judged,
checked relevant attributes of the line graph, identifying and naming the
dimensions, the units, ranges of values and - this is of particular interest
- some trends. Low ability subjects in contrast scarcely verbalized
graphical information before reading the verbal statements.
Consequently they had to spend more time and effort in the verification
procedure, localizing and identifying the graphical information needed
in order to judge each of the five verbal statements. These findings
strengthen the hypothesis that good graph readers use a line graph
schema, which enables them to recognize quickly which type of graph is
currently being viewed, and which directs their attention automatically
to typical line-graph-information.

Given our initial argument that, when a line graph schema is activated,
the assessment of trend information should be enhanced and thus readily

available whereas absolute value information should be available only with additional cognitive effort, good graph readers should have more difficulty in extracting and comparing point values than in extracting and comparing trend information; furthermore trend comparisons should be less effortful to them than to low level ability subjects. Poor graph readers on the other side, who are supposed to use a general rather than a specific graph schema, should behave in an opposite way, needing more mental effort in order to verify trend comparisons than point value comparisons. The findings of the present study largely confirm this prediction. Protocol analysis indicated that for good graph readers quantitative trend comparisons were significantly less effortful and thus easier than for poor ones, and that comparisons of point values was the most effortful procedure for good graph readers; protocol analysis revealed many identification and localization processes, strengthening the hypothesis that the whole procedure had a cognitive controlled status as opposed to the more automatic status of the quantitative trend comparison procedure.

Contrary to our prediction, results suggest that qualitative comparisons of trends covering the same period of time are easily extracted both by good and poor graph readers; for both groups this procedure seemed to be highly automated, so that only few steps were available for verbal reports. This result is consistent with findings presented by Simcox (1983), where he documented that readers are able to infer qualitative trend information directly from the geometric features representing them. Simcox, furthermore, demonstrated that even uninterpreted stimuli resembling line graphs are automatically encoded in terms of their slopes.

An implication of the present theory is that the growth of graph comprehension ability can be viewed as the development of successively higher level codes which enables the graph reader to translate higher-order perceptual patterns, such as pairs of lines, directly into the quantitative trend information that it symbolizes, reducing the amount of information processing that is necessary to answer questions and to solve problems posed in graphic formats.

Ericsson & Simon (1984) point out that the thinking aloud method can help to identify the degree of expertise in a particular domain of knowledge. They cite some findings indicating that the concurrent verbalizations of highly skilled individuals answering questions and solving problems, are less complete than those of less skilled ones; the researchers argue that with increase in experience, the same process should move from cognitively controlled to automatic status, so that what is avaible to the novice may be unavailable to the experienced subject. Our findings confirm this assumption, showing that good and poor graph readers differ with respect to the amount of verbalization within a task. Thus, qualitative analysis of thinking aloud protocols can be seen as basis for a deeper understanding of individual differences in a domain which only recently has been dealt with in research on perception and cognition.

Conclusions

As far as the results of these explorative studies can be generalized, the differences revealed between good and poor graph readers' cognitive processes while reading and interpreting line graphs have implications for instructional practice as well as for test development and validation. If an investigator aims at developing a graph comprehension test which effectly discriminates between good and poor graph readers, he/she will have to create tasks which are performed by good graph readers more successfully and/or with less mental effort than by poor graph readers. If we assume that subjects with a high level of graph comprehension ability use a specific graph schema, parsing the line graph into the right units and directing their attention automatically to relevant line graph information whereas low level ability subjects use a general graph schema, "line graph items" should be designed in such way that good graph readers are in fact able to use their line graph schema. Our findings suggest that such tasks should require operations with quantitative rather than qualitative trend information and/or absolute value information and longitudinal rather than cross-sectional data.

The same findings have implications for instructional practice as well. Teaching students to read and interpret graphs flexibly and skillfully is a particular challenge to anyone seriously concerned with good education for students who live in an increasingly technological society. In school, the arrival of microcomputers increases the importance of graph comprehension ability, especially comprehension of line graphs, since the output of simulations which are widely used in science, mathematics, and social science instruction usually has the format of a line graph (time plot). As Rumelhart & Ortony (1977) point out, schemata develop as they become more elaborate and more specific. Given our initial assumption that less experienced graph readers use a graph schema embodying only general knowledge of what graphs are for and how they are interpreted in general, improvements in the ability to read line graphs should be expected from explicit instruction aiming at elaborating and specifying students' general graph schema. We assume that such improvements should come, (1) with instruction about how to perceive the graph, that is, how to parse it perceptually into adequate units, and (2) with instruction of how visual patterns (such as parallel versus converging lines) correspond with line graph information represented by such visual patterns (such as additive versus interactive effects of two variables), and (3) with practice at doing so, transforming the encoding and interpreting processes from cognitively controlled to automatic status.

RÉSUMÉ

Cet article décrit la façon dont des bons et des mauvais lecteurs de graphiques raisonnent quand ils interprètent des graphiques représentant des données scientifiques multidimensionnelles. La compétence de lycéens dans la lecture de graphiques était estimée à l'aide d'un test normalisé approprié dans lequel les performances des sujets étaient comparées selon, (1) la quantité et le type d'informations extraits spontanément des graphiques, (2) la séquence et le type d'information pris en compte et verbalisés au cours de la vérification d'énoncés verbaux se rapportant à l'information présentée graphiquement.

Les résultats montrent que les bons lecteurs de graphiques extraient les informations à un niveau de complexité plus élevé que les mauvais lecteurs. L'analyse des protocoles verbaux indiquent qu'ils utilisent un schéma spécifique au graphique, qui focalise leur attention sur les informations typiques des graphiques, notamment les tendances quantitatives. Les résultats sont envisagés dans le cadre d'une théorie de la compréhension de graphiques et les implications concernant l'évaluation ainsi que le développement des compétences de compréhension de graphiques sont esquissées.

References

Bell, A., & Janvier, C. (1981). *The interpretation of graphs representing situations.* University of Nottingham, Shell Centre for Mathematical Education.

Clement, J. (1988). *The concept of variation and misconceptions in Cartesian graphing* (Paper No. 175). University of Massachusetts, Scientific Reasoning Research Institute.

Culbertson, H.M., & Powers, R.D. (1959). A study of graph comprehension difficulties. *Audio Visual Communication Review, 7,* 97-100.

Ericsson, K.A., & Simon, H.A. (1984). *Protocol analysis. Verbal reports as data.* Cambridge: MIT Press.

Maichle, U. (1992). Zur Trainierbarkeit des Textverstehens und des schlußfolgernden Denkens im medizinisch-naturwissenschaftlichen Bereich. In H. Mandl & H.F. Friedrich (Eds.), *Lern- und Denkstrategien. Analyse und Intervention* (pp. 167-192). Göttingen: Hogrefe.

McDermott, L., Rosenquist, M., Popp, B., & van Zee, E. (1983). *Student difficulties in connecting graphs, concepts, and physical phenomena.* Paper presented at the American Educational Association meetings, Montreal, Canada.

Pinker, S. (1990). A theory of graph comprehension. In R. Freedle (Ed.), *Artificial intelligence and the future of testing* (pp. 73-126). Hillsdale, N.J.: Lawrence Erlbaum Associates.

Plunkett, S.P.O. (1979). Diagrams. *Mathematical Education for Teaching, 3,* 3-15.

Rumelhart, D.E., & Ortony, A. (1977). The representation of knowledge in memory. In R.C. Anderson, R.J. Spiro & W.E. Montague (Eds.), *Schooling and the acquisition of knowledge.* Hillsdale, N.J.: Lawrence Erlbaum Associates.

Simcox, W.A. (1983). *A perceptual analysis of graphic information processing.* Unpublished doctoral dissertation. Tufts University, Medford, MA.

Trost, G. (1989). A nationwide testing program for admission to Medical School in West Germany. In R.C. King & J.K. Collins (Eds.), *Social applications and issues in psychology* (pp. 131-137). Amsterdam: North-Holland.

Wainer, H., & Thissen, D. (1981). Graphical data analysis. *Annual Review of Psychology,* 32, 191-241.

Washburne, J.N. (1927). An experimental study of various graphic, tabular, and textual methods of presenting quantitative materials. *Journal of Educational Psychology, 18,* 361-376, 465-476.

Comprehension of Graphics
W. Schnotz and R. W. Kulhavy (Editors)
1994 Elsevier Science B.V.

Chapter 14

On Children's Understanding of an Economic Concept: The Role of Graphics in Evaluation

Camilla Gobbo

University of Padova, Italy

ABSTRACT

The main goal was to study the possibility of utilizing graphical devices in evaluating 12 year-olds' acquisition of economic concepts presented in a lecture. Two line-graphs representing the demand and supply laws, and a chart diagram representing the causal chain of the concepts were used in the evaluation tasks. The tasks involving the chart were a completion, a reconstruction, and a reading task. Subjects were asked to complete the missing values of the concepts, to link the concepts positioning in the chart, and to read the chart. Furthermore, students were required to state the law represented in each line-graph, and to choose the correct formulation of the law among three alternatives. Several patterns of responses, showing the subjects' misconceptions and misunderstandings of the laws, were revealed. Some patterns were found to be more typical than other ones; moreover, the appeared to vary, depending on the task structure and demand. Some difficulties were found in reading the line-graphs, which should be taken into account when they are utilized in teaching. Although the specific patterns could vary across tasks, significant correlations were found among performances, suggesting the usefulness of the graphics in evaluating students' learning.

This research is part of a study in progress on children's learning of the economic concepts related to market price, involving the two laws of demand and supply. The few studies available on students' representation of this domain, e.g. Shute, Glaser and Raghavan (1989) carried out with college students, and Berti and Grivet (1990) carried out with children, showed that some subjects had specific misconceptions. For example, instead of thinking that an increase in price determines an increase of the quantity supplied, they think that when more quantity is supplied the price should decrease, because, by selling a greater quantity the suppliers should be satisfied with a lower selling price. In the context of the present research the interest in children's spontaneous ideas was restricted to seeing whether their performance after the teaching session could be related to their previous representation. In particular this paper addressed the question whether it is feasible to utilize graphic tools in evaluating children's understanding.

Two types of graphs were utilized, line-graphs and a chart diagram. The line-graphs presented linear functions representing the so-called demand and supply curves (henceforth referred to as curves), showing the relationship between price (vertical axis) and quantity (horizontal axis) either demanded or supplied. According to the two laws, the higher the price the lower the quantity demanded (law of demand: line-graph with a negative slope), but the higher the price the higher the quantity supplied (law of supply: line-graph with a positive slope). In the present research the line-graphs were presented to the subjects both in the lecture and in testing their acquisition of the two laws. Line-graphs are considered a useful "tool for reasoning in economics" (Larkin & Simon, 1987, p. 94) and their use "requires no special knowledge" (Marshall, 1890, quoted by Larkin & Simon, p. 95). However, students have been shown to hold specific misconceptions and difficulties in the area of functions and graphs (for a good review see Leinhardt, Zavlasky, and Stein, 1990). Examples are students' tendency to represent a function in terms of a linear graph (e.g. Lovell, 1971), confusion between continuous versus discrete graphs (e.g. Kerslake, 1981), tendency to deal with single points rather than with intervals (Bell and Janvier, 1982), difficulty in moving from a graph to an equation (e.g. Zavlasky, 1988), and difficulty in constructing the axes (Vergnaud and Errecalde, 1980).

In the case of the present research the use of the line-graphs did not require a sophisticated knowledge of graph construction and interpretation. There were reasons to believe that subjects in the age group considered (12 years old) would be competent at understanding the graphs and in handling the tasks. Children as young as 6 years are able to extrapolate straight lines (e.g. from an axis to the function line and from the function line to an axis); for example in order to find the value on the vertical axis corresponding to the value on the horizontal axis (Bryant & Sommerville, 1985; Sommerville & Bryant, 1985). Moreover, while 7 and 9 year old children often did not understand the two axes as a place where the values of each variables are displayed, and the function line was interpreted in terms of a visual metaphor of increase and decrease, the great majority of 12 year olds were able to interpret and construct simple line-graphs (Gobbo & Boder, 1987) like those we utilize. On the basis of these findings, this age group was chosen for this study. To detect possible problems in a preliminary session subjects were presented with a set of tasks dealing with line-graphs.

The other type of graph utilized in the evaluation session was a chart diagram representing the causal chain of the main concepts explained during the lecture. Some researches have studied the effect of using chart diagrams (tree diagrams or knowledge maps) as a text replacement or supplement. For example, when a chart diagram was used as a review device, a positive effect was detected in students' performance on inferential, problem-solving questions, while no such benefit was found in recall of explicit information or in recognition tasks (Lambiotte, Peel & Dansereau, 1989). Moreover, subjects seemed to benefit from the use of a tree diagram when they could use it freely along with the text, rather than when forced to find a match between diagram and text paragraphs (Moore & Scevak, 1992). In general these findings suggest that chart diagrams provide explicit links between interrelated concepts, helping the student to achieve a better integration of the to-be-learned material.

However, as Winn (1990) proposes, the way concepts are grouped and sequenced in a graphic does not always reflect the natural tendency to read it. Moreover, although an important component of a chart diagram is represented by the interrelationships between the concepts, there is no guarantee that the subjects will fully process that information, as in the case of the present research where it was presented for the first time after the lecture. Knowledge of the material is assumed to guide the reading and interpretation of the chart diagram, so that performance should reflect possible misunderstandings or poor knowledge representation.

Thus, the major aim of this paper was to see whether tasks using graphical devices, such as line-graphs and a chart diagram would allow detection of individual differences highlighting the children's understanding. Five tasks were devised in order to see whether the same patterns of responses would be found in students' performance across tasks, and whether some tasks were more useful than other ones in assessing students' difficulties.

Method

Subjects. A total of 35 Italian seventh graders (approximately half males and half females), mean age 12 years 3 months, participated in the pre-test on graph understanding. They all attended the same school in a town near Padova. The number of children attending the subsequent sessions dropped to 32. An evaluation of school achievement was based on the tests routinely taken in the school: 18 subjects scored at the medium-to-high level, 14 at the low level.

Material. The questionnaire devised to tap children's spontaneous ideas involved three questions dealing with the law of supply (e.g. "If at a certain time the price of motorbikes decreases, would the suppliers decide to produce more, fewer, or the same quantity of motorbikes than before? Why?") and three questions dealing with the law of demand (e.g. "If the price of a product decreases, would the buyers be willing to buy more, less or the same quantity as before?"). For the pre-test on line-graph understanding a booklet of 5 pages was prepared, each page containing one line-graph and a set of questions, except for the fifth page that contained 2 graphs. The graphs are presented in Figure 1, bold faced line.

Graphs 1, 3 and 4 presented linear functions, whereas graph 2 presented an irregular trend. With the graphs from 1 to 4 (pre-test 1), the children were asked to interpret each function line and to find the x (or y) value corresponding to a given y (or x) value. In addition, with graphs 2 and 3, children, given the values of the two variables, were also asked to complete the trend (Graph 2, dashed line). The last task (pre-test 2) asked to compare graph 5a (which looks like a rectangular hyperbola) and 5b (linear function, negative slope) with respect to the quantity sold over the years.

A 2 page text was constructed on the basis of two economics textbooks (Napoleoni, 1972; Stanlake, 1989). It explained the concept of market in terms of the interaction between all the suppliers and the buyers of a certain product, and it introduced the law of demand followed by the law of supply. The two linear graphs (similar to graphs 1 and 4 of the

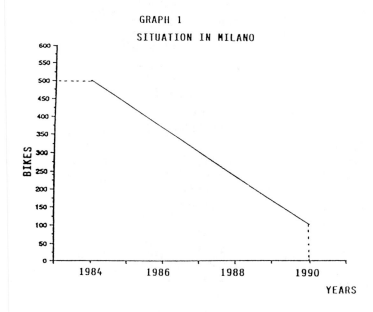

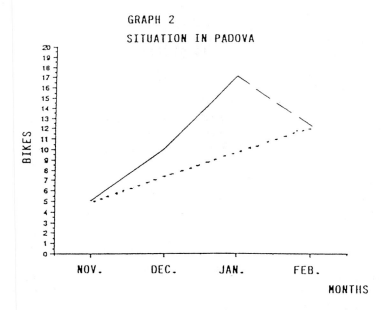

Figure 1. Line-graphs presented in the pre-test (dashed lines: segments to be constructed by the subject; dotted lines: examples of errors).

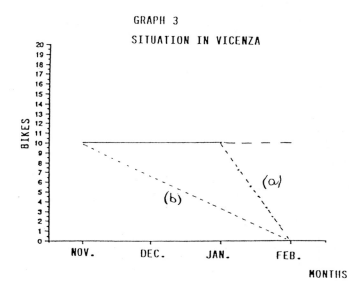

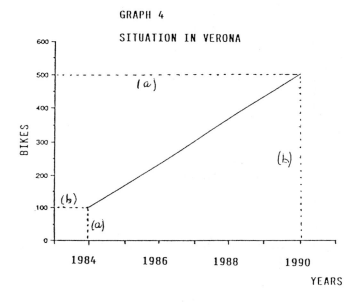

Figure 1 (continued).

GRAPH 5a

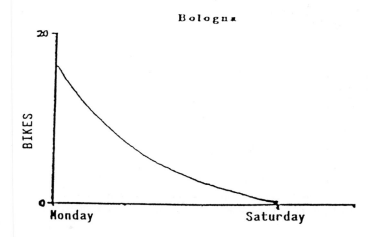

GRAPH 5b

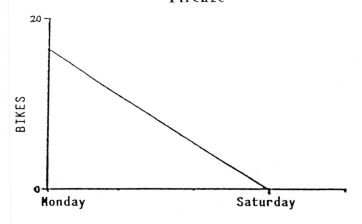

Figure 1 (continued).

pre-test) were also inserted, where quantity was listed on the x axis (from 0 to 25) and price on the y axis (from 0 to 500). Then, holding other factors constant, followed the variations in the quantity demanded and supplied as a result of setting the price too high or too low and the consequence of it in terms of disequilibrium in the market, either as shortage or surplus of a product. Finally, the concept of equilibrium price was introduced, in terms of price adjustment making the quantity demanded equal to the quantity supplied. Price was the only factor introduced to account for changes in the quantity demanded and supplied, in order not to overload the children.

To test children's understanding of the lecture, 5 post-tests were presented. The first 3 tasks involved the use of a chart diagram, where the main concepts from the lecture were graphically presented in a causal chain. Each concept was written in a box and the links were represented by arrows. Its complete form (as utilized in post-test 3) is reported in Figure 2. Post-test 1 was a "cloze" task presenting the chart with a slot in each box: the child had to fill it by choosing between two alternatives written on a side (e.g. for the box "Quantity demanded.....", the alternatives were: does it increase or decrease?). Post-test 2 was a reconstruction task: the chart was presented with empty boxes except the fifth one, dealing with price. The task required children to insert in the chart the concepts randomly displayed. Post-test 3 was a reading task: children were asked to provide a written description of the chart, paying attention both to the concepts and the links. In post-test 4, two linear graphs (one with positive and the other with negative slope) were presented; the subjects had to decide which law was represented by each of them, and to justify their answers. With respect to the curves presented in the lecture, the values of the two variables changed, i.e. quantity ranged from 0 to 50 and price from 0 to 1000. Finally, post-test 5 was a multiple choice task, asking children to underline the correct statement representing each law, choosing among three alternatives: one was correct (for the demand: "If the price increases, then the quantity demanded decreases" (P+ --> D-), one presented an inversion of the relationship (P+ --> D+) and the other one reversed the direction of the if-then terms (D --> P).

Procedure. First, children were presented with the pre-test on line-graph comprehension and were asked to answer one page at a time. Approximately 10 days later, they were presented with the questions to tap their spontaneous ideas (there was no time limit). Two weeks later, the teacher gave the lecture in the classroom. She was asked to give the children a copy of the written text, and to introduce the concepts

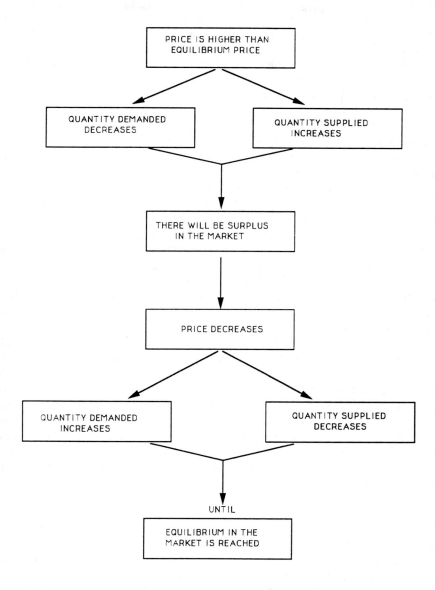

Figure 2. The complete form of the chart diagram used in the post-tests.

making strict reference to the text to help children to pay close attention. She also drew and described the two linear graphs, representing the two curves of demand and supply on the blackboard. After the lecture, children were asked to perform the tasks.

All tasks in each session were performed in a written form in the classroom; children were asked to work alone, and told that their performance would not be evaluated by their teacher.

Results and Discussion

All pre-tests and post-tests were analyzed by two independent judges, reaching an agreement of 96% in the pre-tests on graphs and post-test 4, 97% in post-test 3 and 100% in the remaining tests. Discrepancies were resolved by discussion.

Questionnaire on children's spontaneous ideas

The subjects' answers revealed understanding of the relationship between price and quantity demanded: 26 subjects answered all questions correctly, and the other 6 subjects made an inversion (P+ --> D+) in only one question. More problems were detected for questions dealing with the relationship between price and quantity supplied: none of the subjects answered all questions correctly and only 30% of the answers were correct. The most typical pattern of answers reflected a consistent misconception similar to that found in previous research, that is: "At a lower price the quantity supplied must be greater because, when a product is cheaper, more quantity will be sold so the suppliers gain more". For those children, a change in price causes the same variation in both quantities demanded and supplied. Subjects clearly did not take into account the production costs, and confused proceeds with earnings. Six subjects showed a "moralistic" thinking, that is "If people need more at a lower price, the supplier should offer a larger quantity.

Pre-tests on line-graph understanding

The performance on line-graphs from 1 to 4 (pre-test 1) showed that 65.7% of the subjects were able to perform correctly all tasks; altogether, 13 reading and 7 production errors were made by 12 subjects, the great majority being low achieving students. The most common error patterns revealed lack of understanding of the function line: instead of being considered as the sum of the intercepts, or as the sum of the segments connecting two intercepts, the function line was often taken as a link connecting the two axes at its end points. In reading graph 1, for example, 7 subjects stated that the bike selling is going well. A typical justification was: "In 1990 they sold 500 bikes"; the time value was found extrapolating a straight line from the right-end point of the function line to the x axis, while the quantity value was found extrapolating a straight line from the left-end point of the function line to the y axis (for examples of this pattern of error, see graphs 1 and 4, dotted lines).

Two subjects showed problems in reading the quantity values in graph 2. However, all subjects but one were successful in finding the intercepts.

The errors made in the production tasks with graphs 2 and 3 revealed a lack of understanding similar to the reading task. To show that the number of bikes sold in February was 12 in graph 2 and 10 in graph 3, the subjects either drew a segment connecting the right-end point or the left-end point of the trend (which represented the quantity value) to the time value on the x axis (see graph 3, dotted lines a and b) or a new trend was created connecting the intercept to the left-end point of the trend (graph 2, dotted line).

As far as the comparison task dealing with graphs 5a and 5b is concerned (pre-test 2), 15 subjects acknowledged that the quantity sold was greater in 5b than in 5a, but only 6 of them gave a plausible justification (a mathematical analysis of the functions obviously was not expected); for example: "In Firenze from Tuesday to Friday the selling has decreased less than in Bologna". More than half the subjects either stated that there was no difference (13 subjects) or could not identify the direction (9 subjects), although most of them differentiated the description of the two graphs, e.g.: "In Bologna there is a hurry whereas in Firenze it is slower". This task seemed more difficult than the previous ones; the subjects had some intuitions but they often read the trends as visual metaphors. This might be partly due to the fact that the values were not listed on the axes. The comparison task could perhaps be too demanding with respect to the subjects' level of mastering. The performance on this task was useful also in helping to choose the type of line-graph to be used during the lecture to represent the curves of demand and supply. Economics textbooks make use of either a linear function or a rectangular hyperbola. In the case of the present study the teaching of the two laws did not include concepts such as elasticity of demand and supply; given that fewer reading problems were shown with the linear graphs, these would be utilized during teaching.

Table 1. Frequencies of incorrect patterns of responses related to the two laws in the post-tests. Post-test 4 responses are divided according to performance in graph reading.

	Incorrect Laws					
Post-tests	(a) P^a+-->D+	(b) D-->P	(c) D/D	(d) D-->S	(e) P-->D=S	other
1 Cloze	3	-	-	-	10	-
2 Reconstr.	3	-	-	-	7	2
3 Reading	-	2	2	9	-	1
4 Line-graph						
Graph+	2	2+1^b	-	-	-	-
Graph-	3	3^b	4	2	-	-
Graph?	3	-	-	-	-	-
5 Mult. Choice	4	4+4^b	-	-	8	-

a: P price; + : higher / increases; D: quantity demanded; S: quantity supplied.
b: Number of subjects combining this pattern with another one.

Line graph post-test

On Post-test 4, students were asked to decide which of the two curves represents the law of demand and the law of supply and to justify the answer. The test was analyzed first in order to compare more easily the students' performance with the one offered on the pre-test with line-graphs. The performance was analyzed looking at whether the students (a) labeled each curve with the corresponding law, and/or stated the laws correctly, (b) made explicit reference to the line-graph in their justification, in which case it was possible to discriminate whether their difficulties were due to problems with graph reading or to lack of knowledge of the two laws. Out of the 16 students stating the laws and/or labeling the curves correctly (Law+), 8 read the graphs correctly making explicit reference to changes in the variables of price and quantity and commenting on the function line (Graph+), and 5 subjects labeled the curves but did not justify their answer, thus making no reference to the graphs (Graph?). Three subjects, although stating the laws correctly, labeled the curves incorrectly, showing errors in reading the graphs (Graph-), e.g. "It (curve of demand) represents the quantity supplied because it is clear that when the price goes up to 1000 (the highest price value) they supply 50 pieces (the highest quantity value)" (for a similar pattern, see Figure 1, graph 1, dotted lines). The remaining 16 subjects stated the laws and/or labeled the curves incorrectly (Law-). Four patterns of responses have been identified in post-test 4. They are shown in Table 1, divided according to the accuracy in graph reading.

Eight subjects fell in pattern (a), inversion in both laws (P+ --> D+ and P+ --> S-). In particular, 2 subjects labeled the curves incorrectly, while reading the graphs correctly (Graph+): "It (curve of demand) is the supply curve; I can see that at higher prices the quantity decreases"; other 3 subjects (Graph-), correct in labeling the curves, ended up making an inversion due to a graph reading error: "It is the curve of demand because when the price goes up to 1000 the quantity demanded is 50" (for a similar pattern, see Figure 1, graph 1, dotted lines). Three subjects (Graph?) produced an incorrect labeling with no reference to the line-graphs, thus it cannot be decided whether the error was due to difficulty with graph reading. Pattern (b) consisted of reversing the direction of the relation (D-->P), thus it is the change of quantity that affects the change of price rather than the reverse: this was the only error in 2 subjects, and it was combined with an "inversion" error in other 4 subjects. In pattern (c) both curves represented the law of demand (D/D): for example, for 2 subjects each curve presented a specific variation of price, while quantity was read just in terms of the function line going down or up: "(Curve of demand) At the higher price the quantity demanded is less; (curve of supply) When the price is lower the quantity demanded is more" (a pattern shown in Figure 1, graph 4 dotted lines, b). According to the 2 subjects falling in pattern (d), changes in quantity demanded are caused by changes in quantity supplied (D --> S): one axis represents the quantity demanded and the other the one supplied.

To summarize, only one fourth of the subjects were completely successful in this task, being accurate both in graph reading and in stating the laws. Some children did not understand the laws, and/or showed problems in reading the graphs. A few children limited their performance to labeling the curves, without stating the laws, not allowing further analysis of their performance. Errors in graph reading were offered also by some high achieving students.

A correlational analysis was run on the performance in post-test 4 and in pre-tests 1 and 2 dealing with graphs, on the basis of accuracy and level of justifications (when required by the task). In particular, in pre-test 1 a 1 to 3 point scale was used, where 1 point was assigned to subjects correct in all tasks and 3 points to the ones making 2 or more errors. Pre-test 2 performances were ranked using a scale from 1 to 4 (1 was assigned to a correct response, 2 to a correct one but without justification, 3 when the subject aknowledged the difference between the two graphs without being able to tell which one presented the greater quantity, and 4 when the two graphs were considered equivalent). Ranks assigned to post-test 4 penalized errors in graph reading rather than in law statements. Thus, regardless of the accuracy in stating the laws, rank 1 was assigned to those offering a correct reading of the graphs (12 subjects Graph+), rank 2 to those not referring directly to the graphs (8 subjects Graph?), and rank 3 to the subjects making errors in graph reading (12 subjects Graph-). A Spearman correlational analysis was run (interval scale points were converted into ranks) and it showed that post-test 4 significantly correlated only with pre-test 2 (r=.406 p<.02). The cognitive load of pre-test 2, compared with pre-test 1, was more similar to post-test 4: both required a comparison between two graphs rather than a plain reading of them, thus it was more likely for the performances to correspond.

Chart-diagram post-test
These post-tests (1 close, 2 reconstruction, 3 reading will be first analyzed as far as the performance related to the components dealing with the laws of demand and supply are concerned, i.e. the relational unit linking price with quantity demanded and supplied. The patterns of incorrect responses are reported in Table 1.

In post-tests 1 and 2 students were required to complete the value of the concepts, and to order the concepts in sequence, respectively, two main patterns of errors were detected. Few subjects showed the inversion error typical of pattern (a) discussed above, so that a higher price will cause the quantity demanded to increase and the quantity supplied to decrease. The greater number of inaccurate subjects revealed pattern (e) comparable to the one that emerged in children's spontaneous ideas, according to which price causes the same change in both quantities $(P \rightarrow D=S)$. Thus, for example, given a lower price, both quantities demanded and supplied increase. In post-test 4 this pattern did not emerge; perhaps, having the graphs at hand, the children were reminded of the opposite relationship between price and the two quantities. Other 2 errors were found in post-test 2, where the concept of market was directly linked to quantity supplied. Children were not consistent in the way that they completed the two relational units presented in the chart: some of them made an error in just one unit, others in both units, in which case a majority followed one pattern, and a minority showed both patterns of errors.

In post-test 3, which asked students to read and describe the chart, children were guided by the chart, so that some patterns of errors revealed in other tasks would not be made. However, the majority of the subjects added and/or disregarded concepts and links, providing useful hints for the understanding of comprehension. Most of the inaccurate descriptions of one or both units fell in a pattern similar to (d): changes of quantity supplied were directly linked to quantity demanded rather than to price ("If the price decreases then the quantity demanded increases, but if people buy more, then the quantity supplied decreases"). They took supply as "product in storage".

Few subjects showed patterns similar to (c): "The quantity demanded increases and the request decreases", or to (b), i.e. they disregarded the direction of the links: "The seller rises the price" (vs. price linked with quantity supplied). As for the other two relational units, involving the concepts of disequilibrium in the market and the following change in price, 15 errors in completing the market concept were found in post-test 1, 10 of which after a pattern (e) error in the previous relational unit. 8 errors were made in the concept of "price", thus showing problems with the relation between disequilibrium and price variation. On the whole, in post-test 2 the errors were fewer, but followed a similar trend.

In post-test 3 there were 10 subjects breaking the causal chain as if it were dealing with two isolated episodes ("... But if the price decreases..." vs. stating a causal link between disequilibrium in the market and change in price). Moreover, 4 subjects added new concepts in post-test 3. They were factors introduced to account for the initial disequilibrium in the market or for the change in the quantity offered. Seventeen new links were created by a total of 10 subjects: they connected concepts which were not directly linked in the chart; they were introduced in subjects' elaborations to directly compare different states of the market, to explain the difference between quantity supplied in different market conditions, and to point out the consequences of different market prices.

In post-test 5, which asked students to choose the correct formulation of each law among three alternatives, 16 subjects chose one or both incorrect formulations. In particular, 4 subjects accepted for both laws the statement following pattern (a), inversion; 8 subjects inverted just one law, thus falling in pattern (e): 8 subjects fell in pattern (b) in one or both laws (D --> P), for 4 of them it was the only error.

One point of interest was to see whether the subjects' performance showed some consistency across the tasks in order to be better able to comment on the usefulness of the tasks in highlighting students' difficulties. Thus, a Spearman correlational analysis was computed. Performances of post-tests 1, 2 and 5 were evaluated using interval scales, whereas post-tests 3 and 4 performances were ranked. In particular, in post-tests 1 and 2 performances were assigned point 1 to 5 according to the number of relational units failed (1 all correct and 5 all incorrect). In post-test 3, rank 1 was assigned to subjects stating all the concepts and links and constructing a coherent description; they often elaborated and expanded the chart information; rank 2 when concepts and links were present but links were weak, temporal rather than causal and no elaborations were offered. Subjects assigned rank 3 either produced an erroneous pattern in one relational unit or interrupted the causal chain dividing it in two separate episodes, while subjects with rank 4 presented both problems. As far as post-test 4 dealing with the line-graphs is concerned, inaccuracy in stating the laws was here penalized more than errors in reading the graphs: rank 1 when the laws were correct, rank 2 when either the subject labeled the curves without justification or when their justification pointed out graph reading problems; rank 3 when the laws and/or the labeling were incorrect. Finally, in post-test 5, points 1 to 3 were assigned according to whether both alternatives chosen were correct, only one was correct, or both were incorrect. The frequencies of subjects assigned to each rank or point in the five post-tests are presented in Table 2.

The results showed that post-test 1 significantly correlated with post-tests 2, 3, and 4. Moreover, post-test 2 significantly correlated with post-test 5; post-test 3 also correlated with post-tests 4, and, finally post-test 4 correlated with post-test 5. The correlation coefficients are shown in Table 3.

Table 2. Frequencies of subjects assigned to each point of the scale in the five post-tests (point 1 represents the completely accurate performance).

	Post-tests				
Points	1 Cloze	2 Reconstr.	3 Reading	4 Line-graph	5 Mult. Choice
1	15	22	5	8	16
2	5	-	7	8	10
3	6	2	13	16	6
4	4	5	7	/	/
5	2	3	/	/	/

Table 3. Correlation coefficients of the five post-tests

	1 Cloze	2 Reconstr.	3 Reading	4 Line-graph	5 Mult. Choice
1 Cloze	1.000				
2 Reconstr.	.518**	1.000			
3 Reading	.380**	.164	1.000		
4 Line-graph	.282	.158	.594**	1.000	
5 Mult.Ch.	.205	.401*	.284	.368*	1.000

$** p < .01; * p < .05$

Subjects' accuracy was generally consistent across the different tasks, although the consistency was by no means complete due to the different requirements of the tasks. These results allow a better analysis of the tasks utilized. As can be seen in the first row of Table 2, the subjects failed more often with the tasks required them to describe the chart diagram (post-test 3) and the line-graphs (post-test 4). These tasks were both "reading" tasks, that asked students to read and elaborate the given material. The difficulties encountered in post-test 4 were due partly to problems in reading the graphs, partly to children's problems with understanding the laws. A result revealed also by other tasks. Post-test 1 and 2 are both "production" tasks, requiring students to provide information to complete the chart. The sizeable number of correct responses on post-test 2, compared with post-test 1, could be attributed to an effect of practice due to the children's memory of the sequence seen in the previous task. It was always presented second because of difficulties in understanding the task. For this reason, it seems advisable to rely more on information derived from post-test 1. As far as post-test 5 is concerned, it did not add much information: the alternatives were blocked and some children might have chosen the one that "sounded" closer to their understanding.

General Discussion

One issue addressed in this paper concerned the usefulness of graphic tools in evaluating learning. In this particular case, subjects were asked to work with a chart diagram, novel to them since it was not presented during the lecture. More is known about the efficacy of a chart diagram as a study aid rather than how students process such a device. Although the "ingredients" in the chart, i.e. boxes and arrows, are familiar, to follow the exact sequence and to extract meaning from it require some processing. One aspect this research attempted to address was whether the processing is affected by the individual's knowledge. Should this be the case, then the way one elaborates the chart information could be taken as an indication of the level of his/her understanding. For this reason three tasks were devised, asking the subjects first to select a specific value of the concepts forming the causal chain outlined in the chart, second to recall the links between the concepts, and finally to read the chart in order to explain it. Thus, given that the tasks themselves involved different types of processing, a direct match among performance was not expected. However, it was expected that subjects' performances would correlate across tasks. For example, a subject with a lower level of understanding would neither be able to fill the chart with appropriate information nor to interpret the information accurately. The results supported this prediction and gave some suggestions on the type of difficulty each task could highlight. Problems with the two laws of demand and supply were detected in all tasks, but the specific patterns that emerged varied with the task. This means, on the one hand, that by using one of the tasks one can immediately detect the presence of difficulties; on the other hand, by using more tasks one interested in devising repair strategies can gain a better picture of the different sources and components of misunderstandings.

Given that inaccuracy with the chart diagram might be partly due to the specific way the information was outlined in the chart (Winn, 1990) rather than to the subjects' lack of knowledge, two other tasks required the subjects to provide information on the same content. One task involved reading two linear graphs, those presented during the lecture, and stating the laws. Looking at the results, two considerations are in order. On the one hand, the data showed the presence of misunderstandings, thus giving external support to the diagnostic potential of the other tasks. On the other hand, it was often possible to discriminate graph reading from conceptual difficulties. The relatively low performance in post-test 4 with respect to the one in pre-test 1, may be ascribed to two sources: (a) perhaps some children did not store the match between laws and graphs; (b) children were transitional in their ability to read graphs. When the task demanded a greater cognitive effort, they could not concentrate both on graph reading and on producing the laws. This result suggests that using line-graphs does not necessarily help understanding. Unless students have complete mastery of these devices, understanding line-graphs can become a task by itself, thus caution should be taken when using them in teaching and evaluating.

Overall, performance on the post-tests seemed to provide useful information on children's learning from the lecture. In particular, some subjects seemed to have changed their spontaneous representation; however, more than half the subjects showed problems in stating the two laws. In general, fewer problems were found related to the comprehension of the law of demand, with some variations depending on the task. Several patterns of responses were identified. For some children the quantity supplied and the quantity demanded held the same relationship with price. Thus, when the price is low, people ask for more, so a greater quantity should be supplied (and vice versa); this appears to correspond to children's spontaneous idea. According to some other responses, it is a change in quantity that affects a change in price, rather than the reverse. This pattern, although plausible in a different context, where other factors were introduced, does not reflect the formal laws of demand and supply. Some students, by relating a change in quantity supplied directly to a change in quantity demanded, understood supply exclusively as the product in storage. When the quantity demanded increases, then the storage is reduced, whereas a decrease in quantity demanded causes the quantity supplied to "increase", that is "there is more of that product left unsold in the storage". It is a plausible but incomplete answer, showing a weak reference to the two laws. A few protocols clearly showed a lack of understanding of the meaning of the word "supply" itself, taken as another way to say "demand" (pattern c). Finally, some subjects inverted the laws, probably guided by the information recalled that price held an opposite relationship with the two quantities. Another source of difficulty, found in the three post-tests involving the chart, was related to the understanding that a change of state in the market is both a consequence of a disequilibrium price and a cause of re-adjustment of price in order to reach a new equilibrium price.

In conclusion, the results of this research suggest that the use of graphical tools can be effective in detecting children's difficulties with the to-be-learned material. Different patterns of responses were found within the same task, showing a wide range of individual differences. Moreover, different patterns were revealed by different tasks, each task involving different guidelines and constraints on the child's production. The data showed for some subjects the persistence of spontaneous ideas. Other subjects showed a novel conceptualization which is the result of a mediation between a naive representation and the formal information provided by the task, while the performance of a few subjects corresponded to the taught information. Given that these post-tests involved a different cognitive demand, resulting in different patterns of responses, the choice of the task should be related to the type of intervention, possibly following the detection of misunderstandings. More research needs to be done on the processing of graphical devices; it would help to understand which characteristics they should have in order to be effectively processed and which relationship they should have with the text; in turn, this would give us useful information on how they can be utilized in evaluation.

RÉSUMÉ

L'objectif principal de cette recherche est d'étudier la possibilité d'utiliser des moyens graphiques pour évaluer l'acquisition, chez des enfants de 12 ans, de concepts d'économie présentés dans un cours. Deux courbes représentant les lois de l'offre et de la demande, et un diagramme représentant la chaine causale des concepts ont été utilisés dans des tâches d'évaluation. Les tâches impliquant le diagramme étaient des tâches de complètement, de reconstruction et de lecture. On demandait aux sujets de compléter les valeurs manquantes des concepts, de relier les positions des concepts dans le diagramme, et de lire le diagramme. De plus, les étudiants devaient établir la loi représentée par chaque courbe et choisir la formulation correcte de la loi parmi trois possibilités.

Plusieurs patterns de réponses sont apparus, révélant les idées fausses et les erreurs des sujets concernant les lois. Certains patterns se sont révélés plus typiques que d'autres. De plus, il est apparu que ces patterns varient selon la structure et les exigences de la tâche. Un certain nombre de difficultés sont apparues dans la lecture des courbes, qui devraient être prises en compte quand on veut utiliser ces graphiques dans l'enseignement. Bien que les patterns spécifiques puissent varier selon les tâches, des corrélations significatives sont trouvées entre les performances, suggérant l'utilité des graphiques dans l'évaluation de l'apprentissage.

Notes

I wish to thank Annalia Calcagno for her help in collecting the data, Luciano Arcuri and Tom Trabasso for useful discussions. A special thanks also to the children, the teachers and the director of the school of Vigonza (Padova) for their collaboration.

References

Bell, A., & Janvier, C. (1982). The interpretation of graphs representing situations. *For the Learning of Mathematics*, 2, 34-42.

Berti, A.E., & Grivet, A. (1990). The development of economic reasoning in children from 8 to 13 years old: price mechanism. *Contributi dei Dipartimenti Italiani di Psicologia*, 3, 37-47.

Bryant, P.E., & Sommerville, S.C. (1985). *Children's extrapolations of lines to and from coordinates*. Presented at the Biennial Meetings SRCD, Toronto.

Gobbo, C., & Boder, A. (1987). *On children's understanding of line-graphs*. Presented at the Annual Meetings SIPs, Padova, 1987.

Kerslake, D. (1981). Graphs. In K.M. Hart (Ed.), *Children's understanding of mathematics concepts*. London: John Murray.

Lambiotte, J.G., Peel, J., & Dansereau, D.F. (1989). *Knowledge maps as review devices: Like ém or not*. Paper presented at the annual meeting of the American Educational research Association, San Francisco.

Larkin, J.H., & Simon, H.A. (1987). Why a diagram is (sometimes) worth ten thousand words? *Cognitive Science*, 11, 65-99.

Leinhardt, G., Zavlasky, O., & Stein, M.K. (1990). Functions, graphs, and graphing: Tasks, learning, and Teaching. *Review of Educational Research*, 60, 1-64.

Lovell, K. (1971). Some aspects of growth of the concept of a function. In M.F. Rosskopf, L.P. Steffe & S. Taback (Eds.), *Piagetian cognitive development research and mathematical education*. Washington DC: National Council of Teachers of Mathematics.

Moore, P.J., & Scevak, J.J. (1992). *"Tracing" as forced processing: Integration or matching*? Paper presented at National Consortium for Instruction and Cognition Annual Convention, San Francisco.

Napoleoni, C. (1972). *Elementi di economia politica*. Firenze: La Nuova Italia.

Shute, V.J., Glaser, R., & Raghavan, K. (1989). Inference and discovery in an exploratory laboratory. In P.L. Ackermann & R.J. Sternberg (Eds.), *Learning and individual differences*. New York: W.H. Freeman.

Sommerville, S.C., & Bryant, P.E. (1985). Young children's use of spatial coordinates. *Child Development*, 56, 604-613.

Stanlake, G.F. (1989). *Introductory economics* (5th edition), London: Longman Group UK Limited.

Vergnaud, G., & Errecalde, P. (1980). Some steps in the understanding and the use of scales and axis by 10-13 year-old students. In R. Karglus (Ed.), *Proceeding of the fourth international conference for the Psychology of Mathematics Education.* Berkeley, University of California.

Winn, W.D. (1990). A thoretical framework for research on learning from graphics. *International Journal of Educational Research, 6,* 553-564.

Zasvlasky, O. (1988). *Conceptual obstacles in the learning of quadratic functions.* Unpublished doctoral dissertation, Technion, Haifa, Israel.

Chapter 15

Visualized Analogies and Memory for New Information in First Graders

Marie-Dominique Gineste

Laboratoire de Psychologie de l'Université Paris XIII
et
Centre d'Etudes de Psychologie Cognitive, Orsay Cedex, France

ABSTRACT

This study investigated what kind of knowledge children construct when processing analogous information in the form of verbal analogy, pictorial analogy or picturo-acting analogy. Sixty first grade children were assigned to the three analogy conditions and to a control No-Analogy condition. Results show that children can process analogies, with better performance for visualized than for purely verbal analogy formats. A qualitative analysis of verbalizations examines inference patterns and sheds light on the nature of the enriched representational model and the stages involved in the development of analogical processing.

Over the last ten years, numerous experiments in cognitive psychology have approached the issue of the cognitive function of analogies. Most have centered on problem solving and a minority have dealt with memorization and acquisition of new knowledge. Few studies however have been conducted in this area on young school age children, despite the fact that analogy is one of the main techniques used in textbooks or introductory science books in the classroom.

Analogies used to introduce a new fact, complex object or concept can be presented in the form of verbal statements, or through pictures (known as pictorial analogies). Aside from work by Issing in this area

(Issing, 1987, 1990), few accounts of the cognitive processes implemented in this type of situation have been reported. The present study, part of a more extensive program on analogy issues in general, explores memorization of information presented by verbal or pictorial analogy in young school age children, and the representations children build up from these analogies.

Analogies, knowledge structures and processes mechanisms

Theoretical work on the nature of analogy indicate that two domains of knowledge are analogous if they are characterized by a structural similarity between the relationships connecting their components (Gentner, 1983, 1989 ; Holyoak, 1984 ; and Indurkhya, 1992). The term "source domain" or the domain of reference, is reserved for the domain which is considered to be more familiar and more well known than the target domain or analog.

The well known domain is used as a model for the target domain because it provides a relational structure for processing the new domain. This structure is mapped onto the concepts or objects in the target domain. In Gentner's famous example (1982), the solar system domain can be used as a model for the atom domain. The argument nodes of the source domain -- the sun and planets -- are mapped onto the argument nodes of the target domain -- the nucleus and electrons. The objects in each domain are different, but their structural roles are identical.

Mastering the source domain is one of the preconditions for transfer. Units of information need to be represented mentally, and must be organized into structured sets. Without a mental representation, a learner cannot interpret new information, or in Rumelhart's (1979), terms, s/he has no framework for understanding.

Analogical transfer is generally believed to depend on factors related to the source domain representation in long term memory, the current representation of the new domain or the new situation (a temporary representation), and cues acting as bridges between the two domains. Studies on analog problem solving have shed the light on the underlying processes, and have led to a successful computer simulation (Falkenhainer, Forbus & Gentner, 1989 ; Holyoak & Thagard, 1989). Studies on adults (Holyoak & Koh, 1987; Novick & Holyoak, 1991) and

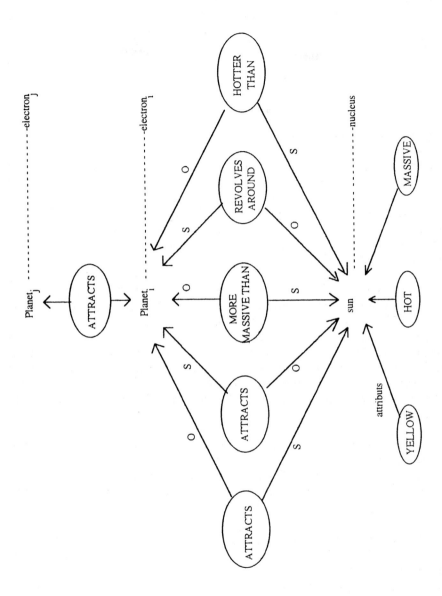

Figure 1. Planetary model of atom: structure mapping for Rutherford analogy (from Gentner, 1982).

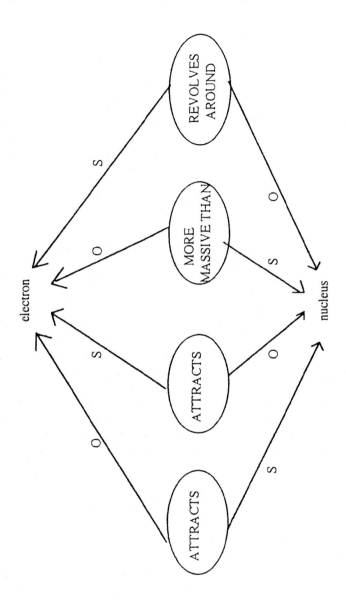

Figure 1 (continued).

young children (Gholson, Dattel, Morgan, & Eymard, 1989), have identified the main processes in problem solving by analogy and indicate that the first problem solved serves to construct a representation of the problem (the "problem schema") at an abstract level where each piece of given information is categorized as goal, initial and final state, and constraints (Gick & Holyoak, 1983). This schema is maintained in memory while a search is conducted for a problem characterized by the same schema (same goal, same states, same constraints). When an analogous situation is found, its solution schema is applied to the target problem. This analog procedure ends here if the target problem is solved. If the solution process fails, search is reinitiated or abandoned. In general, solution elaboration is enhanced by advance notification of a candidate analogy to the solver.

Analogies in the learning process

Analogies are valuable tools for teaching scientific concepts. They are generally used to facilitate understanding and make knowledge acquisition more efficient. The few experimental studies on the role of analogies in understanding and acquiring new knowledge draw on the same theoretical considerations as those found in research on problem solving. They have focused on the role of causal structures in determining judgment of analogy (Gentner & Landers, 1985), the role of analogous domain distance on the comprehension of scientific passages (Halpern, Hansen, & Riefer, 1990), the effect of the reference domain taken as source domain (poetic metaphor without referential function or analogy with referential function; Gineste, 1987). All these studies show a facilitation effect on comprehension or in memory for new facts when a prior analogous domain is available for processing (Curtis, 1986; Gineste, 1991a; Hayes, 1986; Simons, 1982). There is greater facilitation when learners are explicitly prompted to look for or establish structural similarity (Halpern et al., 1990).

Source domain representation and accessibility. In addition to the likelihood of a facilitation effect, the representation of the source domain may play a major role in determining accessibility. In particular, the way information is presented places specific processing demands on learners, and may affect the quality of storage. For example, in a study on the ways in which text material influence information extraction, Waddill, McDaniel, & Einstein (1988) report that picture adjuncts have differential effects depending upon type of text and comprehension skill. The information units depicted in an illustration may enhance recall of these elements, especially in highly skilled comprehenders (Waddill & McDaniel, 1991).

Findings from a previous study on mental representations of an analog domain (Gineste, 1991b) have shown that pictorial support for a text in the source domain assists in the building of a representation in the target domain. The data suggest that because illustrations represent main ideas in the source domain text, they can help learners encode information from this source domain. In comparison to a condition where students were asked to learn and recall material from a text with no illustrations, readers (sixth and eighth graders) easily retrieved the source domain and its structure from a text+pictorial presentation, which could be used to encode new information and recall the main ideas of the text. This suggests that figurative representation of certain items or objects in a domain enhance the vividness of individuals' mental representation of this knowledge. Greater vividness implies that the representation is more salient, and greater salience facilitates retrieval. However, this enhancement of recall was only observed in 8th grade students. Older students were able to retrieve the source domain and maintain the relevant elements in memory to build a representation of the new information.

Analogy and cognitive development. Research on analogical reasoning in children show that even very young children (7 year olds) can benefit from analogy (Vosniadou & Schommer, 1988), as shown by the fact that they can identify the structural similarity of two different domains. Vosniadou's conclusion is that "children can use similarity in salient properties between two systems as a vehicle for discovering structural similarities between them just like adults do .... What develops is not the analogical mechanism itself but the conceptual system upon which this mechanism operates" (Vosniadou, 1989, p. 414).

The present experiment draws on reports of analogical processing by young children, pictorial enhancement of recall for new information and a Piagetian approach. Piaget (1946) argued that the age of 6-7 marks the end of the stage of symbolic and preconceptual thought, which translates by egocentric language where the child is guided by his perceptions of his actions in the here-and-now, and his own representations. The 6-7 year old is on the threshold of the concrete operations stage where there is decentration with respect to personal perceptions and current actions, and hence the possibility to make generalizations. This period heralds the emergence and development of new abilities to manipulate entities that represent objects or actions. This new mastery is a major milestone in the child's understanding of the world, and in particular comprehension of language in all its forms. Children begin to understand metaphors at this age (Winner, 1979; Winner, Engel & Gardner, 1980; Winner, Rosenstiel & Gardner, 1976) although performance is inconsistent. Studies on explication of metaphors have reported understanding in even younger children (Fourment, Emmenecker & Pantz, 1987) provided that the target is concrete and identifiable.

All these findings underscore the importance of studying comprehension and memory for analogous information in 6 year olds, and the need to better describe the cognitive function of the visualization of an analogous domain in understanding new facts. They also suggest the need to differentiate representations built up from discourse (verbally presented information) from representations formed from perceptual information or manipulation (handling of objects). If there is a parallel between understanding of metaphors and analogical transfer, 6 year-old children should benefit more from an "acted analogy" (an analogy presented by or through action), than from a pictorial analogy presented as a static illustration. If a teaching aid is used to make the analogy concrete -- either in the form of an action or an illustration -- performance should be better in these conditions than in a condition without this aid. Winner (1979) shows that younger children's production of metaphors was facilitated when they acted out the action in pretend play, but was only efficient in older children (before acting) on the basis of perceived similarities. Pictorial or acted out analogy as an aid for concretizing unobservable processes and entities should result in better performance than without this aid. Piaget shows that six year olds need concrete objects for building a representation, in particular when the target knowledge domain deals with phenomena that are not directly available to perception. Children at this age cannot yet build up a representation from verbally transmitted information. Hence a concrete aid provided by an analogy, if it refers to a concrete, familiar domain, should result in better performance, in contrast to the no-aid situation. However performance should also be affected by the form or the nature of the analogy, and memorization-performance should adhere to the following pattern: Picturo-Acted analogy > Pictorial Analogy > Verbal Analogy.

Method

Subjects. Subjects were 60 1st grade children (6 and 7 years old), attending a school in the North of Paris.

Design. The design had four conditions, a No-Analogy condition and three Analogy Conditions (Verbal Analogy, Pictorial Analogy, and Picturo-Acting Analogy). In each condition, immediately after having heard a story (repeated twice) about "Infection", children answered six questions orally and then were administered a recall test in the form of an puppet play. One puppet, held by the experimenter, was a child with no knowledge about infection. The other puppet, held by the child, played the role of a child who was knowledgeable about infection. One week later, the same questions were asked and the same puppet game was reenacted. The puppet dialogues were fully transcribed by the experimenter.

Procedure and materials. The target domain was "Infection". The text was a slighty modified version of a passage used by Vosniadou & Schommer (1988). It describes the spread of infection after a finger injury. We learn that "Infection is caused by germs penetrating the body and the body has to react to germs. For example, what happens when a finger is injured? Germs enter the finger and the body reacts to them by using white corpuscles that protect it. White corpuscles are in the blood. The first barrier to infection is the skin. But if germs make their way under the skin, white corpuscles react. More and more germs develop and many white corpuscles disappear. This causes pus, the yellow substance. Then, more and more white corpuscles develop and they go and suppress germs in the finger. Infection is over when there are no more germs."

In the "No Analogy condition", the children were first read a story about infection (twice) and then answered questions and played the puppet game to act out a conversation between two children about the topic of infection. In the "Verbal Analogy Condition", the information from the target domain was presented in a way identical to the No Analogy condition, except that a written comparison of the process of the body fighting an infection with the process occuring in a battle was included. For example, white corpuscles were said to be the "soldiers of the body" and germs the "enemies of the body". A huge battle is described in which several "soldiers of the body" die and the "remaining soldiers are very hungry and destroy all the enemies of the body", etc. ... In the "Pictorial Analogy condition", the target domain presentation was identical to the Verbal Analogy condition, but five drawings illustrating the processes in a battle were included.

In the "Picturo-Acting Analogy condition", the experimenter displayed a board depicting a cut finger on a table. He then acted out a battle between "soldiers" and "enemies of the body" by moving tiny figurines representing (a) germs (enemies of the body) and (b) leucocytes (soldiers of the body).

Scoring. Questions were scored 0 for no answer or inadequate answer. Correct answers were scored 2. A correct answer was defined as an answer providing the target term or the target explanation. A score of 1 was assigned when the answer was incomplete or contained an explanation of the target in terms of the source domain, i.e, in an analogical way. The transcription of the puppet play were scored for five pieces of information: actors in the Infection story (germs and white corpuscules), the infection process (germs entering the body, white corpuscules reacting to germs) and cure (no more germs). The maximum score was 22. Verbalizations on the puppet play were analyzed qualitatively to a greater extent than quantitatively, to explore the content of the children's mental representations.

Results

A 4 x 2 ANOVA was performed on the totals to determine the effects of conditions on memory in immediate and delayed recall.

Analysis of variance (1) reveals a positive effect of conditions ($F(3, 56) = 14.82$, $p<.001$, MSe $=346.76$) and recall ($F(1, 56) = 12.94$, $p<.001$, MSe $= 45.63$). An interaction between these two factors was observed ($F(3, 56) = 3.67$, $.01<p<.05$, MSe $= 12.94$). Young children perform better when they can use an analogy to grasp new information, but the decrease in recall was not identical across conditions.

A finer analysis was conducted to tease out the role of analogy as a function of type (verbal, pictorial or picturo-acting). Comparison of the No-Analogy condition to the three other conditions shows an overall positive effect for analogy ($F(1, 56) = 34.36$, $p<.001$, MSe $=23.39$),and Recall ($F(1, 56) = 12.93$, $p<.001$, MSe $= 3.52$). When this effect is decomposed to assess impact of each mode of analogy, the data show

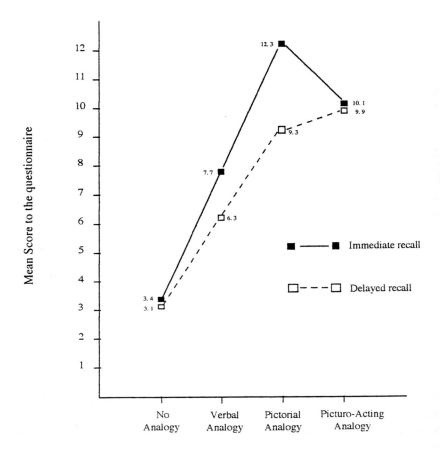

Figure 2. Mean score to the questionnaire as a function of Analogy-conditions and delay of recalls.

that verbal analogy was less useful to the subjects than forms of analogy where they could see the analogy --pictures or enactment-- $(F(1,41) =7,57, .001< p <.01, MSe = 29,96)$. The difference between pictorial and picturo-acting analogies was significant for immediate recall and for delayed recall; the recall and condition effects went in opposite directions - the interaction was significant: $(F(1,28) = 6.47, .001< p <.01, MSe = 4.54$, as well as the Recall effect $(F(1,28) = 8.45, .001< p< .01, MSe = 4.54)$.

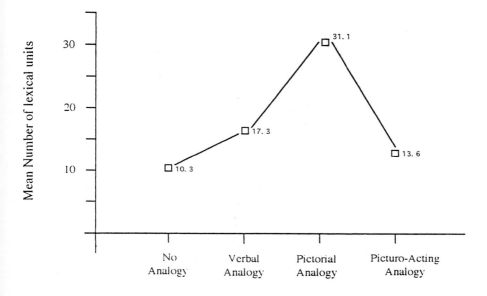

Figure 3. Mean number of lexical units produced in "No-Analogy" and "Analogy" conditions.

In the quantitative analysis above, a clearcut increase in performance was observed when these scores were calculated on the basis of responses to the six questions and responses in the puppet play. More detailed analysis of responses on the puppet play provides more insight into the children's behavior. First of all, some children were unable to verbalize at the start of the puppet play whereas all answered (correctly or erroneously) to the questions which preceded the game. More children showed initial hesitation in the No-Analogy condition (6/15) than in the Verbal Analogy (5/15) the Pictorial Analogy (1/15) or the Picturo-Acted Analogy (3/15). This suggests that a concrete basis for illustration and object handling provides children with a foundation for building a mental representation which he or she can then verbalize when requested to do so by the experimenter.

In terms of number of verbalizations, a tabulation of explicit verbal items (excluding interjections, "there are ..." and non-specific pronouns) indicates more output in the Verbal and Pictorial Analogy conditions than in the No-Analogy condition.

These differences prompted categorizing the subjects' response "styles" as a function of source and target analogy content. Two categories were defined: a) response on the target domain, with exclusive use of arguments and predicates from the target domain; b) analogy using a combination of concepts from the source and target domains (with explicit or implicit association of domains). More than 90% of the children used analog expressions in the Analogy conditions as compared to 45% in the No-Analogy condition. Children made analogies from source to target domain in several ways:

1. The child designated the arguments "germs", "white corpuscles", by the corresponding arguments in the source domain ("enemies", "soldiers") and used predicates such as "invade", "fight", "die", "destroy" (source domain) instead of "penetrate", "react", "disappear" and "suppress" (target domain). These arguments and predicates were provided by the adult in the presentation of the target domain. The child thus repeated items in the test material. An example of this type is as follows: "An infection is germs that want to invade the body. Like a war when there are corpuscles, soldiers who want to protect the body make traps to kill the body's enemies" (Subject 2, Verbal Analogy).

2. The child extends the analogy by assigning moral intentions to the agents of infection. There are genuine inferences made on the basis of the protagonists in the infection story. "There are enemies and they are mean and they want to get into your finger" (Subject 8, Pictorial Analogy). "When you get hurt, the bad guys can't get in because the soldiers stop them from going in." (Subject 10, Pictorial Analogy). "When you get hurt, the bad guys come and the nice guys make traps to stop them from getting through." (Subject 10, Picturo-Acted analogy).

3. The child uses other lexical items to designate the white corpuscles, but these verbal labels all belong to the class of "body defenders"; for example "knights", "dukes", "policemen". In contrast, the child does not develop the same type of features to talk about germs. Germs are designated as "bugs", "ants", or "thorns".

4. Labelling of agents in terms of color differences in the figurines or drawings: " The orange go in. The yellow attack." (Subject 7, Pictorial Analogy). "The bad guys attack the yellows." (Subject 2, Pictorial Analogy).

5. In a few cases the child continues the story and adds elements that although connected to the topic have a fully anthromorphic view of the situation. The child derives his or her prolongation of the story from a word or preceding content. "There are soldiers who kill the bad guys. Afterwards they are dead. They are put in the ground..." (Subject 13, pictorial analogy).

These transformations of the target concepts and inferences were especially prevalent in analogy conditions. In contrast, few transformations and inferences were produced spontaneously in the No-analogy condition. When produced however, they were comparable to the inferences occurring in Analogy Conditions; i.e. belonged to the semantic field of war.

Discussion

The findings shed light on young children's cognitive mechanisms and the mental representations they build up from exposure to analogy. Young children recall information about the target domain better from pictorial and picturo-acting analogy than from analogy presented in a verbal form alone. The data show that they can use analogies to process new information. They are sensitive to pictures, perceived actions and the characters in the infection story. Static illustrations as well as moving the characters in tandem with the text provide the children with two basic building blocks for constructing a representation.

The elements in the source story were identifiable and concrete, allowing children to associate new concepts and structure them. Secondly, these objects heightened the salience between the target and source concepts which were materialized by the elements in the drawing and by the movement of the figurines. Verbal analogy alone provides no support for materializing the analogy or for constructing relationships between concepts and insuring the most exhaustive analog transfer between the two domains. This lack of concrete support translates in the data by lower scores. Although performance was better in the other conditions, there was a difference in scores between children presented with analogies in the form of pictures and those who watched an enactment. Children in the pictorial analogy group learned more items of information than those who perceived actions. Delayed recall shows however that they lost more information over time, bringing their level down to scores observed in the picturo-acted group.

This suggests that analog transfer needs to be constructed and that concrete materials enhance effectiveness in six year old children. In the absence of concrete objects, the child literally does not "see" the analogy and hence cannot use it to construct new representations.

The data also suggest that children draw inferences from a variety of sources. They know from daily experience that they can be stung by bugs and that something develops at the site of the bite that can hurt. This lead to the confusion between germs and "bugs". They have also learned or know from personal experience that people are buried after they die. Television or books give them a whole host of fighting heros; they know that dukes and knights are good soldiers fighting for a good cause. They then tend to associate the attributes of these fictional characters to the events in the infection story.

The children's mental representation is thus an enriched model of Infection-as-war, where the enrichment taps a number of knowledge domains. This intermediate-buffer-model needs to be pruned by selecting out the information relevant to the target domain. When this final stage has been reached, children can be considered to have acquired new knowledge.

RÉSUMÉ

La recherche exposée dans cet article étudie le type de connaissance que les enfants construisent lorsqu'ils ont à traiter des informations analogues selon qu'elles sont présentées par un texte (analogie verbale), par une illustration (illustration analogique) ou par une action (illustration analogique et en action). Soixante enfants de cours préparatoire ont été repartis dans quatre conditions expérimentales, une condition contrôle sans analogie et trois conditions d'analogie. Les résultats indiquent que les enfants traitent bien les analogies et que leur performance est meilleure dans le cas où ces analogies sont présentées visuellement que lorsqu'elles sont présentées sous la simple forme verbale. Une analyse qualitative des verbalisations s'attache à décrire les inférences produites et apporte quelques éclaircissements sur la nature de la représentation "enrichie" et sur les phases impliquées dans la genèse du traitement de l'analogie. Visualized analogies and memory.

Notes

1 Analysis run on VAR3, a program developed by D. Lépine, H. Rouanet & M. O. Lebeaux, Groupe Mathématiques et Psychologie, Université Paris V, 12 rue Cujas, 75005 Paris, France.

Acknowledgements

We thank Anne Pérez for aid in collecting data. We thank also Ric Lowe, Wolfgang Schnotz and an anonymous reviewer for their fruitful comments on the first draft of this paper.

References

Curtis, R.V. (1986). *The analogy as an instructional design strategy in text*. Paper presented at the meeting of the American Educational Research Association, San Francisco, April 1986.

Falkenhainer, B., Forbus, K., & Gentner, D. (1989). The structure-mapping engine: algorithm and examples. *Artificial Intelligence*, *41*, 1-63.

Fourment, M.Cl., Emmenecker, N., & Pantz, V. (1987). Etude de la production de métaphores chez des enfants de 3 à 7 ans. [A study of metaphors production on 3 to 7 years old children]. *L'Année Psychologique*, *87*, 535-551.

Gentner, D. (1982). Are Scientific Analogies Metaphors ? In D.S. Miall (Ed.), *Metaphor: problems and perspectives*. Brighton, Sussex: Harvester Press.

Gentner, D. (1983). Structure Mapping: a theoretical framework for analogy. *Cognitive Science*, *7*, 155-170.

Gentner, D. (1989). The mechanisms of analogical learning. In S. Vosniadou & A. Ortony (Eds), *Similarity and Analogical Reasoning*. Cambridge, England: Cambridge University Press.

Gentner, D., & Landers, R. (1985). Analogical reminding: a good match is hard to find. *Proceedings of the International Conference on Systems, Man and Cybernetics.* Tucson, AZ.

Gholson, B., Dattel, A.R., Morgan, D., & Eymard L.A. (1989). Problem solving, recall, and mapping relations in isomorphic transfer and nonisomorphic transfer among preschoolers and elementary school children. *Child Development, 60,* 1172-1187.

Gick, M., & Holyoak, K.J. (1983). Schema induction and analogical transfer. *Cognitive Psychology, 15,* 1-38.

Gineste, M.D. (1986-1987). Les analogies et les métaphores: leur rôle dans la compréhension de textes informatifs. [Analogies and metaphors: their role in expository text understanding]. *Bulletin de Psychologie, 40,* 473-479.

Gineste, M.D. (1991a). *Analogies and learning of scientific Concepts.* Document CEPCO n°66, Orsay.

Gineste, M.D. (1991b). *Analogies and illustrations: their role in text understanding and memory.* Paper presented at the Fourth European Conference for Learning and Instruction, 24-28 August, Turku, Finland.

Halpern, D.F., Hansen, C., & Riefer, D. (1990). Analogies as an aid to understanding and memory. *Journal of Educational Psychology, 82,* 2, 298-305.

Hayes, D.A. (1986). *Readers' use of analogic and visual aids for understanding and remembering complex prose.* Paper presented at the meeting of the American Educational Resarch Association, San Francisco, April 1986.

Holyoak, K.J. (1984). Analogical thinking and human intelligence. In R.J. Sternberg (Ed.), *Advances in the Psychology of Human Intelligence,* Vol. 2. Hillsdale, New Jersey: Lawrence Erlbaum Associates.

Holyoak, K.J., & Koh, K. (1987). Surface and structural similarity in 'analogical transfer. *Memory and Cognition, 15,* 332-340.

Holyoak, K.J., & Thagard, P.R. (1989). A computational model of analogical problem solving. In S. Vosniadou & A. Ortony (Eds), *Similarity and Analogical Reasoning.* Cambridge, England: Cambridge University Press.

Indurkhya, B. (1992). *Metaphor and Cognition.* Dordrecht, The Netherlands: Kluwer Academic Press.

Issing, L.J. (1987). *Visualization by pictorial analogies in understanding expository text.* Paper presented at the Second European Conference for Research on Learning and Instruction, Tübingen, Germany, September, 1987.

Issing, L.J. (1990). Learning from pictorial analogies. *European journal of Psychology of education, 5*, 4, 489-499.

Novick, L., & Holyoak, K.J. (1991). Mathematical problem solving by analogy. *Journal of Experimental Psychology: Learning, Memory, and Cognition, 17*, 3, 398-415.

Piaget, J. (1946). *La formation du symbole chez l'enfant.* [The formation of symbol in the child]. Neuchâtel, Delachaux & Niestlé.

Rumelhart, D.E. (1979). Some problems with the notion of literal meaning. In A. Ortony (Ed.), *Metaphor and Thought.* Cambridge, England: Cambridge University Press.

Simons, P.R. (1982). Concrete analogies as aids in learning from texts. In A. Flammer & W. Kintsch (Eds.), *Discourse processing.* Amsterdam, The Netherlands: North Holland Publishing Company.

Vosniadou, S. (1989). Analogical reasoning as a mechanism in knowledge acquisition: a developmental point of view. In S. Vosniadou & A. Ortony (Eds.), *Similarity and Analogical Reasoning.* Cambridge, England: Cambridge University Press.

Vosniadou, S., & Schommer, M. (1988). Explanatory analogies can help children acquire information from expository text. *Journal of Educational Psychology, 80*, 524-536.

Waddill, P.J., & McDaniel, M.A. (1991). *Pictorial enhancement of text memory: Limitations imposed by picture type and comprehension skill.* Paper presented at the Workshop "Comprehension of Graphics", Tübingen, Germany, 29-30 October.

Waddill, P.J., McDaniel, M.A. & Einstein, G.O. (1988). Illustrations as adjuncts to prose: A text appropriate processing approach. *Journal of Educational Psychology, 80*, 457-464.

Winner, E. (1979). New names for old things: the emergence of the metaphorical language. *Journal of Child Language, 6*, 469-491.

Winner, E., Engel, M., & Gardner, H. (1980). Misunderstanding metaphor: what's the problem ? *Journal of Experimental Child Psychology, 30*, 22-32.

Winner, E., Rosenstiel, A.K., & Gardner, H. (1976). The development of metaphoric understanding. *Developmental Psychology, 2*, 289-297.

Appendix

Questionnaire

1. Quand il y a une infection, contre quoi se défend le corps?
    When there is an infection, how does the body defend itself?
2. Est-ce-que le corps a plusieurs moyens de se défendre, plusieurs
    façons pour se défendre? Does the body have different ways and
    means of defending itself?
    Donne-moi un exemple. Give me an example.
3. Comment s'appellent ceux qui défendent le corps? What is the
    name for the things that defend the body?
4. Comment s'appellent ceux qui envahissent le corps? What do we
    call the things that invade the body?
5. Le pus: qu'est-ce que c'est ? D'où ça vient? What is pus? Where
    does it come from?
6. S'il n'y a plus de défenseurs du corps, est-ce que l'infection guérit?
    If there are no more body defenders, does the infection get better?
    Pourquoi? Why ?

PART IV

INSTRUCTIONAL ASPECTS

Comprehension of Graphics
W. Schnotz and R. W. Kulhavy (Editors)
© 1994 Elsevier Science B.V. All rights reserved.

Chapter 16

The Supplantation of Mental Images through Graphics: Instructional Effects on Spatial Visualization Skills of Adults

Norbert M. Seel[1] & Günter Dörr[2]

[1]Technical University of Dresden, FRG &
[2]College of Education of Weingarten, FRG

ABSTRACT

This study supposes that the ability of spatial imagery is a trait which, even though often only acquired in the course of informal learning, can be further developed by adequate instruction. Thus, the purpose of this study was to investigate the effectivity of a special training program on spatial visualization skills of female students who had not been trained in technical drawing. Performance differences of the students in a spatial imagery test before and after instruction through a special computer-based training program were explored. For this purpose, the training program which consisted of transforming three-dimensional objects with the help of a supplantation condition was contrasted with a simple imagery condition. The most important result of this investigation was that, after instruction, the students gained significantly from the training program in both spatial visualization programs. The effects of instruction, which consisted in improved spatial visualization skills, provide support for the notion that these skills are teachable and can be learned even in crash-courses. However, the specific skills underlying the ability of spatial visualization only improved with practice.

Reading and understanding technical drawings are important skills, and both the ability to draw objects and the ability to read drawings are a necessity for skilled workers. They are required to mentally manipulate, rotate, twist, or invert pictorially presented stimulus objects when performing spatial transformations on diagrams of three-dimensional structures. Cultivating the ability to perform technical drawings is obviously an essential part of vocational training, but not of general education. Thus, spatial understanding of these tasks is primarily informally acquired. In order to understand or to draw technical drawings, students must be able to "think" in spatial terms. That means, they must be able to mentally "look" at pictorially presented three-dimensional objects from different perspectives ("front view", "top view", "side view"). Because of the great importance of technical drawings for technical-scientific occupations (especially engineering), it is almost self-evident that instructional psychology is concerned with the question of how the ability of spatial imagination required for the understanding of technical drawings can be enhanced by special training.

A review of the related literature reveals the typical, but not universal, finding, that spatial visualization tasks which can be efficiently solved by using a mental rotation strategy, yield small but consistent sex and culture differences (Ben-Chaim, Lappan, & Houang, 1988; Harris, 1981; Linn & Petersen, 1985; Seddon, Tariq & Dos Santos Veiga, 1982; Sherman, 1980). There are various theoretical explanations concerning these differences in spatial visualization - some authors emphasize the relevance of biological factors, others emphasize the role of learning, practice, and socialization (Harris, 1981; Linn & Petersen, 1985). The latter corresponds with the assumption of a functional incorporation of communication codes into the domain of mental representation, and it suggests the need to explore whether the ability to use mental images for understanding technical drawings can be influenced by various learning environments.

Mental representation and semiotics

The question of how knowledge about facts, events, actions, and plans is organized and represented in memory, has been recognized as central to both the construction of cognitive theories (such as ACT* of Anderson, 1983) and to educational psychology. Among the different possibilities to analyze knowledge and its representation, respectively (Brachman & Levesque, 1985), functional approaches are particularly relevant for educational psychology. In accordance with cognitive science (e.g., Fodor & Pylyshyn, 1988), functional approaches to mental representation postulate that human thinking is necessarily a symbol manipulating process: The use of symbolic "languages" enables an individual to express subjective experiences, feelings and thoughts. According to this view, we comprehend mental representation as a relation or function which allows an "operative mapping" of experiences in such a way that the internal manipulation of symbols will be possible during thinking. This argumentation is based on a broad concept which considers symbols as standing for something else (cf. Quine, 1987). In the terminology of Peirce, we could also use the concept "sign". However, cognitive sciencists often operate with the concept "symbol" in the broader sense (Aebli, 1981; Seel, 1991).

Following Piaget (1969), mental representation requires the functional incorporation of communication codes as "vehicles" for thinking. This internalization or "adaptation of the external for the internal use" (Salomon, 1979) essentially consists of the abstracting transposition of imitation activities with object-related nature into the "space" of mental representations. The result of this process are several so-called semiotic functions. The most important "semiotic functions" named by Piaget are "delayed imitation", "symbolic play", "drawings", "mental images", and "language" (Piaget & Inhelder, 1971). They are not components of the thinking process but rather aids for imagining the knowledge people have about the world (Seel, 1991). It is not difficult to assign the Piagetian semiotic functions to the fundamental codes differentiated by semiotics of Peirce, namely "index", "icon", and "abstract symbol". Founded on Piaget's theory, other authors talk about "enactive", "iconic", and "symbolic formats" of representation (Aebli, 1981; Bruner, 1970), and Anderson's (1983) "tricode theory of knowledge representation" is partly overlapping.

However, contrary to Anderson (1983) who considers knowledge as a structural element of the architecture of cognition, Piaget has an ontogenetic perspective as basis for his differentiation of "semiotic functions". Following this perspective, the process of internalization serving the development of the ability to mentally manipulate symbols involves two aspects, namely

(a) a figurative aspect based upon the continuous transposition of imitation activities (e.g., pictorial or linguistic signs), and

(b) an operative aspect which assigns meaning to symbols by categorizing the represented objects into a conceptual class (e.g., a pictorially presented object is classified as a "cube").

This process of internalization constitutes the basis for the mental representation by bringing about the transition from the senso-motoric level into the "world of imagination". This requires, however, that the cognitive operations be increasingly removed from perception and are realized only through imagination. Thus, representational codes and semiotic functions evolve from the capability of an individual to differentiate between symbol and denotation, between meaning and phenomenon, between linguistic expressions and their content. Accordingly, different semiotic functions are predominant as representational formats at different times in cognitive development. However, dependent on the demands of a situation or task, an individual might fall back upon representational formats which ontogenetically have been developed earlier. As a consequence, a second main characteristic of functional approaches to mental representation consists in the employment of multiple representational codes or formats in order to adjust to the requirements of specific situations or tasks.

Since information processing not only implies the internalization of contents but also the internalization of the modalities of information presentation we have grounds for believing that the formats of representation are directly related to information presentation through different media. This is very important in relation to educational psychology because there exists the possibility for influencing the modality of mental representation by choosing specific formats when presenting information.

Implications for instructional psychology

Following Piaget's theory, we fundamentally assume that the development of semiotic functions is a life-long process and, to a high degree, affected by learning and practice. Therefore, we maintain that it is possible to influence the application of several different representational codes for representing human knowledge, depending upon a specific situation, or task and its requirements (Gardner, 1985; Glucksberg, 1984). Returning to the basic assumption that students are able to use different representational codes to adjust to the requirements of a learning task, we are concerned with spatial visualization tasks such as technical drawings which require the ability to mentally manipulate (i.e., rotate, twist, or invert) pictorially presented stimulus objects (cf. Anderson, 1983; Shepard & Metzler, 1971). Anderson (1983) referred to this type of tasks as good examples for demonstrating the existence of "spatial images" as a specific representational format which is dominated by the figurative aspect of the internalization process.

In accordance with the "supplantation hypothesis" of Salomon (1972, 1979) we assume that the correct execution of specific spatial operations such as mental rotations which are involved in the visualization task of orthogonal projection must correspond to the perception of external objects and its spatial transformations. Salomon (1979) defines "supplantation" as a specific kind of skill-cultivation in which a particular internal process (e.g., the mental rotation or transformation of a spatial image) is overtly simulated (e.g., by specific media). Two mechanisms or procedures through which external symbol systems and specific coding elements can affect spatial visualization are elementary: Either they activate preexisting mental skills and, by exercising these skills, they cultivate skill-mastery (comparable to the process of "proceduralization" in Anderson's theory), or they overtly "supplant" mental skills, and, by modeling these skills, the external symbols and communication codes (e.g., pictorial and linguistic signs) are functionally incorporated. When the mediated model overtly "supplants" mental processes, these can be acquired only by observation. That means: Individuals prefer to represent information in the same modality which was originally used for presenting the information to them (Mani & Johnson-Laird, 1982; Reeves, Chaffee & Tims, 1982).

Related to the "supplantation hypothesis" of Salomon (1972, 1979) we assume that computer-based learning environments can efficiently support such a supplantation. The experiment described in this paper investigates the effectivity and efficiency of a supplantation procedure realized by a relative simple computer-based learning environment on the basis of Hypercard. The main goal consists of investigating the possibility to train the application of spatial images for visualizing the effects of transformations of technical drawings.

Method

Subjects

In order to avoid sex differences, only female students took part in the experiment. The subjects (n = 52) were students of various colleges and of the University of Saarbrücken; all students were between 20 and 24 years old, and none of them had specific prior experiences with technical drawings and orthogonal projections.

Materials

The material consisted of a special HyperCardTM learning program (developed by Bresser, Seel & Dörr, 1991) divided into four experimental conditions. Following a common "introduction" which explains the technique of orthogonal projection, two main conditions were differentiated, namely

(a) a simple "imagery condition" asking the students to mentally imagine the solution of 8 tasks demanding an orthogonal projection, and

(b) a "supplantation condition" providing several aids for the solution of the same 8 tasks.

Each main condition was divided in two sub-conditions. In the first condition, three-dimensional objects were presented and the correct orthogonal projection had to be provided (through "top view", "side view", and "front view"). In the second condition, the orthogonal projections were pictorially presented, followed by the task to find the corresponding three-dimensional object.

Both groups of the imagery condition could watch either the drawing of a three-dimensional object on the screen and should then imagine the corresponding orthogonal projection; or they could watch the drawing of orthogonal projection and had to imagine the correspondent three-dimensional object. As soon as the subjects believed that they had solved the task they should indicate their solution by a mouse-click. And then they could compare their individual solution with the correct program solution on the screen. Figure 1 illustrates this screen display of the imagery conditions.

In the supplantation conditions the subjects solved the same tasks. Here, they additionally could call for several aids. In the sequence "from objects to perspectives" the subjects could choose among two combined views (front view and side view; front view and top view; or side view and top view) presented on the screen (see Figure 2).

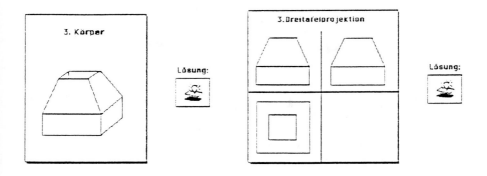

Figure 1. Screen display in the imagery conditions.

The subjects could, but did not have to call for the aids. As soon as they believed that they had solved the task they should indicate their solution by a mouse-click. And then they could compare their individual solution with the correct program solution on the screen. In the sequence "from perspectives to objects", the program offered three different results of putting together two views (see Figure 3).

In this experimental session, the subjects also could, but did not have to call for the aids. As soon as they believed that they had solved the task they should indicate their solution by a mouse-click. And then they could compare their individual solution with the correct program solution on the screen.

Procedure

The basic plan was a pretest-treatment-posttest-design. First, it was necessary to administer two pretests measuring the vividness of students' imagery (by a questionnaire developed by Marks, 1972) as well as the ability of students to understand technical drawings. Following the pretests, there was a random assignment to the different experimental conditions. In order to measure the treatments' effectivity, we administered two post-tests (with regard to two dependent variables). The first one consisted of 10 drawings of three-dimensional objects, and the subjects had to select the correct orthogonal projection

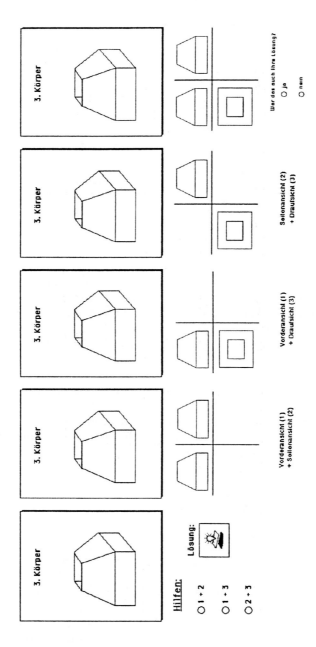

Figure 2. Different combined views which could be chosen by the subjects in the "from objects to perspectives" condition.

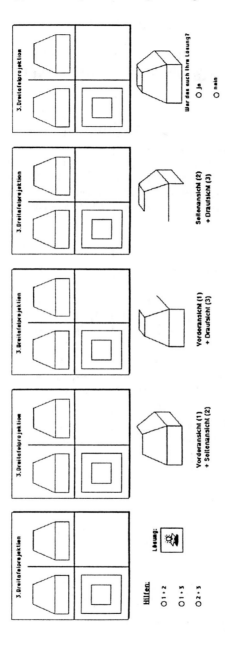

Figure 3. Different combined views which could be chosen by the subjects in the "from perspectives to objects" condition.

out of four alternatives. The second post-test consisted of 10 orthogonal projections, and the subjects had to select the correct drawing of a three-dimensional object out of four alternatives. Furthermore, we recorded the time needed for performing the learning tasks.

Results

As a first step in our analysis, we controlled the initial vividness of students' imagery. The results gained by the questionnaire of Marks (1972) indicate a great homogeneity of the selected students: There was no significant difference between the four experimental groups.

Instructional effects

The most important result of this investigation was that after instruction the students gained significantly from training in both spatial visualization programs (see Table 1). All t-tests were significant (p < .01).

Now, some of the results in more detail, using residuals as the dependent variable and as an indicator of the increase in learning. Residuals are defined as the difference between posttest-score and predicted posttest-score based upon the empirical correlation of pre- and posttest (cf. Klauer, 1975). The computation is based on the formula: $g = y_i - y - b(x_i - x)$. The results of the experimental groups are reported in Table 2.

We analyzed the data with 2 x 2 - ANOVAs with the factors "treatment" (imagery vs. supplantation), and "instructional sequence" (from objects to perspectives vs. from perspectives to objects). The results are reported in Table 3.

In both ANOVAs, the main effect of the factor "treatment" was significant. The supplantation condition evidently was superior to the imagery condition, independently from the test sequence. There were no significant main effects of the factor "instructional sequence" and also there was no significant interaction.

Table 1. Means and standard deviations of the pre- and post-test results (* : p < .01).

Group	Rate 1 Test Sequence 1 Object - Perspectives Pre-Test Post-Test		Rate 2 Test Sequence 2 Perspectives - Objects Pre-Test Post-Test	
Instructional Sequence				
1. Imagery: Objects - Perspectives	M = 6.14 SD = 2.28	M = 8.43* SD = 1.34	M = 6.36 SD = 1.91	M = 8.50* SD = 1.40
2. Imagery: Perspectives - Objects	M = 5.64 SD = 2.25	M = 8.00* SD = 1.10	M = 6.36 SD = 1.75	M = 8.82* SD = 0.87
3. Supplantation Objects - Perspectives	M = 6.00 SD = 1.41	M = 9.57* SD = 0.51	M = 7.07 SD = 0.92	M = 9.79* SD = 0.43
4. Supplantation Perspectives - Objects	M = 6.08 SD = 1.26	M = 8.69* SD = 1.25	M = 6.54 SD = 1.05	M = 9.62* SD = 0.51

For both treatments, especially for the supplantation condition, a more detailed analysis of Table 2 indicates differences of the residuals in dependence on the test sequence. When instructional and test sequences were identical, the results generally were better than when differentinstructional and test sequences were used. In order to specify these results statistically we computed t-tests for dependent samples with regard to rate 1 and 2. There were significant differences only in both supplantation conditions (group 3: t = -2.343, df = 11, p < .05; group 4:t = 2.459, df = 11, p < .05). Obviously, the subjects of the

Table 2. Means and standard deviations of the residuals for the experimental groups (* : p < .05).

Group	Rate 1 Test Sequence Object - Perspectives	Rate 2 Perspectives - Objects
Instructional Sequence		
1. Imagery Objects - Perspectives	M = -.39 SD = 1.58	M = -.52 SD = 1.22
2. Imagery Perspectives - Objects	M = -.46 SD = 1.34	M = -.27 SD = 1.24
3. Supplantation: Objects - Perspectives	M = .85 SD = .72	M = .37* SD = .51
4. Supplantation: Perspectives - Objects	M = -.08 SD = .95	M = .45* SD = .65

supplantation conditions could better solve those test tasks which had the same sequence as the instruction. In the case of an incongruent sequence between test and instructional conditions, a transfer could not be found. One possible interpretation for this result is that the mental effort required by overt supplantation is not sufficient for the development of the required spatial visualization skills. Therefore, we plan to complete this study with a more tutorial instruction condition.

Table 3. Results of the analysis of variance of Rate 1 (A) and Rate 2 (B).

(A)

Effects	SS	df	MS	F	p
A: Treatment	8.45557	1	8.45557	5.95711	.017
B: Sequence	3.20837	1	3.20837	2.26036	.136
A X B	2.43961	1	2.43961	1.71875	.193
Within	68.13155	48	1.41941		

(B)

Effects	SS	df	MS	F	p
A: Treatment	8.24999	1	8.24999	9.12399	.004
B: Sequence	.34492	1	.34492	.38146	.547
A X B	.08285	1	.08285	.09162	.757
Within	43.40202	48	.90421		

Furthermore, our data may indicate a trend for the factor "instructional sequence" (cf., Table 3 (a)). That means, that, at least for the supplantation condition, the instructional sequence "from objects to perspectives" was more effective than the reverse sequence.

The main results consisted in a significant difference between the groups 3 and 4 in regard to rate 1, but not in regard to rate 2 of the increase in learning. That means, the instructional sequence "from objects to perspectives" (group 3) surpassed the sequence "from perspectives to objects" (group 4) in that test which had the same sequence, namely from objects to the perspectives (t = 2.885, df = 25; p = .008). A corresponding result could not be observed for rate 2: The instructional sequence "from perspectives to objects" did not produce any effect in the related test condition (rate 2).

The instructional sequence "from objects to perspectives" is more effective than the reverse sequence, but only in the "congruent" test condition. In contrast, the instructional sequence "from perspectives to objects" is not more effective than the reverse sequence in the related ("congruent") test.

We believe to have good reasons for assuming that it is obviously easier to conclude from pictorially presented three-dimensional objects to two-dimensional perspectives (of technical drawings). That's plausible because of the students' greater familiarity with three-dimensional objects from everyday experience.

Time effects

We also analyzed the amount of time our students spent on performing the learning tasks. These amounts of learning time were recorded by a Hypercard program. We assumed that the factors, especially the quality of instruction, work as trigger mechanisms in regard to the motivation of students to perform the demanded spatial visualization tasks. First, we analyzed the amount of time the students spent on the introduction to the program (see Table 4). Here, we did not find any significant difference between the experimental groups. A corresponding 2 X 2 - ANOVA did not produce any significant effects. Secondly, we analyzed the time needed for performing the learning tasks in the different experimental groups (see Table 4). The corresponding 2 X 2 - ANOVA only produced a significant main effect for the factor "treatment" (see Table 5).

The difference between the imagery condition and the supplantation condition was significant: The students of both supplantation groups (3 and 4) spent twice as much time performing the demanded spatial transformations than the students of both imagery groups (1 and 2). A possible explanation of this result could be that the students actually

Table 4. Means and standard deviations of the needed learning time (in seconds).

	Rate 1	Rate 2
Group	Introduction	Learning program
Instructional Sequence		
1. Imagery: Objects - Perspectives	M = 134 SD = 80	M = 314 SD = 99
2. Imagery: Perspectives - Objects	M = 131 SD = 45	M = 277 SD = 79
3. Supplantation: Objects - Perspectives	M = 174 SD = 74	M = 675 SD = 333
4. Supplantation: Perspectives - Objects	M = 136 SD = 67	M = 662 SD = 560

used the more comprehensive learning material of the supplantation condition and the involved learning aids, respectively.

Discussion

Based upon a functional perspective with regard to the relevance of different representational formats we suppose that individuals apply those formats dependending on the requirements of the learning tasks.

Table 5. Results of the variance analysis of the needed learning time.

Effects	SS	df	MS	F	p
A: Treatment	1570034	1	1570034	13.61082	.001
B: Sequence	6993	1	6993	.06062	.794
A X B	1877	1	1877	.01627	.86
Within	4844781	42	115352		

Therefore, we investigated in this study whether and how a specific format of mental representation, namely spatial images, can increase the learning efficiency in a well-defined domain.

The results of this investigation generally indicate that the ability of spatial imagery is a trait that, even though often only acquired in the course of informal learning, can be further developed by adequate instruction. The most important result was that after instruction the female students which were not trained in technical drawing gained significantly from the computer-based training in both spatial visualization programs. The positive effects on spatial visualization skills provide evidence to support the notion that these skills are teachable and can be learned in adequate learning environments.

However, the specific skills involved in spatial visualization improved with an "overt supplantation" condition significantly more than with an imagery condition. The results of this study conform to the "supplantation hypothesis" of Salomon (1979) and provide strong support for the assumption that "overt supplantation" increases the ability of adult learners to perform those spatial transformations which are involved in technical drawing. The overt supplantation also produced specific effects with regard to the time students actually spent with learning. This finding supports the assumption that a stimulating learning environment can increase the motivation of students and, as a consequence, their capability to perform learning tasks such as technical drawing. With reference to Bloom's taxonomy, a plausible explanation of this finding may consist in the special nature of spatial visualization tasks which require mental operations on higher taxonomic levels (Kunen, Cohen & Solman, 1981).

Apart from these results, the investigation reported in this article reveals the consistent finding, that the adult learners obviously could easier perform those spatial visualizations which proceed from a three-dimensional object to the corresponding orthogonal projection. In contrast, the students could not so effectively perform the spatial visualization tasks proceeding from the different orthogonal views to the corresponding object. In accordance with Rubinstein's (1977) conception of human thinking we argue that spatial visualization tasks (like technical drawings) require both analysis and synthesis. "Analysis" requires to cognitively parse an object and to bring out its elements, parts, or features. "Synthesis" restores the entity of an object and uncovers the essential relationships between analyzed elements.

Spatial understanding of technical drawings requires the ability to analyze a three-dimensional object with regard to specific aspects or perspectives. At the same time, such an understanding requires that the learner be able to synthesize the results of the analysis through arranging top view, side view and front view in such a way that the result is a spatial image of a three-dimensional object. The results of our investigation support the assumption that the spatial imagery of the adult learners was dominated by analysis. From the perspective of Bloom's taxonomy, we can propose that synthesis is located on a higher taxonomic level (Kunen et al., 1981) and requires, therefore, more mental effort than analysis. An alternative explanation of this finding can be based on the widely accepted definition of imagery as the mental simulation of cognitive operations involved in perception (Finke, 1989; Seel, 1991). Following this definition, we can conclude that imagery is primarily object-related and, consequently, more analytic. On the other hand, spatial visualization tasks that proceed from the orthogonal projection to the object, obviously require more synthesis which involves more constructive inference processes than imagery. However, with regard to the results of our study this explanation is a little speculative. In order to clarify the situation, we plan to conduct a further experiment focussing on a systematic investigation of the mental efforts involved in performing spatial transformations, proceeding from orthogonal projection to three-dimensional objects.

RÉSUMÉ

Cette étude suppose que la capacité d'imagerie spatiale est un trait qui, bien que souvent acquis au cours d'un apprentissage informel, peut être davantage développé par un enseignement adéquat. L'objectif de cette recherche est donc d'étudier l'efficacité d'un programme spécial d'entraînement sur les capacités de visualisation spatiale d'étudiantes non entraînées au dessin technique. On a cherché à mettre en évidence les différences de performances des étudiantes à un test d'imagerie spatiale avant et après enseignement par le biais d'un programme spécial d'entraînement sur ordinateur. A cette fin, le programme d'entraînement, qui consistait à transformer des objets tri-dimensionnels à l'aide d'une condition de supplantation, était contrasté avec une condition d'imagerie simple. Le résultat le plus important de cette étude est qu'avec enseignement, les étudiantes bénéficient de l'entraînement dans les deux programmes de visualisation. Les effets de l'enseignement, qui se traduisent par de meilleures capacités de visualisation spatiale, contribuent à postuler que ces capacités sont éducables et peuvent être acquises même en cours intensifs. Cependant, les capacités spécifiques sous-tendant la capacité de visualisation spatiale ne sont améliorées qu'avec la pratique.

Acknowledgements

The authors wish to thank the editors for their helpful comments on a former draft of this article.

References

Aebli, H. (1981). *Denken: Das Ordnen des Tuns*. Band II: Denkprozesse. Stuttgart: Klett-Cotta.
Anderson, J.R. (1983). *The architecture of cognition*. Cambridge, MA: Harvard University Press.

Ben-Chaim, D., Lappan, G., & Houang, R.T. (1988). The effect of instruction on spatial visualization skills of middle school boys and girls. *American Educational Research Journal, 25* (1), 61-71.

Brachman, R.J., & Levesque, H.L. (Eds.) (1985). *Readings in knowledge representation.* Los Altos, CA: Kaufmann.

Bresser, M., Seel, N.M., & Dörr, G. (1991). *"Dreitafel-Projektion".* Tübingen: DIFF.

Bruner, J.S. (1970). *Der Prozeß der Erziehung.* Düsseldorf: Schwann.

Finke, R.A. (1989). *Principles of mental imagery.* Cambridge, MA: The MIT Press.

Fodor, J.A., & Pylyshyn, Z.W. (1988). Connectionism and cognitive architecture: A critical analysis. *Cognition, 28,* 3-72.

Gardner, H. (1985). Die Entwicklung von Symbolkompetenz bei Kindern. *Zeitschrift für Semiotik, 7,* 319-333.

Glucksberg, S. (1984). Commentary: The functional equivalence of common and multiple codes. *Journal of Verbal Learning and Verbal Behavior, 23,* 100-104.

Harris, L.J. (1981). Sex-related variations in spatial skill. In L.S. Liben, A.H. Patterson, & N. Newcombe (Eds.), *Spatial representation and behavior across the life span: Theory and application* (pp. 83-125). New York: Academic Press.

Klauer, K.J. (1975). *Intelligenztraining im Kindesalter.* Weinheim: Beltz.

Kunen, S., Cohen, R., & Solman, R. (1981). A levels-of-processing analysis of Bloom's taxonomy. *Journal of Educational Psychology, 73,* 202-211.

Linn, M.C., & Petersen, A.C. (1985). Emergence and characterization of sex differences in spatial ability: A meta-analysis. *Child Development, 56,* 1479-1498.

Mani, K., & Johnson-Laird, P.N. (1982). The mental representation of spatial descriptions. *Memory and Cognition, 10,* 181-187.

Marks, D.F. (1972). Individual differences in the vividness of visual imagery and their effect on function. In P.W. Sheehan (Ed.), *The function and nature of imagery* (pp. 83-108). New York: Academic Press.

Piaget, J. (1969). *Nachahmung, Spiel und Traum. Die Entwicklung der Symbolfunktion beim Kinde.* Stuttgart: Klett.

Piaget, J., & Inhelder, B. (1971). *Mental imagery in the child.* London: Routledge & Kegan Paul.

Quine, W.V. (1987). Symbol. In R.L. Gregory (Ed.), *The Oxford Companion to the Mind* (pp. 763-765). Oxford: Oxford University Press.

Reeves, B., Chaffee, S.H., & Tims, A. (1982). Social cognition and mass communication research. In M.R. Roloff, & C.R. Berger (Eds.), *Social cognition and communication* (pp. 287-326). Beverly Hills: Sage Publ.

Rubinstein, S.L. (1979). *Grundlagen der Allgemeinen Psychologie.* Berlin: VEB Volk und Wissen.

Salomon, G. (1972). Can we affect cognitive skills through visual media? An hypothesis and initial findings. *AV Communication Review, 20* (4), 401-422.

Salomon, G. (1979). *Interaction of media, cognition, and learning.* San Francisco: Jossey Bass.

Seddon, G.M., Tariq, R.H., & Dos Santos Veiga, J. (1982). The visualization of spatial transformations in diagrams of molecular structures. *European Journal of Science Education, 4,* 409-420.

Seel, N.M. (1991). *Weltwissen und mentale Modelle.* Göttingen: Hogrefe.

Shepard, R.N., & Metzler, J. (1971). Mental rotation of three-dimensional objects. *Science, 171,* 701-703.

Sherman, J.A. (1980). Mathematics, spatial visualization, and related factors: Changes in girls and boys, grades 8-11. *Journal of Educational Psychology, 72,* 476-482.

Comprehension of Graphics
W. Schnotz and R. W. Kulhavy (Editors)
© 1994 Elsevier Science B.V. All rights reserved.

Chapter 17

Enhancing Graphic-Effects in Instructional Texts: Influencing Learning Activities

Joan Peeck

University of Utrecht, The Netherlands

ABSTRACT

Although positive effects of graphics in instructional text have often been documented, there is a reason to fear that in actual educational practice the benefits of text illustrations will often be disappointing, due to students' superficial or otherwise inadequate processing of the graphics concerned. The present chapter examines what can be done to make learning activities more suitable for bringing about graphic effects. It presents the results of a study that shows benefical effects of instructing readers what to look for in illustrations in text, it discusses the outcome of related work, and suggests ways of dealing with the problem that readers may be unable or unwilling to follow graphic-processing instructions.

When we look at the literature on text illustrations over the last two or three decades, an interesting development may be discerned. In educational psychology research around 1970 there was not much interest in text illustrations - nor in text, for that matter -, and, inasmuch as there was an interest, people did not appear to think much of the contributions of illustrations to instructional texts. Characteristic of this position was the much quoted review by Samuels (1970) in which he concluded, on the basis of the few (mostly retention!) studies then available, "that pictures used as adjunct aids to the printed text, do not facilitate comprehension". (p. 405). Then in the seventies and early eighties a considerable number of empirical studies and review-papers appeared, and generally a much more positive view developed. Initially the tone was still somewhat defensive, and positive effects were contingent upon strict conditions (see, for instance, Levin and Lesgold's (1978) groundrules), but gradually the case for text illustrations was put forward more assertively, and some of the earlier conditions were attenuated. And now in the early nineties the mood seems to be a bit more pessimistic again, in that awareness has grown that, though the instructional potential of illustrations tends to be widely acknowledged, in daily educational practice too little of that potential is generally realized. An important and characteristic paper in this respect was Weidenmann's contribution to the Tübingen Symposium on Knowledge Acquisition from Text and Pictures in 1986 (subsequently published in Mandl and Levin (1989)). In his paper Weidenmann discusses how text illustrations will often be undervalued and encoded at a superficial level, with the result that quite frequently, as Weidenmann puts it, 'good pictures fail' in achieving any contribution to the instructional process.

A number of factors may be responsible for this undervaluation of picture informativeness. The overall meaning, the 'gist' of a picture can generally be attained in any easy and rapid way (often in as little as 300 milliseconds, (cf, Biederman, 1981); "this subjective ease of encoding (...) may lead the learner to the illusion of a full understanding" (Weidenmann, 1989, p. 163), or suggest an educational more requiring little cognitive effort (cf. Salomon, 1984). The informativeness of pictures may be undervalued because of literate bias of schooling (Olson, 1977), and so on.

In view of the asserted lack of impact of text illustrations I recently reviewed a number of measures that could be tried to remedy this state of affairs and make text illustrations more effective in the educational process (Peeck, 1991). As a framework for the review I used Bransford's version of Jenkins's well-known tetrahedron model (Jenkins, 1978) that allows for a systematic treatment of questions about learning, understanding and remembering (Bransford, 1979). The framework identifies four basic factors to be taken into account in any learning event: (a) Criterial tasks, (b) Nature of the materials, (c) Characteristics of the learner, and (d) Learning activities. In the present paper, I want to concentrate on the fourth factor in this framework, and explore more extensively how learning activities may be manipulated to enhance the effectiveness of text illustrations. One approach to dealing with the learning activities is to affect them indirectly, through the other factors in Bransford's model. For instance, learners could perhaps be made more skillful in dealing with text illustrations, and motivated to do so, by training and coaching (factor c), the processing of illustrations could be improved by explanatory captions, attention-focussing arrows, and so on (factor b), or by attention to pictorial information in posttests (factor a). Though such indirect procedures are valuable and important, the present paper will focus on more direct ways of manipulating learning acitivities, and explore how specific instructions and tasks may enhance picture effectiveness.

Perhaps the most obvious of these more direct ways is to simply ask learners to pay attention to text illustrations, or, somewhat more forceful, to urge or to tell them to do so. Inspection of educational material reveals that such more or less general admonitions are, indeed, quite common, and in the research literature too, many examples may be found. In most cases, it is impossible to decide whether or not anything was gained by including such instructions, because it is not known how much would have been learned from the pictures without the intervention. From the few studies (Hayes & Readence, 1983; Rasco, Tennyson & Boutwell, 1975) that allow of such a comparison, however, it may be concluded that if gains there were, they can only have been slight: neither in Hayes and Readence, nor in Rasco et al. was a significant increase in picture effectiveness obtained by telling subjects to attend to the illustrations. In view of the paucity of research data, however, Hayes and Readence nevertheless indicated that "as a matter of sound educational practice, teachers would be well advised to continue to call readers' attention to illustrations in their text" (Hayes and Readence, 1983, p. 248). In a recent study by Reinking, Hayes, and McEneaney (1988) support for this position was obtained when it was shown that poor readers -- a category not included in the earlier Hayes and Readence study -- did in fact benefit from such general cuing of graphic aids.

An important problem vis à vis these general admonitions, cues or instructions is that they are probably not specific enough, that is, they do not adequately specify what to look for in the pictures. In the next paragraph I will report on a study designed to investigate the effects of making a general (i.e., generally usuable) instruction more specific.

An experimental study of directing learning activities

Subjects in the study, that I did with Huib Vlam, were 45 students of Utrecht University who were paid for their participation. The learning material was a 3000-word text (adapted from an article in the Scientific American) that dealt with population density and behavioral pathology in colonies of rats. In two conditions (TP and TP+) the text was presented with two illustrations, in the third, control condition (T) the text was presented without. One of the illustrations was a drawn overview of the experimental setting that provided the reader with a number of important elements from the experiment concerned, e.g., the dwelling units (pens), ramps connecting the pens, food hoppers and drinking throughs. The other picture was a graphic display of some of the results of the experiment reported in the article. In all three conditions the subjects were instructed to read the text thoroughly in view of a test that would be given three days later. In one of the illustration conditions, (TP+), subjects were also told to pay attention to the illustrations by checking carefully 'which information from the text is depicted in the illustration, and how this is done'; in the other illustration-condition (TP) no mention of the illustrations was made. Subjects were tested individually; their reading time was recorded. Immediately after reading the text, the subjects filled out a questionnaire that dealt with characteristics of the learners (e.g., interest in the topic of the studied text, prior knowledge), an evaluation of the text (e.g., level of difficulty, liveliness), and the amount of invested mental effort (AIME), according to a procedure developed by Salomon (1984). Salomon defines AIME as "the number of non automatic mental elaborations applied to a unit of material" (1984, p.648). Following Salomon, AIME was measured by giving subjects a brief questionnaire about, for example, their effort in understanding and concentrating, and by asking them to indicate their responses on a 4-point rating scale. Three days later the subjects came back and took a set of 22 multiple-choice questions (4 alternatives), some of which covered illustrated text content while others dealt with content that was not illustrated in any of the three conditions. Subjects were told to add to each response a rating of their confidence on a 4-point rating scale, and to indicate whether they had derived their response from the text, from the illustrations, or from both (by putting, respectively, T, P, or TP in the margin).

The results of the posttest are presented in Table 1. They show for non-illustrated text content and for illustrated text content the mean number of items answered correctly, the mean confidence ratings for the correctly answered items, and - in percentages - the source that subjects in the illustrated text conditions used in answering these items. As Table 1 indicates, subjects in the three conditions did not differ in their performance on the non-illustrated text content: the mean scores for items correct, and for confidence ratings are highly similar (F's<1.0). The origin of correctly answered posttest items was almost invariably ascribed to the text.

Table 1. Post test results for non-illustrated (top) and illustrated (bottom) text content.

Condition	Mean Score		Confidence		Response source(%)		
	M	SD	M	SD	T	TP	P
T	7.87	1.78	2.15	.54	-	-	-
TP	7.73	1.88	2.12	.44	96	2	2
TP+	8.07	1.88	2.17	.34	95	2	3
T	5.47	1.36	2.23	.18	-	-	-
TP	5.80	1.76	2.40	.49	65	18	16
TP+	7.73	2.08	2.48	.40	34	36	30

As can also be seen in Table 1 however, for illustrated text content several differences between the conditions occurred. The differences for posttest means were significant (F (2,42) = 6.79, MSe = 3.31, p<.01) with subjects in condition TP+ outperforming subjects in both other conditions. As for the confidence ratings, the differences, though somewhat larger than for non-illustrated text content, were not significant. Comparison of the mean confidence ratings for the two types of question within each condition, however, showed for TP+ subjects a significant greater confidence for illustrated (2.48) than for non-illustrated (2.17) testitems (t (14) = 2.39; p <.05). In the TP condition there was a similar trend (2.40 vs 2.12), but this difference did not reach significance. Finally, with regard to the origin of the correct responses on illustrated-text questions again a clear difference was found. Subjects not specifically instructed to inspect the illustrations indicated they had derived their responses mainly from the text, whereas the TP+ subjects indicated illustrations significantly more often as the source of their responses (t (28) = 3.44; p<.05).

On none of the other measures did differences between the conditions occur: so no differences in rated difficulty level of the text, interest in the topic, and so on, no differences in the ratings of amount of invested mental effort, nor in the registered reading time.

The results of this study show that -- in comparison with a no-instruction condition -- a significant increase in picture effectiveness can indeed be achieved when a general instruction is made more specific by indicating what the learner should look for in the pictures. That inspection of the illustrations did actually occur and did help subjects at the test to bring target knowledge to mind, is shown by the source data obtained in the two picture conditions.

Before I go on to discuss other, and probably more effective ways of manipulating learning activities, a brief comment on another outcome of this study may be appropriate. While it proved possible to boost performance in the TP+ condition, relative to the TP condition, there was a noticeable failure to find performance facilitation in TP subjects relative to controls. This outcome provides an eloquent demonstration of Weidenmann's assertion that quite often 'good pictures fail', even though, as the level of responding at the posttest indicates, subjects could clearly have benefitted from the information the pictures provided. Several of the reasons why pictures fail, mentioned above, will have operated here: undervaluation and superficial encoding of the pictures, over-reliance on textual information -- especially for these highly skilled readers! -- etcetera. The relative neglect of the illustrations is nicely illustrated by the source data in Table 1 which shows the dominant position of the text as knowledge base for TP subjects.

At the same time this result may come as a surprise in the light of reviews such as the one by Levie and Lentz (1982) who found that "Learning illustrated text information was better with illustrated text than with text alone in 98% of the [46] experimental comparisons. For 81% of the comparisons the difference was statistically significant" (p. 213). A number of variables may account for this apparent anomaly: instructional variables (it is, for instance, not known to what extent in the reviewed studies attention was drawn to the pictures by instruction), textual variables (many experiments used relatively short narratives rather than an extended expository text), subject variables (few of the reported studies used university students as subjects), etcetera. Apart from that, it may be suspected that published research does not present an accurate impression of the real occurrence of the phenomenon: Journal-reviewers and editors may have been inclined to reject studies that do not come up with a significant difference, and experimenters may have decided not to submit failures-to-find-differences, so that even in laboratory experimentation the phenomenon is perhaps less pervasive than the reviews suggest.

Further measures to enhance picture effectiveness

Although the results of the study reported above showed a boost in performance, a form of instruction, or a task, that specifies for a particular illustration what information is to be extracted, may be even more helpful to the learner. Indirect evidence for this assumption comes from various studies. A number of earlier investigations, for instance, has shown how encoding and retention of picture content is affected by the presence of verbal descriptions that accompany the pictures (e.g., Bacharach, Carr & Mehner, 1976). Further indirect evidence comes from the classic experiments by Yarbus (1967) that showed how eyemovement patterns of subjects viewing a painting varied with instructions to look for different types of information (e.g., 'give the ages of the people in the painting' or 'estimate the material circumstances of the family"). Even though in Yarbus's research no recall or recognition of the inspected scene was measured, there is little doubt that retention patterns corresponding to the viewing patterns could have been obtained (e.g., Nelson & Loftus, 1980).

More direct evidence for the facilitative effects of instructive captions that specify what to look for in text illustrations, what information to focus, extract, or remember, has recently been presented in studies by Reinking, Hayes and McEneaney (1988), Weidenmann (1989), and Bernard (1990). In all three studies, specific picture-oriented instructions or cues enhanced the effect of text illustrations in comparison with conditions that did not offer these instructions or cues. Apparently, the instructions "increase [the subjects'] attention to graphic aids to the extent that they are able to recall more information presented in graphic aids" (Reinking et al., 1988, p. 239).

Even though such results are of considerable educational importance in that they convincingly show that the instructional benefits of text illustrations can be enhanced, and how this may be done, the interventions will only be successful if the learners are willing to follow the directions. In laboratory studies these conditions are probably easily met. For instance, when required to trace the pathway of pain through the nervous system, and told 'While you trace the route, describe it in your own words to help you remember it', subjects (nursing students) in the Bernard study probably did more or less what the experimenter asked them, though it should be realized that we do not really know much about the nature of their learning activities.

The processing instructions could, however, also be easily ignored, and in actual educational practice such instructional interventions may turn out to be considerably less successful, unless, somehow, more control over the learning activities can be achieved. One way to do this, is to require learners to come up with an external and controllable product or response to the picture-oriented instructions. Several studies have demonstrated the viability of this approach. In one recent study, for instance, Hayes and Reinking (1991) found that adjunct study materials which required eight graders to act on the information given in graphic aids to expository passages, significantly increased students' attention to, and learning from these aids compared to students who studied the text in the absence of these materials. Other ways of promoting effortful processing of the information contained in the illustrations, or in relating it to information contained in the text have also been subject of experimental investigation. Several studies, for instance, have looked at the effect of requiring students to label features of an illustration that accompanies text to be learned. In a study by Dean and Kulhavy (1981, experiment 2), for instance, subjects (undergraduates) benefitted more from a map showing topological features from a text when they were required -- under supervision -- to label each feature than when the map was presented with the labels already provided. A similar result with fifth and sixth graders was obtained by Verhaegen (1983) with a text on airballoons. Children who studied the text with a drawing that showed a balloon with 15 labeled parts discussed in the text, remembered less of the location of these parts than subjects who were given the illustration and told to put in the labels themselves. In an earlier study (Peeck, 1980, Experiment 2) with roughly the same material, however, subjects required to complete the outline drawing of an airballoon by drawing and labeling the parts, were slightly inferior on a cued recall test of the text than children who had seen the complete and labeled illustration. Inspection of the children's drawings revealed that the quality of the students' drawings was often poor: many balloon parts were omitted, wrongly located or incorrectly labeled. Additional analyses of each child's drawing in relation to his or her testperformance showed that test questions on balloon parts were answered correctly more often when the pertinent part had been drawn and labeled correctly than when it had not (for fifth graders, 71% vs. 13%, for sixth graders 71% vs. 24%, respectively).

This suggests a second problem with instructions or tasks that require students to act on the information presented in a text illustration: the student may be willing to comply but unable to do so. Inability to respond adequately may easily occur in tasks, as in Peeck (1980), where students are required to construct illustrations themselves, though some studies (e.g. Alesandrini, 1981; Dean & Kulhavy, 1981, Experiment 1) indicate that for older students this procedure does have promise as an adjunct aid to text processing. For younger learners, however, a good deal of training and coaching may be necessary before the procedures become effective and efficient. Finally, it should be noted that by their very proneness to error, these learner-generated procedures create the possibility of detecting at a relatively early stage in the learning process misconceptions and failures to comprehend the learning material. This will enable corrective intervention so that misunderstandings can be clarified and erroneous visualizations can be remedied before they affect the learning result adversely (cf. Peeck, 1986).

RÉSUMÉ

Bien que les effets bénéfiques des graphiques dans des textes instructionnels aient souvent été rapportés dans la littérature, il existe des raisons de craindre que dans la pratique éducative réelle, le bénéfice des illustrations de textes soit souvent décevant, les étudiants traitant les graphiques concernés superficiellement ou bien de façon inadéquate. Ce chapitre examine ce qui peut être fait pour rendre les activités d'apprentissage plus appropriées pour conduire à des effets des graphiques.

On présente les résultats d'une recherche montrant qu'instruire les lecteurs sur ce qu'il faut chercher dans les illustrations de texte a des effets bénéfiques. Les résultats de travaux voisins sont discutés, et on suggère des moyens de palier le refus ou l'incapacité des lecteurs à suivre les instructions de traitement de graphique.

References

Alesandrini, K.L. (1981). Pictorial-verbal and analytic-holistic learning strategies in science learning. *Journal of Educational Psychology*, *73*, 358-368.

Bacharach, V.R., Carr, T.H., & Mehner, D.S. (1976). Interactive and independent contributions of verbal descriptions to children's picture memory. *Journal of Experimental Child Psychology*, *22*, 492-498.

Bernard, R.M. (1990). Using extended captions to improve learning from instructional illustrations. *British Journal of Educational Technology*, *21*, 215-225.

Biederman, I. (1981). On the semantics of a glance at a scene. In M. Kubovy & J.R. Pomerantz (Eds.), *Perceptual organization* (pp. 213-253). Hillsdale. NJ: Erlbaum.

Bransford, J.D. (1979). *Human cognition: Learning, understanding, and remembering*. Belmont, CA: Wadsworth.

Dean, R.S., & Kulhavy, R.W. (1981). The influence of spatial organization in prose learning. *Journal of Educational Psychology*, *73*, 57-64.

Hayes, D.A., & Readence, J.E. (1983). Transfer of learning from illustration dependent text. *Journal of Educational Research*, *76*, 245-248.

Hayes, D.A., & Reinking, D.R. (1991). Good and poor readers' use of graphic aids cued in texts and in adjunct study materials. *Contemporary Educational Psychology*, *16*, 391-398.

Jenkins, J.J. (1978). Four points to remember: A tetrahedron model of memory experiments. In L.S. Cermak and F.I.M. Craik (Eds.), *Levels of processing and human memory*. Hillsdale, N.J.: Erlbaum.

Levie, W.H., & Lentz, R. (1982). Effects of text illustrations: a review of research. *Educational Communication and Technology Journal*, *30*, 195-232.

Levin, J.R., & Lesgold, A.M. (1978). On pictures in prose. *Educational Communication and Technology Journal*, *26*, 233-243.

Mandl, H., & Levin, J.R. (Eds.) (1989). *Knowledge acquisition from text and pictures*. Amsterdam: Elsevier.

Nelson, W.W., & Loftus, G.R. (1980). The functional visual field during picture viewing. *Journal of Experimental Psychology: Human Learning and Memory*, *6*, 391-399.

Olson, D.R. (1977). The language of instruction: The literate bias of schooling. In R.C. Anderson, R.J. Spiro & W.E. Montague (Eds.), *Schooling and the acquisition of knowledge* (pp. 65-89). Hillsdale, NJ: Erlbaum.

Peeck, J. (1980). *Experimenter-provided and learner-generated pictures in learning from text.* Paper presented at the annual meeting of American Educational Research Association, Boston.

Peeck, J. (1986). Het maken van tekeningen als hulpmiddel bij het verwerken van teksten. [Drawing as an aid to text-processing], *Tijdschrift voor Taalbeheersing, 8,* 81-93.

Peeck, J. (1991). *Increasing picture effects in learning from illustrated text.* Paper presented at the Fourth European Conference for Research on Learning and Instruction, Turku, Finland, August.

Rasco, R.W., Tennyson, R.D., & Boutwell, R.C. (1975). Imagery instructions and drawings in learning prose. *Journal of Educational Psychology, 67,* 188-192.

Reinking, D.R., Hayes, D.A., & McEneaney, J.E. (1988). Good and poor readers' use of explicitly cued graphic aids. *Journal of Reading Behavior, 20,* 229-247.

Salomon, G. (1984). Television is "easy" and print is "tough": The differential investment of mental effort in learning as a function of perceptions and attributions. *Journal of Educational Psychology, 76,* 647-658.

Samuels, S.J. (1970). Effects of pictures on learning to read, comprehension and attitudes. *Review of Educational Research,* 40, 397-407.

Verhaegen, I.J.J. (1983). *Visuele hulpmiddelen bij het lezen van teksten* [Visual aids for the reading of text]. Unpublished master's thesis, University of Utrecht, Psychological Laboratory.

Weidenmann, B. (1989). When good pictures fail: An information processing approach to the effects of illustrations. In H. Mandl & J.R. Levin (Eds.), *Knowledge acquisition from text and pictures* (pp 157-171). North Holland: Elsevier.

Yarbus, A.L. (1967). *Eyemovement and vision.* New York: Plenum Press.

Comprehension of Graphics
W. Schnotz and R. W. Kulhavy (Editors)
© 1994 Elsevier Science B.V. All rights reserved.

Chapter 18

Systematic Forced Processing of Text and Graphic Information

Phillip J. Moore and Jill J. Scevak

University of Newcastle, Shortland, Australia

ABSTRACT

This paper examines the effects of forced processing of a tree diagram on comprehension of redundant and non-redundant information at both detail and main idea levels of abstraction. Also of concern was the role of reading ability in such processing. High school students read a social studies text under one of three conditions: text without tree diagram; text plus tree diagram; text plus tree diagram and forced processing. In the forced processing condition, subjects were required to integrate text and tree diagram information using a trace method developed by Kloster and Winne (1989). This method provides an index of text-diagram integration during reading. Comprehension was assessed using a multiple choice format with questions addressing redundant and non-redundant details and main ideas. Diagram subjects also completed a post-test diagram task. Correlational results showed tracing scores significantly related to comprehension, particularly for average ability subjects. However, the analyses of variance results showed the forced processing to be harmful to overall and detail level comprehension. Diagram task analyses revealed firm memories for the structure of the diagram but comparatively little memory of its semantic content.

Diagrams, charts, maps and other forms of spatially representing information are often incorporated into textbooks as ways of potentially increasing learning. While there is a growing research base indicating that text illustrations can have important effects upon learning (e.g Mandl & Levin, 1989), there is less research examining the ways in which such spatial aids are used by readers (e.g. Moore, Chan & Au, 1990) and less instructionally oriented research investigating how readers might be encouraged to more systematically process these aids (e.g. Moore, 1991; Peeck, 1991; Weidenmann, 1989).

In this paper we focus on one particular form of spatial organiser, the tree diagram, and we examine the effects of a particular form of systematic forced processing, linking text and diagram information, by having subjects complete a "trace" (Kloster & Winne, 1989). Trace was originally employed in the Kloster and Winne study to assess the ways in which readers understood the relationships between a text and its corresponding verbal advance organiser. While reading, the subjects were required to leave a "trace" of their cognitions by indicating, at the end of each paragraph, whether or not the information contained in that paragraph was related to any part of the advance organiser (parts of the organiser were numbered). In this way, Kloster and Winne were able to ascertain the degree to which readers linked text and organiser information. Importantly Kloster and Winne showed that subjects with higher trace scores were better comprehenders of text information and also that subjects of higher academic ability were more likely to have higher trace scores.

We were prompted by the Kloster and Winne (1989) research to ask several questions. The first question was whether or not the trace method, as employed for verbal advance organisers, would provide a reliable index of linking in the context of a spatial organiser, a tree diagram. In other words, would subjects with higher trace scores comprehend the text information more so than those who had lower trace scores? Determining whether or not a paragraph is related to part of the tree diagram should prove beneficial to comprehension in that the reader has to actually process the two representations and then make a decision about the relationship between the two before progressing to the next paragraph in the text. A high trace score should represent a coherent linking of the two sets of information with the additional spatial organisation of the diagram providing potential for conjoint retention (Dean & Kulhavy, 1981; Kulhavy, Stock & Caterino, 1991). Conjoint retention theory would predict that redundant information, information expressed both in the diagram and the text, would have dual codes for such information. By way of contrast, non-redundant information which is expressed only in the text would be coded essentially via verbal processes.

Levels of abstraction of comprehension could also be influenced by tracing operations. As tree diagrams tend to express main ideas and supporting details (Guri-Rozenblit,1989), it is likely that the major effects of tracing would be at the main idea rather than the detail level but this would of course depend upon the nature of the diagram and whether or not it represented the whole of or a proportion of the text. Hence the first objective of this study was to examine the relationship between trace performance and subsequent comprehension in a group of students forced to link text with tree diagram information during reading. The diagram was designed to represent approximately half of the text's main ideas and a summary of their supporting details so that the comprehension of both redundant and non-redundant information could be assessed at both the main idea and detail levels.

The second question we were prompted to ask about tracing was an extension of the first. As Kloster and Winne (1989) had no "text-only" condition (all treatments included an organiser), it is not clear as to the overall effects of tracing on comprehension. While Kloster and Winne demonstrated that those who left a "better" trace were better comprehenders, we were left considering whether or not such forced processing was indeed beneficial (or harmful) to comprehension when compared to "normal" reader text/spatial organiser processing. We have argued above that the explicit examination of the relationship between the two aspects of the material to be learned should prove beneficial to comprehension. An alternative hypothesis, however, suggests itself. Tracing may be intrusive and lead to lower levels of comprehension when compared to treatments where readers can employ their own, idiosyncratic strategies. Automated strategies normally employed while reading may have to be modified, or even abandoned when readers are placed in the situation of having to examine the relationship of paragraphs to segments of a diagram as they progress through a text. The literature (e.g. Moore, Chan & Au, 1990) suggests that readers do not examine the relationships between texts and diagrams in any systematic manner and the novelty of having to make such connections may disturb the development of a coherent mental representation of the material being read. Hence, the second objective of this study was to compare the comprehension performance of subjects forced to process the diagram by tracing with subjects in a text plus diagram treatment and a control treatment of text only.

In the context of these two questions we were also interested in the role of reading ability. Readers who have well learned and automated reading-specific strategies would require little of working memory capacity for text processing leaving residual capacity for the explicit linking of text and diagram information. For the less competent reader, though, we can envisage at least two likely outcomes. On the one hand, the explicit linking of both types of information may provide scaffolding in strategy use. Forcing readers to be strategic in this manner may prove beneficial to comprehension. On the other hand, the movement from text to diagram at the end of each paragraph may prove disruptive to the generation of a coherent text representation for the less competent reader, the trace actually interfering with comprehension.

In summary, as an overriding theme this study sought to examine the effects on comprehension of forcing readers to link text and diagram information by using a trace technique developed by Kloster and Winne (1989). More specifically, it sought to investigate: (1) the relationships between performances in tracing and comprehension of both redundant and non-redundant information at detail and main idea levels of abstraction; (2) the relative benefits to comprehension of such forced processing when compared to a traditional text-diagram presentation and a text without-diagram presentation; and (3) the likely interactive role of reading ability in tracing and text-diagram comprehension.

Method

Design and Subjects

The design of the experiment was a 3 group (Control, Diagram, Trace) x 2 ability (High, Average) analysis of variance with dependent measures on total multiple choice, redundant details, non-redundant details, redundant main ideas and non-redundant main ideas.A further 2 group (Diagram, Trace) x 2 ability (High, Average) analysis of variance with scores on the diagram task as the dependent measure was also conducted. The subjects in the study were 95 tenth grade students (15-16 years old) from a secondary school in Gosford, NSW. The students constituted the top four classes in English in the grade and thus represented average and high ability students. A stratified random sampling procedure, based on reading ability, was used to assign subjects to either the Control group, Diagram group or Trace group. Mean reading ability of the Control group as measured by the Gapadol Reading Comprehension Test, Form Y, (McLeod & Anderson, 1972) was 52.20 (9.95), for the Diagram group 51.86 (11.06), and 51.10

(9.98) for the Trace group. There were 33 subjects in the Control group, 29 in the Diagram and 33 in the Trace groups.

All groups received the same text. Both the Diagram and the Trace groups' texts were accompanied by a tree diagram. The Trace group's text differed from the texts of the other two groups in one way. Although the content was exactly the same, their text had a small box at the end of each paragraph in the text (following Kloster & Winne 1989). This box was used to record their traces.

Materials

Texts. A 1200 word passage about The Great Depression in the U.S.A. was constructed as the main text for the study. This text presents two basic strands: (i) the economic conditions prior to the Great Depression and; (ii) the causes and outcomes of the Great Depression. Readability of the text as measured by Rix (Anderson, 1981) was Year 8 level. The text read by the Trace group had a 1cm x 1cm box (to be used to code the paragraph) at the bottom right hand corner at the end of each paragraph.

An additional, a much shorter text was constructed for the purposes of acquainting Trace subjects with the trace procedure before they were involved in the experiment proper. Some paragraphs were related to the numbered parts of the attached tree diagram, some were not. The diagram represented the main ideas and details of the text and each section of the diagram was numbered.

Diagram. A diagram (see Figure 1) representing the second strand of the text, the causes and outcomes of the Great Depression, accompanied the text for both the Diagram and Trace groups. The diagram represented the eight main ideas and 20 supporting details of this part of the text and each section of the diagram was numbered (1-8). The wording in the boxes was obtained from the topic sentences in each paragraph represented in the diagram, hence representing redundant information at both main idea and detail levels. It was permanently available for reference during reading as part of the booklet.

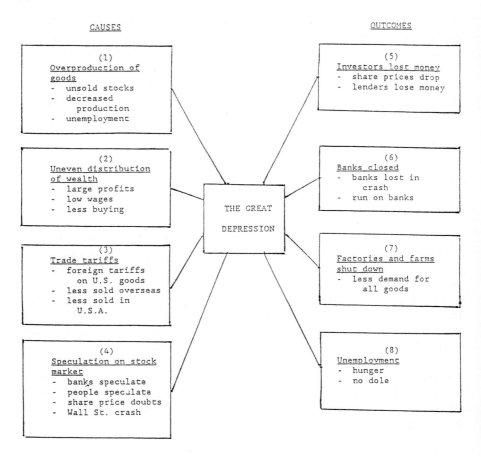

Figure 1. Tree diagram.

Measures of comprehension

Trace Score. The trace score for each subject in the Trace group was the number of correct traces. A score of 1 was given for each correct answer, with a maximum of 20.

Multiple Choice Questions. Comprehension was assessed by twenty multiple choice questions. Of the twenty questions, ten were aimed at assessing comprehension at the detail level and ten at the main idea level. It will be remembered that the diagram expressed ideas for approximately half of the text and consequently, at the main idea level, five questions tested redundant information (i.e. information which appeared in the text and the diagram) and five questions tested non-redundant information (i.e. information which appeared only in the text). For details, a similar pattern applied of five redundant and five non-redundant questions. A score of 1 was assigned for each correct answer with a maximum of 20 for total comprehension.

Diagram Task

To assess memory for the diagram and the information contained in it, subjects were asked to draw as much of the diagram as they could after they had completed reading the text and answering the multiple choice questions. Only the Diagram and Trace groups completed this task.

Three scores were obtained from the diagram. An organisational score represented the accuracy of replicating the structure of the diagram. The headings "Causes" and "Outcomes" were also scored as part of the organisational pattern. The maximum organisation score was 11 (9 boxes & 2 headings, see Figure 1). The main idea score represented the number of main ideas included (maximum of 8). For a main idea to be included it had to be on the correct side of the diagram. A detail score represented the number of details included (maximum of 20). To be scored as correct, details had to be placed on the correct side and under the relevant main idea.

Procedure

Prior to the investigation proper data were gathered on the students' reading ability. Trace subjects were given a 10 minute training programme prior to reading The Great Depression text. During this time they read the practice text and they were instructed in tracing. All subjects mastered the tracing procedure during practice.

For testing, subjects were given 20 minutes to study the main text. Subjects in the Control group had the text only and they were instructed to study the material as they would be tested on it later. Subjects in the Diagram group were instructed to study the text and the diagram as they would be tested on it later. Subjects in the Trace group were given the same instructions as those in the Diagram group, but in addition they had to fill in the trace boxes at the end of each paragraph of the text. They were required to code each paragraph in the text by writing the number (0-8) of the matching diagram section in the box at the end of each paragraph of the text, a zero representing no match. At the end of the 20 minute study period all materials were collected and all subjects in the three groups completed a five minute filler task designed to remove any surface memory of the text (and diagram). Subjects then completed a 20 item multiple choice test. Ten minutes were allowed. Subjects in the Diagram and Trace groups then completed the diagram task for which five minutes were allowed. All subjects completed the tasks in the allocated times.

Results

Trace Group

The mean and standard deviation for total trace are 13.03 and 2.91 respectively. As for the ANOVA the Trace group was divided into 2 (High, Average) ability reading groups. For High ability readers the mean total trace score was 14.07, standard deviation 2.40. For Average ability readers the mean total trace and standard deviation were 12.17 and 3.07 respectively.

Correlations were computed between trace and comprehension scores and these are presented in Table 1. The correlations between mean total trace and all measures of comprehension are positive, significant in the case of total multiple choice and non-redundant main ideas. The High ability group show substantially lower levels of relationship between mean total trace and all comprehension measures, whereas the Average ability correlations are stronger particularly between total mean trace and total multiple choice and non-redundant main ideas.

For the Trace group the mean and standard deviations for the organisation score are 9.24 and 1.80, for main idea score 2.67 and 1.81 and for detail score 4.24 and 3.12. Correlations between mean total trace and organisation, main ideas and details scores from the diagram task are 0.18, 0.38 and 0.36 respectively, the latter two proving to be reliable.

Table 1. Correlations of Trace Scores and Comprehension Scores of Details (Redundant, Non-redundant) and Main Ideas (Redundant, Non-redundant) for Total Trace Group and High and Average Ability Trace Subjects.

		comprehension			
Trace Score	Total	Redundant Details	Non-Redundant Details	Redundant Main Ideas	Non-Redundant Main Ideas
Trace (Whole group)	.43*	.28	.32	.24	.43*
Trace (High ability)	.18	.13	.10	.13	.10
Trace (Average ability)	.38	.13	.25	.17	.49*

* sig < .05

Control, Diagram and Trace Group Comparison

A series of 3 x 2 analysis of variance were conducted with group (Control, Diagram and Trace) as the first factor, reading ability (High, Average) as the second factor and total multiple choice, redundant and non-redundant details and main ideas as the dependent measures. Table 2 shows the means and standard deviations for all groups.

The first analysis involving total multiple choice as the dependent measure yielded significant group $F(2,89) = 4.0$, MSe = 39.53, P<.02) and ability $F(1,89) = 16.18$, MSe = 159.90, P<.0001 main effects. The

Table 2. *Means and Standard Deviations for Total comprehension, Detail comprehension (Redundant, Non-redundant) and Main Idea comprehension (Redundant, Non-redundant) by Group (Control, Diagram, Trace) by Ability (High, Average).*

Group	Control		Diagram		Trace	
Ability	High	Average	High	Average	High	Average
Total multiple choice	12.94 (3.42)	12.18 (2.43)	14.43 (3.27)	11.60 (3.72)	13.00 (2.67)	8.78 (3.23)
Redundant Details	3.13 (1.31)	2.65 (1.22)	3.21 (1.31)	2.80 (1.32)	2.87 (1.19)	1.56 (0.92)
Non-Redundant Details	3.13 (1.41)	3.18 (0.95)	3.57 (0.94)	3.13 (1.13)	2.93 (0.96)	1.83 (1.10)
Redundant Main Ideas	3.25 (1.00)	2.88 (1.05)	3.71 (0.83)	3.07 (1.39)	3.67 (0.98)	2.89 (1.41)
Non-Redundant Main Ideas	3.44 (1.21)	3.47 (1.23)	3.93 (1.38)	2.60 (1.72)	3.53 (1.06)	2.50 (1.20)

(Standard deviations in parentheses)

group x ability interaction approached significance at the .08 level. The interaction suggests that Average ability subjects in the Trace group were disadvantaged by tracing. A Scheffe test showed the Diagram group scoring significantly higher than the Trace group at the .05 level. No other differences were significant.

The second analysis involving redundant details as the dependent measure yielded significant group $F(2,89) = 3.98$, MSe = 5.84, P<.02) and ability $F(1,89) = 8.67$, MSe = 12.72, P<.004) main effects. A Scheffe test showed the Diagram group scored significantly higher than

Table 3. Means and Standard Deviations for Diagram Recall of Organization Main Ideas and Details by Group (Diagram, Trace) by Ability (High, Average).

Group	Diagram		Trace	
Ability	High	Average	High	Average
Organisation	9.86 (1.35)	9.13 (2.10)	9.93 (1.44)	8.67 (1.91)
Main Idea	3.50 (3.06)	1.46 (2.00)	3.47 (1.60)	2.00 (1.75)
Details	3.36 (2.93)	2.00 (2.10)	5.07 (3.10)	3.56 (3.05)

(Standard deviations in parentheses)

the Trace group at the .05 level. No other differences proved to be significant.

The third analysis involving non-redundant details as the dependent measure yielded significant group $F(2,89) = 6.89$, MSe $= 8.26$, P$<$.001 and ability $F(1,89) = 4.83$, MSe $= 5.79$, P$<$.03) main effects. Once again the Diagram group scored significantly higher than the Trace group at the .05 level using a Scheffe test. No other differences proved to be significant.

The fourth analysis involving redundant main ideas as the dependent measure yielded a significant ability effect $F(1,89) = 6.48$, MSe $= 8.42$, P$<$.01, with High ability subjects scoring higher than Average ability subjects. No other effects were significant.

The fifth analysis involving non-redundant main ideas as the dependent measure yielded a significant ability effect $F(1.89) = 8.27$, MSe $=$

14.21, P<.005, with High ability subjects scoring higher than Average ability subjects. There were no other significant effects.

Diagram Task

A series of 2 group (Diagram, Trace) x 2 ability (High, Average) analysis of variance with dependent measures on organisation, main idea and detail scores was conducted.

Table 3 shows the means and standard deviations from these analyses. The organisation analysis yielded a significant ability effect, $F(1,58) = 5.00$, $p<.05$, $MSe = 15.22$, a finding replicated in the main ideas analysis, $F(1,58) = 10.30$, $p<.05$, $MSe = 47.06$, and the detail level analysis, $F(1,58) = 3.93$, $p=.05$, $MSe = 31.60$. In each case the higher ability subjects recalled more than the Average ability subjects. The only other significant effect was for Group on the detail level score, $F(1,58) = 5.09$, $MSe = 40.95$, with the Trace subjects recalling more details than Diagram subjects.

Discussion

Two interrelated research questions drove this research examining the effects of forcing readers to link text and tree diagram information. Also of interest was the role of reading ability in any such effects. The first question was concerned with the relationship between trace scores and comprehension of information of different types (redundant, non-redundant) and of differing levels of abstraction (main ideas, details). The second question focused upon the comparative effects of tracing on comprehension.

The answer to the question of the relationship between trace scores and comprehension was found from the within-group analyses of the Trace group. The correlational data for the Trace group as a whole showed that subjects with higher trace scores had higher overall comprehension, a finding that is consistent with the verbal organiser results reported by Kloster and Winne (1989). Trace scores were positively correlated with comprehension scores for details and main ideas (both redundant and non-redundant) but only the non-redundant main ideas correlation proved to be significant.

These findings indicate the Trace subjects processed both the text and its accompanying diagram, and that those who were more competent in determining whether or not there was a relationship between the text segment being read and the diagram gained a better grasp of the text. The finding of the strongest relationship with recognition of non-redundant main ideas suggests that the making of decisions of no link, a zero trace, may require more processing than a situation in which matching is achievable. Indeed, given the nature of the "considerateness" (Armbruster & Anderson, 1988) of both our text and the diagram (e.g. topic sentences, sub-headings, topic sentences summarised in the diagram), this hypothesis seems plausible.

To further examine the role of reading ability in tracing and comprehension, we examined separately the correlational pattern for the high and average students in the Trace group. For the high ability students, the results clearly demonstrated little relationship between trace scores and the various comprehension scores suggesting that the strategies the students had in their repertoire were well automated and they did not require the potential strategy scaffolding from the forced linking. Alternatively, if the tracing process were potentially disruptive, these higher ability subjects had sufficient mental capacity to do such tracing without disruption to comprehension.

On the other hand, for those of average ability, trace was a consistent predictor of comprehension, particularly of non-redundant main ideas. The provision of explicit cues to examine links between text and diagram information, when done competently, was shown to be positively related to comprehension for the average ability students. Presumably, the deeper processing required in the linking process played a substantial part in these effects. However, the answer to our second question raises some doubts about the level of processing.

The second question was concerned with comparing Trace subjects' performance with those who read a text with a diagram and those who had read the text without a diagram. The answer to this question provides a somewhat different perspective on the effects of tracing. For overall comprehension, the Trace group's performance was significantly less than that of the Diagram group but not significantly different from the Control group's scores. The major source of this difference can be seen in the trend for the average ability subjects in the Trace group to perform poorly on overall comprehension. When levels of abstraction were considered though, trace was shown to have little impact on main ideas but a harmful effect upon comprehension of details. These comparative data, then, illustrate that tracing had harmful effects on average ability students and also, irrespective of ability, negative effects on detail level comprehension.

Competition for mental resources are implicated in both of these findings. For the average ability student with a reasonable repertoire of strategies for dealing with texts, and perhaps little knowledge of how to process diagrams (see Moore, Chan & Au, 1990), the constant movement from text to diagram may have disrupted the formation of a coherent text base in memory. Tracing for such students seems intrusive, and indeed may have led to a segment-by-segment approach to text analysis not allowing full benefit of the diagram to be realised. Thus, in the competition to examine the relationships between text main ideas, text details and those represented in the diagram, details were casualties. The diagram task results showed the Trace group with superior detail scores when compared to the Diagram group, although both groups' scores were relatively low. This finding suggests that the exercise of linking, for at least some of the average ability readers, may have been done utilising an item-by-item approach rather than an integrative process (Lowe, 1991). Indeed, the organisational and detail/main idea scores from the diagram task show that the subjects remembered the structure of the diagram but not much of its semantic content (Winn, 1991).

In terms of the instructional implications of this study, the importance lies in the principles rather then the details of the tracing procedure. Students need to appreciate that there are substantial relationships between texts and their accompanying graphics, and that an understanding of those links will positively influence their level of learning. Graphics can be employed to not only reinforce text information but also as retrieval devices, through imagery, of conjointly retained information. We would argue that comprehensive strategy training in the use of graphics should become an integral part of classroom instruction in the various content areas. It is not as if this is a difficult task to achieve. A training programme developed for understanding links between maps and texts based upon the strategies of summarising, explicit linking of texts and maps (by active processing), imagery, and checking for understanding has been shown to be beneficial for high school students' learning in History (Scevak & Moore, 1990). It is likely that these strategies can be generalised to other content areas and other types of graphics (Moore, 1991).

In sum, our trace results are consistent with verbal advance organiser research (Kloster & Winne, 1989) in that those subjects who were able to correctly link text and organiser information were better comprehenders. This was particularly the case for the average ability readers. However, when comparisons were made between those who had been forced to process the diagram-text relationships and those in text only and text-plus-diagram conditions, the findings clearly indicated that tracing was harmful to detail level comprehension and, for the average ability readers, harmful to overall comprehension. Future research may wish to examine the manner in which links are made in such forced processing. An obvious question relates to levels of processing. Is tracing, in the Kloster and Winne (1989) sense, merely matching or something more integrative when used with redundant diagrams?

RÉSUMÉ

Cet article examine les effets du traitement forcé d'un diagramme arborescent sur la compréhension d'informations redondantes et non redondantes, à deux niveaux d'abstraction: les idées principales et les détails. La question du rôle des capacités de lecture et de compréhension dans ces traitements est aussi abordée. Des lycéens lisaient un texte portant sur des études sociales selon une des trois conditions ; texte sans diagramme, texte accompagné d'un diagramme arborescent, texte avec diagramme arborescent et traitement forcé. Dans la condition de traitement forcé, les sujets devaient intégrer les informations du texte et du diagramme en utilisant une méthode de trace développée par Kloster et Winne (1989). Cette méthode fournit un indice de l'intégration texte/diagramme au cours de la lecture. La compréhension était évaluée à l'aide de questions à choix multiples, abordant les détails redondants, non redondants et les idées principales. Les sujets avec diagramme ont aussi, en post-test, complété une tâche de diagramme. Les corrélations observées montrent que les scores de tracing sont reliés significativement à la compréhension, particulièrement pour les sujets dont les capacités de lecture sont moyennes. Toutefois, les résultats des analyses de variance montrent que le traitement forcé est défavorable à la compréhension du niveau global et de détail. Les analyses des tâches de diagramme révèlent une bonne rétention de la structure du diagramme mais, comparativement, une rétention faible de son contenu sémantique.

Acknowledgments

The staff and students at Lisarow High School are thanked for their involvement in this research. We are particularly indebted to Deb McPherson.

References

Anderson, J. (1981). Lix and Rix: Variations on a little known readability index. *Journal of Reading, 26,* 490-496.

Armbruster, B.B., & Anderson, T.H. (1988). On selecting "considerate" content area textbooks. *Remedial and Special Education, 9,* 47-52.

Dean, R.S., & Kulhavy, R.W. (1981). Influence of spatial organisation on prose learning. *Journal of Educational Psychology, 73,* 57-64.

Guri-Rozenblit, S. (1989). Effects of a tree diagram on students' comprehension of main ideas in a multi-thematic expository text. *Reading Research Quarterly, 24,* 236- 247.

Kloster, A., & Winne, P. (1989). Effects of different types of organisers on students' learning from text. *Journal of Educational Psychology, 81,* 9-15.

Kulhavy, R.W., Stock, W.A., & Caterino, L. (1991). *Reference maps as a graphic framework for comprehending text.* Paper presented at the workshop comprehension of Graphics, University of Tübingen, Germany, October.

Lowe, R. (1991). *Scientists and non-scientists' mental representations of graphic material in technical diagrams.* Paper presented at the Fourth European Conference for Research on Learning and Instruction, Turku, Finland, August.

McLeod, J., & Anderson, J. (1972). *GAPADOL Reading comprehension (Form Y).* Richmond: Heinemann.

Mandl, H., & Levin, J. (Eds.) (1989). *Knowledge acquisition from text and pictures*. North Holland: Elsevier.

Moore, P.J. (1991). *Effective learning in text and spatial organiser contexts*. Paper presented at the comprehension of Graphics and Texts Symposium at the Fourth European Conference for Research on Learning and Instruction, Turku, Finland, August.

Moore, P.J., Chan, L.K.S., & Au, W. (1990). *High School students' use of diagrams during reading*. Paper presented at the 22nd International Congress of Applied Psychology, Kyoto, July.

Peeck, J. (1991). *Increasing picture effects in learning from illustrated text*. Paper presented at the Fourth European Conference for Research on Learning and Instruction, Turku, Finland, August.

Scevak, J.J., & Moore, P.J. (1990). Effective processing of visual information. *Reading*, *24*, 28-36.

Weidenmann, B. (1989). When good pictures fail: An information-processing approach to the effects of illustrations. In H. Mandl & J.R. Levin (Eds.), *Knowledge acquisition from text and pictures* (pp. 157-171). North Holland: Elsevier.

Winn, W. (1991). *Contributions of structural and semantic components of graphics to their interpretation*. Paper presented at the workshop comprehension of Graphics, University of Tubingen, Germany, October.

Concluding Remarks

Research on cognition and learning clearly demonstrates that there is no such thing as direct knowledge transfer from one individual to another. People acquire knowledge within an active processing framework, and what individuals actually learn is determined by prior experience with the stimuli, task expectations, and ability. This general view of knowledge acqustion as a process of constructing meaning applies directly to the comprehension of graphics. As the papers in this volume demonstrate, graphs, charts, diagrams, maps, and other visual displays have a variety of functions, depending on the processing characteristics of the learner. For example, the evidence reported here suggests that such displays can serve diverse functions like simply depicting data, explaining complex relationships, organizing information, improving memory for facts, and influencing problem solving. However, these functions are not inherent in graphics themselves, but result from the constructive interaction of the individual with the particular stimulus in question. The contributions in this volume are not concerned with how particular graphics influence learning, but with the ways in which such graphic are are processed cognitively, and under what conditions this processing leads to successful comprehension.

The section on Graphical Codes and Graphics Processing in this volume summarizes numerous theoretical and empirical approaches describing the interaction between graphic stimuli and the human cognitive system. This section also reminds us of the many related questions yet to be ansered. Generally, graphics convey information by associating the functional characteristics of the visual system with the conceptual knowledge of the individual. However, while there has been extensive research on the mechanisms of visual perception, we know relatively little about the higher semantic processes involved in the comprehension of graphics. For example, we have only a vague idea about how the principles of visual perception interact with particular graphic formats, e.g., how graphs or flow charts are semantically processed and how the resulting cognitive schemes interact (cf. Pinker, 1990). Also, we are only beginning to understand how directing codes in graphics interact with cognitive processes to influence semantic processes and activate appropriate processing strategies. A detailed analysis of the codes used in graphics must also consider the fact that graphics function as communicative instruments, where the visual presentation of facts consists of both the author's perspective and an implicit request for the learner to carry out specific types of cognitive processing (cf. Bühler, 1934). Of special interest here are questions concerning how concepts from procedural semantics can be used to explain the comprehension of graphics (Woods, 1981).

A central question for further research concerns the types of knowledge structures people construct when they attempt to comprehend graphic stimuli. The section on Graphics and Mental Representations suggests that graphic comprehension is associated with multiple types of mental representations, each of which is constructed to meet a specific demand. Research over the past decade has produced theoretical frameworks with considerably more explanatory power that the basic dual coding positions developed by Paivio (1986) and others. The act of understanding graphics and texts is more complex that the simple visual-verbal code comparisons which underlie dual coding. Rather, there are two representational principles which differ in quality, and when the two combine or interact with one another they produce new entities which are the raw material from which graphic comprehension is produced. The distinction between the two basic representations is simliar to Palmer's (1978) concept of extrinsic and intrinsic representations, where there are symbolic representations with explicit relational elements, and analogous models containing relevant structural characteristics but not explicit relational elements. In such analogous models, relations are made explicit when they are actually read from the representation. The distinction between symbolic/analogous and extrinsic/intrinsic representations is the essential basis for differentiating between propositional representations on one hand and mental models on the other. Propositional representations are a kind of mental language in the form of linear symbol chains, whereas mental models are analogous structures (e.g., Johnson-Laird, 1983). The same distinction is also applied in this volume to stimulus differences between texts and graphs.

Given our previous discussion, it becomes easier to understand why the search for a grammar of graphics has been unsuccessful, and why there has been such difficulty in using concepts from structural linguistics to describe graphic representations (cf. Goldsmith, 1987). Because of their different proximity to the propositional representation and associated mental models, texts and graphs tend to vary in the degree to which they can contribute to the construction of knowledge structures. Mental models built from verbal descriptions are constrained by the truth value of the propositions, while the mental models constructued from graphics are based on the structural correspondence between both visuospatial relations and the semantic content of the model itself. In addition, mental models that include spatial display information contain structural properties that influence learning and retention by allowing more efficient processing within the working memory system (Larkin, 1989; Larkin & Simon, 1987).

Until recently, little has been known about how the verbal-visual systems interact during the construction of mental models, or about the specific processes that are involved in such construction. The main question here is how specific forms of graphic stimuli influence the construction of mental models so that cognitive processing is either facilitated or degraded. A related question concerns the degree to which a given graphic can be used to construct more than one type of mental model, and under what conditions a graphic may actually interfere with model building. Finally, research needs doing that evaluates the effects of prior experience with specific graphic presentations, and ways in which familiar graphics work to activate interpretation and comprehension schemes based on their structure. Such work should relate closely to research on the role of metaphors and analogies in comprehension.

An understanding of relevant individual differences is essential for describing the process of comprehending graphs. The papers in the section on Differential and Developmental Aspects indicate that graphic comprehension is influenced by differences in prior knowledge of both the graph and its content, by the types of cognitive strategies the learner employs, and by the student's willingness to use a given form of graphic presentation. Not only do children of different ages vary considerable in their ability to comprehend graphics, but there are also indications that individual differences play a measurable role in adult learners. Future research might concentrate on the types of differences that are important for understanding graphics and how such differences relate to the metacognitive strategies of the population in question. What is needed is a theoretical framework that incorporates both differential and developmental aspects of the graphic learning and interpretation process.

Research on the comprehension of graphics will also need to concentrate on how graphic representations can be designed and used effectively. There is no question that a well designed graphic is worth more than a thousand words--it's simply a question of what one means by "well designed". In the section on Instructional Aspects it becomes clear that many learners do not understand how to get the most out of a graphic stimulus. In some cases learners do not know how to read the graphic, while in other cases they process the information only superficially, or use strategies that are ineffective. Apparently, students need guidance in what aspects of the graphic to attend to, and in how to process the perceptual patterns so that the information can be incorporated into specific semantic structures. This type of training appears to be especially important for learners in the lower ability levels. On the other hand, some graphics are so complex that students expend their processing capacity on the act of interpretation, with very little attempt to comprehend the graphic's content. There needs to be work done on the trade off between the processing of graphic formats and the amount of content depicted in the stimulus.

As various contributions in this volume demonstrate, programs aimed at supporting learning with both graphs and texts often do not yield the expected results. This finding indicates that such programs need to be carefully planned and implemented in such a way that both local and global knowledge structures result. There is not only the general questions of how graphics need to be designed for specific learning conditions, or how they should be tied to texts to insure that knowledge is imparted effectively. But we also need a more exact analysis of how the embedded strategy activators like direction codes, labels, captions, etc. interact with detached strategy activators that give learners direct guidance for interpreting the graphic and relating it to associated semantic material. We need to investigate how much specific transfer developes when one goes from one type of graphic to another.

Graphics that serve as instruments of knowledge acquisition will become important entities in the future. This is true not only for traditional print media, but also for computer-based learning environments, interfaces between individuals and technical systems, and for the development of flexible multimedia systems. At the same time, graphics comprehension is a domain for multidisciplinary cooperation between cognitive science, instructional psychology, semiotics, and artificial intelligence. The common goal is to better understand the cognitive structures and processes which enable an individual to comprehend graphic presentations. The structural characteristics of graphical presentations are probably best understood within a cognitive processing framework related to their stimulus properties. The structural invariants of such presentations are probably related to specific mechanisms that yield efficient processing of the graphic content. A better understanding of the theory underlying the comprehension of graphics will enrich our knowledge base about human cognition, and will also provide a more comprehensive base for the development of empirically based practical guides aimed at both the design and use of graphics. We hope that this book will contribute to achieving this goal.

Wolfgang Schnotz   Raymond W. Kulhavy

References

Bühler, K. (1934). *Sprachtheorie*. Jena: Fischer.

Goldsmith, E. (1987). The analysis of illustration in theory and practice. In H.A. Houghton & D.M. Willows (Eds.), *The psychology of illustration. Vol 2: Instructional issues* (pp. 53-85). New York: Springer.

Johnson-Laird, P.N. (1983). *Mental Models. Towards a cognitive science of language, inference, and consciousness*. Cambridge: Cambridge University Press.

Larkin, J.H. (1989). Display-based problem solving. In D. Klahr & K. Kotovsky (Eds.), *Complex information processing. The impact of Herbert A. Simon* (pp. 319-341). Hillsdale, NJ: Erlbaum.

Larkin, J.H., & Simon, H.A. (1987). Why a diagram is (sometimes) worth ten thousand words. *Cognitive Science, 11,* 65-99.

Paivio, A. (1986). *Mental representations: A dual coding approach*. New York: Oxford University Press.

Palmer, S.E. (1978). Fundamental aspects of cognitive represenation. In E. Rosch & B.B. Lloyd (Eds.), *Cognition and categorization* (pp. 259-303). Hillsdale, NJ: Erlbaum.

Pinker, St. (1990). A theory of graph comprehension. In R. Freedle
    (Ed.), *Artificial intelligence and the future of testing* (pp. 73-
    126), Hillsdale, NJ: Erlbaum.
Woods, W.A. (1981). Waht's in a link: Foundations for semantic
    networks. In D.G. Bobrow & A. Collins (Eds.), *Representation
    and understanding. Studies in cognitive science* (pp. 35-82). New
    York: Academic Press.

Author Index

Subject Index